In June 1941 – during the first week of the Nazi invasion of the Soviet Union – the quiet cornfields and towns of Western Ukraine were awakened by the clanking of steel and thunder of explosions; this was the greatest tank battle of the Second World War. About 3,000 tanks from the Red Army Kiev Special Military District clashed with about 800 German tanks of Heeresgruppe South. Why did the numerically superior Soviets fail? Hundreds of heavy KV-1 and KV-2 tanks, the five-turreted giant T-35 and famous T-34 tanks all failed to stop the Germans. Based on recently released archival sources, Alexei Isaev describes the battle from a new point of view: that in fact it's not the tanks, but armored units, which win or lose battles. During the Blitzkrieg era the Germans had a superior T&OE for their armoured forces. The German Panzer Divisions could defeat their opponents not by using tanks, but by using artillery, which included heavy artillery, motorized infantry and engineers. The Red Army's armored unit – the Mechanized Corps – had a lot of teething troubles, as all of them lacked accompanying infantry and artillery. In 1941 the Soviet Armored Forces had to learn the difficult science – and mostly 'art' – of combined warfare.

Isaev traces the role of these factors in a huge battle around the small Ukrainian town of Dubno. Popular myths about impregnable KV and T-34 tanks are laid to rest. In reality, the Germans in 1941 had the necessary tools to combat them. The author also defines the real achievements on the Soviet side: the Blitzkrieg in the Ukraine had been slowed down. For the Soviet Union, the military situation in June 1941 was much worse than it was for France and Britain during the Western Campaign in 1940. The Red Army wasn't ready to fight as a whole and the border district's armies lacked infantry units, as they were just arriving from the internal regions of the USSR. In this case, the Red Army tanks became the 'Iron Shield' of the Soviet Union; they even operated as fire brigades. In many cases, the German infantry – not tanks – became the main enemy of Soviet armored units in the Dubno battle. Poorly organized, but fierce, tank-based counter-attacks slowed down the German infantry -and while the Soviet tanks lost the battle, they won the war.

Aleksei Isaev was born in 1974. Since 2004 he has written approximately 20 books on the history of the Eastern Front in the Second World War, with a particular emphasis on the events of 1941 and Stalingrad. His particular research interest today is the war's final period. During 2007-2010, he worked as an academic scholar in the Russian Ministry of Defense's Institute of Military History. He was a contributor to the new 12-volume official Russian history of the war. Thanks to the opening of the previously-classified military archives in Russia, he has undertaken a lot of work with the war's documents as an independent scholar.

Kevin Bridge BA MCIL is a Russian to English translator / editor specialising in Aviation & Aeronautics and Russian translation for the publishing sector. He has been working as a translator since October 2007 and to date he has translated 12 books, which have either been serialised in an historical aviation journal, or have been published by leading military history and academic publishers. He has also acted as an interpreter for Russian and Western aircrew at aviation events such as the Farnborough Airshow. He gained a BA Degree in Russian & Soviet Studies from the University of Portsmouth in 1998 and has travelled extensively in Russia. He also worked for a period of five years as a Russian linguist before embarking on translation. He joined the Chartered Institute of Linguists in March 2012 as a full Member (MCIL) and was elected to the Board of Trustees of the Russian Aviation Research Trust (RART), in view of his translation work and Russian language skills in September 2013. Further details about his work can be found via www.bridge-translation.com.

DUBNO 1941

The Greatest Tank Battle of the Second World War

Aleksei Isaev

Translated by Kevin Bridge BA MCIL

Helion & Company

Helion & Company Limited
Unit 8 Amherst Business Centre
Budbrooke Road
Warwick
CV34 5WE
England
Tel. 01926 499 619
Fax 0121 711 4075
Email: info@helion.co.uk
Website: www.helion.co.uk
Twitter: @helionbooks
Visit our blog http://blog.helion.co.uk/

Published by Helion & Company 2017. Reprinted in paperback 2019
Designed and typeset by Mach 3 Solutions Ltd (www.mach3solutions.co.uk)
Cover designed by Paul Hewitt, Battlefield Design (www.battlefield-design.co.uk)
Printed by Hobbs the Printers, Totton, Hampshire

Originally published as *Dubno 1941: Velichaysheye Tankovoye Srazheniye Vtoroy Mirovoy* ['Dubno 1941: The Greatest Tank Battle of World War II'] (Moscow: EKSMO, 2009).

ISBN 978-1-911628-43-9

British Library Cataloguing-in-Publication Data.
A catalogue record for this book is available from the British Library.

Contents

List of Photographs

List of Maps

In colour section

Map Key

A	Army
XVII	German Corps
RC	Rifle Corps
MC	Mechanised Corps
TC	Tank Corps
71	Infantry Division
PzGrp.	Armoured Group
RR	Rifle Regiment
IR	Infantry Regiment
Pz	Armoured
T	Tank
Cav.	Cavalry
(Mot.)	Motorised
(Mtn.)	Mountain
ATAB	Anti-tank Artillery Brigade
MRBn	Motorised Rifle Battalion
AD	Aviation Division
FR	Fighter Aviation Regiment
LRB	Long Range Bomber Air Regiment
SRB	Short Range Bomber Air Regiment
GAR	Ground Attack Air Regiment
RAR	Reconnaissance Air Regiment

List of Tables

Publisher's Note

We have retained the original flavour of the author's text. This includes sometimes partisan statements, such as 'our tanks' or 'our aircraft'. We feel that keeping this benefits the reader's experience, and preserves the spirit of the original Russian edition.

Introduction

At 1645 hrs Berlin time on 21 June 1941 a phrase, which to the uninitiated would have sounded ambiguous, rang out over the radio across Southern Poland: "The tale of the heroes, Votan, Neckar, 15." Encoded in this message however was one of the most terrifying dates in Russian history. The words "The tale of the heroes" meant that the plan to attack the USSR was being implemented, the name of the God "Votan" referring to the date of 22 June, and the name of a river, the "Neckar", which referred to 0300 and a few minutes, were broadcast in plain text. In obeyance of this command grey tanks with crosses on their sides, as well as thousands of vehicles and tractor units headed east. A few hours later they would be crossing the border with the Soviet Union, which was shrouded in smoke from the fires of war. The countdown had begun to the start of one of the largest tank battles in world history. The five Soviet mechanised columns that fought in this battle amounted to approximately 2,800 tanks, while the three motorised German columns—approximately 800 tanks and self-propelled artillery systems. This clash of an enormous number of tanks was accompanied by an intensive air war, during the course of which hundreds of tonnes of bombs were dropped on the armadas of tanks. Both Russian and Western historians, particularly David M. Glantz, acknowledge that the battles of Dubno represented the only Soviet counterattack in the course of the border battle of June 1941 which had a positive effect on what was, overall, an unfortunate course of events in the initial period of the war.

1

Army Group South

Army Group South command appeared in August 1939 and took its name from the southern wing of the front line in the Polish campaign. On 23 October 1939 the command of this army group was renamed and became the uninspiring *Army Group A*, it was under this name that the group participated in combat operations in the West. Finally on 22 April 1941 the army group headquarters arrived at the Soviet-German demarcation line, where up until 21 June 1941 it was known as the *Silesian Sector Headquarters*. On 21 June 1941 the name '*Army Group South*' appears once again in archive documents. Throughout this period the commander of this army group was Gerd Von Rundstedt.

The objectives for Rundstedt's army in Operation Barbarossa, according to a directive from *Wehrmacht* Supreme Command dated 31 January 1941, were allocated as follows:

> *Army Group South* is to attack using its augmented left flank in the general direction of Kiev, with the mobile units out in front. The overall objective is to destroy the Soviet forces in Galicia and Western Ukraine to the west of the river Dniepr and capture the Dniepr river crossings around Kiev in good time, in doing so creating the prerequisites to continue the operation east of the Dniepr. The offensive needs to be carried out in such a way that the mobile forces are concentrated to enable an attack from the area around Lyublin in the direction of Kiev.
>
> In accordance with this objective for the army and *panzer group*, which takes its orders directly from *Army Group South* Command the following tasks need to be completed:
>
> The *11.Armee* is to ensure that the Romanian territory is protected from invasion by Soviet forces, taking into account the critical importance of Romania to the course of the war. During the course of the invasion by the forces of *Army Group South*, the *11.Armee* will contain the attacking enemy forces creating an illusion of a strategic deployment of enormous numbers of troops and depending on how the environment develops will impede an organised retreat of Soviet forces beyond the Dniester river by inflicting, in cooperation with air power, a series of strikes on the retreating forces.
>
> *Panzergruppe 1*, in cooperation with the forces of the *17. and 6. Armees*, will break through the enemy's defences that are concentrated along the border between Rava-Ruska and Kovel, and advance via Berdichev to Zhitomir. In good time it will close in on the Dniepr river close to Kiev, as well as areas further south. Subsequently, and without wasting any time, the advance along the Dniepr river in a south-easterly direction will continue in accordance with the orders issued by *Army Group South* Command, to obstruct the retreat of the Soviet alignment that is active in Western Ukraine, beyond the Dniepr river and to destroy the alignment via the back door.
>
> The *17. Armee* will break through the enemy's defences on the border to the north-west of Lvov, using its strong left flank to advance rapidly, driving the enemy back south-eastwards and destroying them. Subsequently this army, taking advantage of the successful advance by the forces of the *panzer* group, will close in on the area around Vinnytsia and Berdichev and depending on the circumstances, continue its advance either southwards or south-eastwards.

> The *6. Armee*, in conjunction with the formations of the *Panzergruppe 1*, will break through the enemy front line close to Lutsk and in doing so will cover the army group's northern flank from possible attacks from the Pripyat Marshes. The principal forces will depart for Zhitomir as quickly as possible on the trail of the *Panzergruppe*.
>
> The troops in this army should be ready, under orders from army group command, to transfer their principal forces to the south-east, that is to say west of the Dniepr river in order that they would be able, in conjunction with the *Panzergruppe 1* to obstruct a retreat by enemy forces beyond the Dniepr river, and to destroy these forces.

Thus according to the plan drawn up by the German command the operation against the Soviet forces in Ukraine should be akin to an 'assymetric canna', in which one wing of the encircling forces is comprised of mechanised formations, while the other of infantry. This was one of the predominant approaches in German military thinking in the 1940s, which was used on more than one occasion in the course of the *Blitzkriegs*.

The *Panzergruppe 1* became the sole mobile formation in *Army Group South* (see table). Since the German command were very well aware that the troops in the Kiev Special Military District were the most numerous of the Soviet border districts, they did not send a single division into battle with the *Panzergruppe 1* that was equipped with Czech built 35(t) and 38(t) tanks. All the *panzer* formations in the group were divisions made up of two battalions, which were equipped with German materiel. In addition the *Panzergruppe 1* was characterised by the divisions of which it was formed, which were themselves formed in 1940. None of them could boast of their participation in the Polish campaign and only the 9th *Panzer Division* had any experience of the French campaign (up until that time it had been the *4th Light Division*). The latter group however had been formed in Vienna and the combat readiness of the Austrian units had always been significantly less than that of their German counterparts. The main thrust of the Dubno battles was born by the divisions that had arisen from the reorganisation of *panzer* forces which began in July 1940. As a result of this reorganisation the number of *panzer* divisions in the *Wehrmacht* was doubled. This doubling of the number of divisions occurred by dint of the splitting up of the *panzer* brigades in the existing divisions and the creation of new divisions, on the basis of the newly released *panzer* regiments. There was now one *panzer* regiment, that was formed of two or three battalions, across all the *panzer* divisions in the *Wehrmacht* in place of two. To a considerable extent this was balanced by a quantitative and qualitative enhancement in the strike capabilities of the *panzer* companies in these battalions.

Shortly after their formation the *11th* and *14th Panzer Divisions* were given their baptism of fire during Operation Marita in the spring of 1941 in the Balkans. During the course of Marita the *16th Panzer Division* were in reserve, but for the *13th Panzer Division* Barbarossa became their career debut as a *panzer* formation.

Table 1.1 The Composition of the *Panzers* in the divisions of the *Panzergruppe 1*

Division	*Pz.II*	*Pz.III* with a 37mm gun	*Pz.III* with a 50mm gun	Pz.IV	Commanders' tanks	Total
9th Panzer Division	32 (+8 *Pz.I*)	11	60	20	12	143
11th Panzer Division	45	23	48	20	10	146
13th Panzer Division	45	27	44	20	13	149
14th Panzer Division	45	15	56	20	11	147
16th Panzer Division	44	24	47	20	8	143
Total	219	100	255	100	54	728

To a certain extent this was balanced by the fact that these new divisions were formed of infantry formations that had already gained experience in the Polish and French campaigns. Nevertheless the new *13th* and *16th Panzer Divisions* were placed by command in the second echelon.

Naturally if in Soviet terms the *panzer* divisions in the *Panzergruppe 1* were well equipped, there were signs of a high degree of completeness inside the *Wehrmacht* itself. Specifically this related to the mechanised infantry formations being equipped with the half-track '*Hanomag*' armoured personnel carrier. These vehicles were only present at company level in the *panzer* divisions of *Army Group South*. These were: the 1st Company of the *9. Schützen-Brigade*, *9th Panzer Division*, the 1st Company of the *110th Schützen-Regiment*, *11th Panzer Division* and the 1st Company of the *66th Panzergrenadier Regiment*, *13th Panzer Division*. The *Panzergrenadier* company that operated armoured personnel carriers would normally consist of 13 *Sd.Kfz.251* armoured personnel carriers: 10 standard *Sd.Kfz.251/1* and three Sd.Kfz.251/10 platoon commanders' vehicles armed with a 37mm anti-tank gun. There were no armoured personnel carriers at all in the *14th* and *16th Panzer Divisions*. We note that two companies equipped with armoured personnel carriers had appeared in the *16th Panzer Division* by May 1942, but only appeared in battalion strength in 1944. The *11th Panzer Division* advanced outside Kursk with two companies of armoured personnel carriers in the entire division. Put simply the image of the Germans armed across the board with MP-40 sub-machine guns and advancing exclusively in coffin-shaped armoured personnel carriers is no more than a figment of a cinematographer's imagination. The *Hanomag* armoured personnel carrier was a comparatively rare bird and the overwhelming majority of the *Wehrmacht's Panzergrenadiers* moved forward on a march in trucks and, in battle, on their own two feet. Self-propelled artillery in the *panzer* divisions of *Army Group South* was represented by the self-propelled artillery of the *701st Self-Propelled Artillery Company*, which consisted of six 15cm *sIG Sfl. Ausf.Pz.I Ausf.B* (a 150mm heavy infantry gun mounted on a *Pz.I* tank chassis) in the *9th Panzer Division*. Another sign that the Germans were well equipped was the 10cm corps-level artillery, which replaced four of the twelve 15cm heavy howitzers in one artillery regiment. The armour piercing round from the 10cm *K-18* corps-level armament, which weighed 15.56kgs and had a velocity of 827m/sec, could penetrate any Soviet tank up to, and including, an IS-2. According to available data it was only the *16th Panzer Division* that was not equipped with this armament. In an irony of fate it was this very regiment that encountered the newest Soviet tanks on more than one occasion.

Aside from the *panzer* divisions, mechanised infantry divisions entered the line-up of the *Panzergruppe 1*. These were the *16th* and the *25th Motorised Divisions*. In contrast to the standard motorised divisions they had two and not three infantry regiments, which were however fully motorised. The artillery regiments in these motorised divisions were made up of three battalions in contrast to the four battalions in a standard infantry division, although their armament was towed by half-track tractor units. The motorised divisions differed from the *panzer* formations in the *Wehrmacht* and their namesakes in the Red Army by their lack of tanks (they only received them in the shape of a single battalion in 1942). Motorised divisions were intended to cover the flanks of advancing *panzer* divisions. The motorised *SS* divisions were a breed apart from the *Heer*'s motorised infantry divisions. On June 22 1941 two *SS* formations were subordinate to the *Panzergruppe 1*, namely the *SS* motorised infantry brigade the '*Leibstandarte SS Adolf Hitler*' (consisting of four battalions of motorised infantry and a weak artillery regiment consisting of two battalions) and the '*Wiking*' motorised infantry division. '*Wiking*' was considerably more powerful than its army counterparts in as much as it had not two but three motorised infantry regiments each consisting of three battalions. In turn the '*Leibstandarte*' was the only motorised formation in *Army Group South* equipped with tracked armoured vehicles as standard. Back in May 1940 this division had received six examples of the *StuGIII* self-propelled gun and by 19 June 1941 this had risen to seven. '*Wiking*' was only to receive its *Sturmgeschütz* vehicles in September 1941. The '*Leibstandarte*' were characterised by an unprecedentedly powerful anti-tank armament. Each of the four motorised infantry battalions in the brigade had three 50mm *PAK-38* anti-tank weapons and four 37mm *PAK-35/36s*. By way of a comparison: the infantry divisions in the first wave only had two 50mm *PAK-38* guns per regiment. On the minus side the *SS* differed from the *Heer* in terms of their combat training and therefore the preference was for them to be used to solve auxiliary issues.

The commander of the *Panzergruppe 1* was the 60-year-old Colonel-General Ewald von Kleist. As an old cavalry soldier he had commanded a *Panzergruppe* in the French campaign, which was named after him as *Panzergruppe* Kleist. In November 1940 this group was officially named the *Panzergruppe 1* and it was under this name that it participated in combat operations in the Balkans. The divisions that were subordinate to the *Panzergruppe 1* were to have operated under the leadership of a special purpose headquarters group—the motorised corps directorates. There were three of these headquarters at the tank group's disposal: the *III*, *IX*, and *XXXXVIII Armeekorps*. Formally the *panzer*, as well as motorised, divisions could be subordinate to the motorised corps. The name 'motorised' however had an impact on the role of the corps commander. Attempts were made to recruit commanders with experience in the practice of using mobile formations.

The *III Armeekorps (mot)* was led by *General der Kavallerie* Eberhard Von Mackensen. He was clearly weaker as a tactician than his father, August Von Mackensen, who became one of the most famous military leaders of the First World War. However during the course of the war he rose to the position of commander of *1. Panzerarmee*. The commanders of the *13th* and *14th Panzer Divisions*, Duvert and Kuhn, under whom the corps fought the border battle in its entirety, did not earn high praise. Combat operations for the corps began as part of the *14th Panzer* and the *44th* and *298th Infantry Divisions*. The German command, from the very beginning, had drawn up several plans for this action and therefore the final composition of the *III Armeekorps (mot)* was only decided on the first or second day of the war. The table shows the strength of the divisions, which at one time or another were subordinate to Mackensen's corps during the course of the border battle.

Table 1.2 The strength of the formations in the *III Armeekorps (mot)* on 21 June 1941

	13th Panzer Division	*14th Panzer Division*	*25th Motorised Division*	*44th Infantry Division*	*298th Infantry Division*
Gefechtsstaerke	12,516	10,997	12,258	18,697	14,599
Verpflegungsstaerke	13,980	19,580	15,074	21,443	–

Gefechtsstaerke is the total number of fighting elements in the formations, that is to say infantry, *panzer* crews, reconnaissance (*Aufklärungs)* troops, artillerists, sappers, and so on. This indicator should not be confused with the *Kampfstaerke* denoting combat strength, which included officers, non-commissioned officers and rank and file soldiers who participated directly in the battle. An approximate equivalent of the latter term would be the Soviet term 'active soldiers'. The *Verpflegungsstaerke* denotes the 'number of rations' or the number of people 'on rations', including prisoners of war.

Not only did the *XXXXVIII Motorised Corps* become one of the most famous *panzer* formations in the *Wehrmacht* but also assembled a 'stellar team' of German *panzer* commanders. The *XXXXVIII Motorised Corps*, which was subsequently renamed the *XXXXVIII Motorised Corps*, participated in the majority of the large-scale battles on the Eastern Front, including the battles of Stalingrad and of the Kursk salient, and the fighting on the right bank of the Ukraine between autumn 1943–winter 1944–45. The commander of the corps, Werner Kempf, became the commander of an army group in 1942 that was named after him and in 1944 he was to take up command of *Army Group North*.

Table 1.3 The strength of *XXXXVIII Motorised Corps* formations on 22 June 1941

	The combat strength (*Koepfe*) in terms of personnel	Numbers of horses
57th Infantry Division	21,020	6,000
75th Infantry Division	26,030	6,500
11th Panzer Division	18,340	–
Corps units	8,600	–
Total	73,990	12,500

The commander of the *16th Panzer Division*, which shortly after the start of the battle became subordinate to the corps, Hans-Valentin Hube, was to command the *panzer* corps in September 1942 and in October 1943 the *1. Panzerarmee*, the successor to the *Panzergruppe 1*. He would be killed in an air crash in April 1944 at the rank of *Generaloberst*, and as a Chevalier of the Knight's Cross with Oak Leaves, Swords and Diamonds. The second *panzer* battalion of the *2nd Panzer Regiment* in Hube's division was commanded in 1941 by *Major* Hyacinth Graf von Strachwitz, one of the acknowledged German tank aces, who subsequently commanded the *Panzergrenadier Division 'Grossdeutschland'*. The first battalion of the *Panzer Regiment*, *16th Panzer Division* was commanded by *Major* Bernhard Sowan who, in 1943, was the commander of the *505th Panzer Battalion* (Tiger tanks). The second tank formation in the *XXXXVIII Corps*—the *11th Panzer Division*—was led by *Generalmajor* Ludwig Crüwell, a cavalry officer in the Kaiser's army, he saw in the Second Word War in the headquarters of the *6th Panzer Regiment*. He was probably the only commander of this *panzer* division who was mentioned by name in Halder's diary. Back in August 1941 Crüwell had been promoted and attained the rank of *Generalleutnant* and was sent to Africa as a specialist in combat operations in the tropics. Four months later he attained the rank of *General der Panzertruppe*. Crüwell's rapidly advancing career was interrupted in May 1942 when he landed his 'Storch' aircraft on the English lines following a navigational error.

The table shows the strength of this corps in terms of personnel as of the morning of June 22 1941, that is to say two infantry and one *panzer* division. Subsequently the infantry divisions were withdrawn from the line-up and replaced by mobile formations.

By way of a comparison: the strength of the Soviet 5th Army's rifle formations (including fortified sectors), which became one of the enemies of the *XXXXVIII Motorised Corps*, as of 1 June 1941 was 53,163 men.

The *XIV Motorised Corps* led by *General* von Weitersheim spent the majority of the border battle in reserve. This corps was used to control the reserve *panzer* and motorised formations. As they were introduced to operations they were withdrawn from Wietersheim's formation and were transferred to two other motorised corps.

From the air the infantry and motorised formations of *Army Group South* were to have been supported by the *Luftflotte 4* under *General* Alexander Lohr. Specifically the divisions in the *6.* and *17. Armeen* were to be supported by the *V Fliegerkorps* under R von Greim (see the table). One characteristic idiosyncrasy of the *Luftwaffe* participation in the Dubno battles was the lack of the symbol of the *Blitzkriegs* in the shape of the *Ju-87* dive-bombers. The *Fliegerkorps* led by von Greim was equipped with *Ju-88* and *He-111* bombers, which were used universally in the *Luftwaffe*, these very same aircraft flew sorties both to bomb artillery positions and marching reserve columns, as well as carrying out bombing raids on Moscow and London. During raids on the front line the range was converted to loitering capability over the target, when the *'Heinkel'* and the *'Junkers'* were able to loiter in the air for the entire duration of the attack. German command was under no delusion as to the balance of forces in terms of aircraft. Consequently the forces of the *Panzergruppe 1* planned the forthcoming battle as follows:

> The forces must be prepared to counter massive air raids and large-scale tank attacks from a numerically superior enemy. A large number of low level attacks are expected. What is known at present is that 5,000 Russian aircraft are available, of which only 3,000 are combat capable. Since the Russians do not have well organised ground forces comparable to our own, and the repair facilities are centralised in several locations, there will be considerable losses in the course of a few days due to technical reasons. Furthermore the *Luftwaffe* will be focusing their strikes on the repair facilities and achieving air superiority by striking the airfields and will be able to transfer rapidly onto covering or supporting our own forces.[1]

Table 1.4 The composition of *V Fliegerkorps, Luftflotte 4* 22 June 1941

Unit	Airfield	Aircraft		
		Type	Total	Number of aircraft that are combat capable
KG51 Headquarters	Krosno	*Ju 88*	2	2
I/KG51			22	22
II/KG51			36	29
III/KG51	Lezany		32	28
KG54 Headquarters	Lyublin-Svidnik		1	1
I/KG54			34	31
II/KG54			36	33
KG55 Headquarters	Labunie		2	1
I/KG55			27	27
II/KG55		*Bf 110*	24	22
III/KG55	Klemensow	*He 111H*	25	24
JG3 Headquarters	Hostynne		4	4
I/JG3	Dub		35	28
II/JG3	Hostynne	*Bf 109F*	35	32
III/JG3	Moderovka		35	34

As we can see the *Luftwaffe* had a sufficiently well thought out plan to secure air superiority: concentrating the strikes on the airfields whilst striking the Workers' and Peasants' Red Army Air Force's repair centres. It is not clear why the German command anticipated low-level air attacks. It is possible that experience of the war in the West had taught them this. In reality Soviet aircraft operated from an altitude of between 800–1,200m. The ground-attack aircraft, which were to become the calling card of Soviet aviation, were still few in number. The majority of the air fleet was comprised of bombers that were of a completely standard design.

If the number of tanks, armament, aircraft, and so on could be counted in some way or another then the tactical approaches would not lend themselves to a numerical analysis. The only evaluation that can be done here is on a qualitative level. The typical approach for *panzer* and infantry warfare in the *Wehrmacht* was the formation of so-called *kampfgruppen* (combat groups). These

1 NARA T314 R1138 f640.

kampfgruppen represented a temporary formation made up of units from the different branches of the armed forces that formed part of a division.

Either a *panzer* or an infantry regiment would form the core of the combat group, and battalions from an artillery regiment, batteries from an anti-tank battalion, and companies from a sapper battalion would be attached to them. Often reinforcing armament would be attached to a *kampfgruppe* for their disposal from the corps itself. A regimental commander would lead the *kampfgruppe* and, in the case of the *panzer* units, they were either led by the infantry brigade commander or the commander of a *panzer* regiment. This led to a sufficiently compact and mobile group which encompassed all the arms of the division, as well as the reinforcing weaponry of the corps, from 88mm anti-aircraft artillery to the 240mm mortar, inclusive. This solved the question surrounding cooperation between the different forces, and the commander of the *kampfgruppe* would issue orders to the artillerists and sappers without handing requests to the divisional or corps commander. The essence of the *kampfgruppe* concept lay in the fact that they were not identical. That is to say the combat groups across the different formations could differ in terms of their line-up and their strength. This relates to the *kampfgruppen* that were formed within the confines of a single division. Subject to certain conditions any given *kampfgruppe* could be stronger, and the other weaker. Specifically one widely adopted variant was to create both *panzer* and motorised *kampfgruppen*, with the emphasis being on tanks or on infantry. That is to say the '*panzer*' group would be formed predominantly of tanks, while in the 'infantry' groups there was a predominance of motorised infantry, but few tanks.

Another characteristic approach the German forces used in combat would be to employ a *aufklärung* battalion of *panzer* and infantry formations as an independent motorised unit. Aside from their main functions as the 'eyes' of the division the *aufklärung* battalion would be tasked with capturing and holding certain assets. This was particularly characteristic of infantry formations, where the majority of soldiers would move on foot. In fact this was a commonly used formation for a *kampfgruppe*. The core of the combat group would be the *aufklärung* battalion, but armament from the anti-tank division and from artillery would be attached to it.

Another cornerstone of the combat techniques that had been developed by 1941 was the concept of the '*Panzerstrassen*' (literally 'tank roads'), that is to say the identification of roads in the path of a forthcoming offensive, which could serve as the axis for the advance of mechanised formations. Typically this would be a chain of connecting junctions formed of roads and highways. From the start of an operation movement along these roads was strictly forbidden for the infantry divisions. The *Panzerstrassen* could only be used to move the transport for the *panzer* formations. Three of these *Panzerstrassen* were identified by the *Panzergruppe 1* command in the path of the forthcoming advance in Ukraine. The first, which was dubbed the 'northern', ran through Volodymyr-Volynskyi, Lutsk, Rivne, Novograd-Volynsk, Zhitomir and on to Kiev. The second, known as the 'central' *Panzerstrasse,* passed through Sokal, Radzekhov, Berestechko, Dubno, Ostrog and Zhitomir. A third, dubbed the 'southern' *Panzerstrasse,* passed through Rava-Ruska, Zhulkev, Busk, Zolochiv, Ternopil and Proskurov. From the first day of the offensive it was proposed that movement should be along the northern and central *Panzerstrassen.* The motorised *corps*, the *III* and *XXXXVIII* respectively, were to move along each of these *Panzerstrasse.* The *XIV Motorised Corps* were to move along the southern '*Panzerstrasse*'. It was proposed that they would go into battle dependent on the situation after the infantry of the *17. Armee* had taken the area around Rava-Ruska.

An assessment of the enemy conducted by the German command ahead of the forthcoming tank battle was modest. German intelligence did not have accurate information concerning the newest Soviet T-34 and KV tanks. Therefore at a meeting, held on 14 June 1941 in the office of the Chief of Staff of the *Panzergruppe 1,* in view of the enemy's potential for conducting a tank war, it was announced that:

> There are around 900 tanks ahead of the *6. Armee*. A further 1,000 tanks are concentrated in the Russian motorised strike groups. Approximately 80 percent of the enemy's tanks are of inferior quality with armour between 15–18mm in thickness, which can be penetrated by any anti-tank armament. Leaflets concerning the battle with the enemy's tanks will be issued by the *Panzergruppe 1.*[2]

Shortly they would have to ascertain which tanks the remaining 20 percent were made up of, and check whether their assessment of the combat strength of the tank fleet in the Kiev Special Military District differed significantly from the actual state of affairs. In all fairness the Germans already had experience of fighting heavy tanks (the B1bis in the French campaign). Therefore there was a material readiness, at least, for the forthcoming battle. Overall combat experience was one of the strongest vectors for the Germans in the battle that lay ahead.

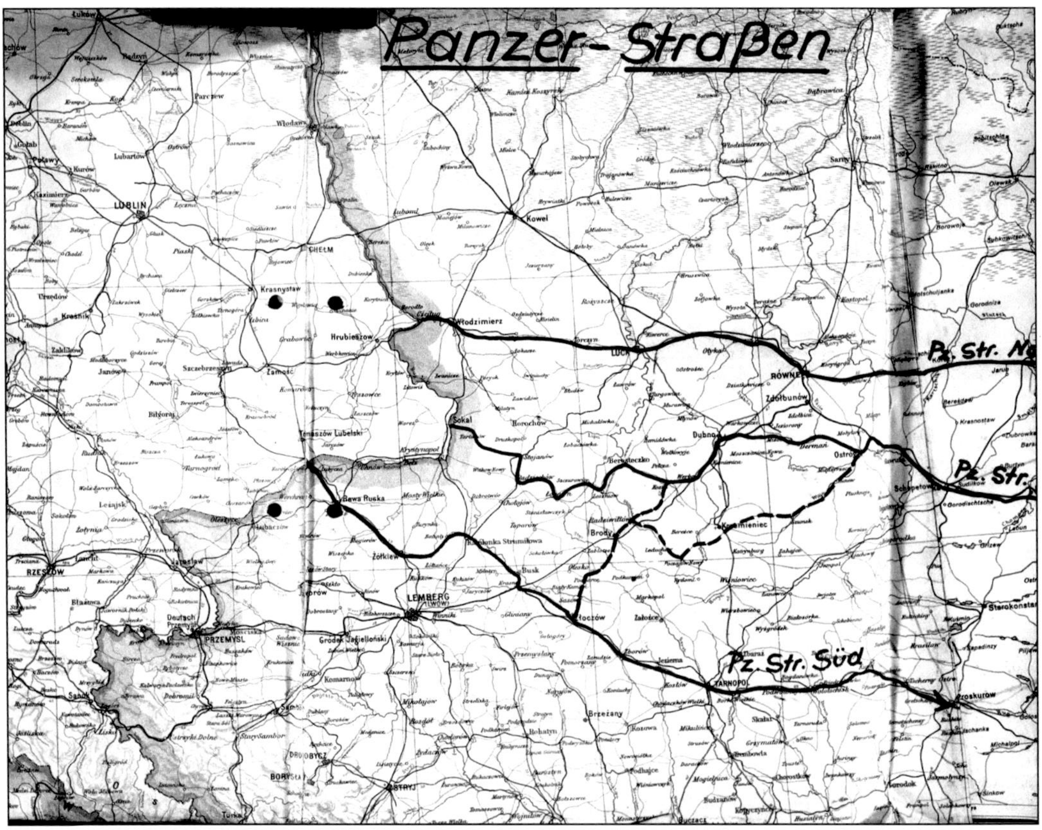

A map of the *Panzerstrassen* (Tank roads) used by the *Panzergruppe 1*. A large number of the techniques that the tank formations of the *Wehrmacht* employed required them to choose highways with hard surfaces for their mobility and infantry were forbidden to use *Panzerstrassen*. These were selected in the territory of the USSR ahead of time.

2 NARA T314 R1138 f640.

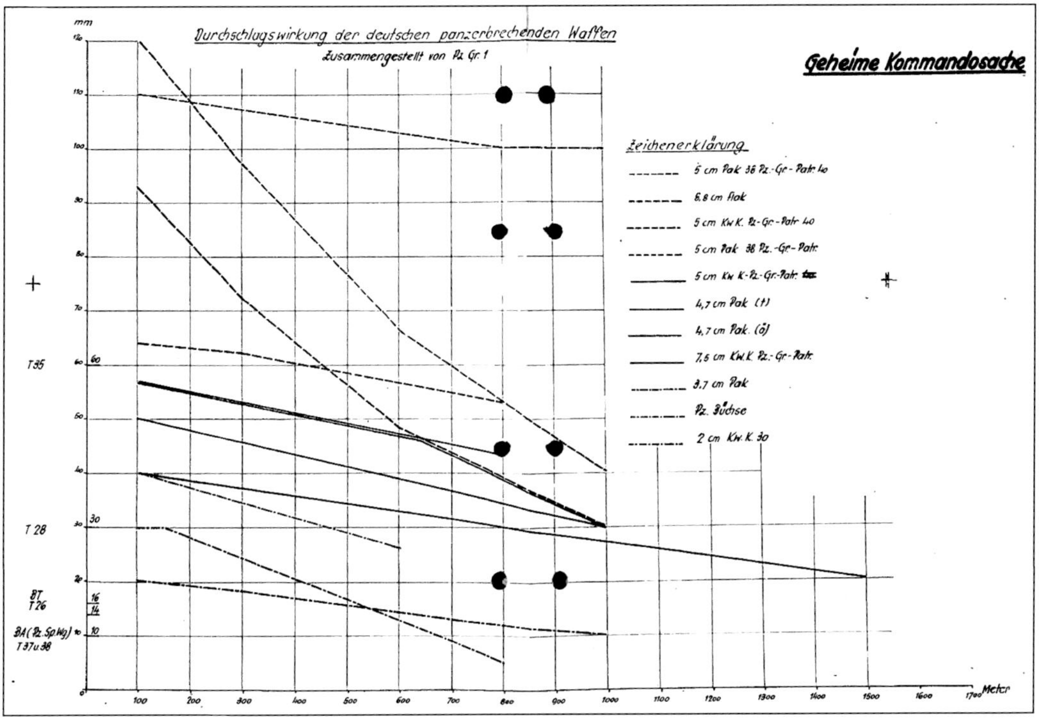

A diagram of the armour piercing capabilities of the German anti-tank armament (NARA). What is evident is that at short distances the 50mm sub-calibre rounds gave an advantage known as 'eight-eight'. Despite the absence of information about the Soviet tanks the Germans already had the means to hit them.

A German *Pz.III* tank, fitted with a 37mm gun, on the move. Judging by the symbols on the front plate of the main body, this tank belongs to the *9th Panzer Division*.

Soldaten der Ostfront!

Von schweren Sorgen bedrückt, zu monatelangem Schweigen verurteilt, ist nun die Stunde gekommen, in der ich zu Euch, meine Soldaten, offen sprechen kann.

Als das Deutsche Reich am 3. September 1939 die englische Kriegserklärung erhielt, wiederholte sich aufs neue der britische Versuch, jeden Beginn einer Konsolidierung und damit eines Aufstiegs Europas durch den Kampf gegen die stärkste Macht des Kontinents zu vereiteln.

So hat England einst in vielen Kriegen Spanien zugrunde gerichtet.

So führte es seine Kriege gegen Holland.

So bekämpfte es mit Hilfe von ganz Europa später Frankreich.

Und so begann es um die Jahrhundertwende die Einkreisung des damaligen Deutschen Reiches und im Jahr 1914 den Weltkrieg.

Nur durch seine innere Uneinigkeit ist Deutschland im Jahre 1918 unterlegen.

Die Folgen waren furchtbar.

Nachdem man erst heuchlerisch erklärte, allein gegen den Kaiser und sein Regime gekämpft zu haben, begann man nach der Waffenniederlegung des deutschen Heeres mit der planmäßigen Vernichtung des Deutschen Reiches. Während sich die Prophezeiungen eines französischen Staatsmannes, daß in Deutschland 20 Millionen Menschen zuviel seien, dh. durch Hunger, Krankheiten oder Auswanderung beseitigt werden müßten, scheinbar wörtlich erfüllten, begann die nationalsozialistische Bewegung ihr Einigungswerk des deutschen Volkes und damit den Wiederaufstieg des Reiches einzuleiten.

Diese neue Erhebung unseres Volkes aus Not, Elend und schmählicher Mißachtung stand im Zeichen einer rein inneren Wiedergeburt.

Besonders England wurde dadurch nicht berührt oder gar bedroht.

Trotzdem setzte die neue haßerfüllte Einkreisungspolitik gegen Deutschland augenblicklich wieder ein. Innen und außen kam es zu jenem uns bekannten Komplott zwischen Juden und Demokraten, Bolschewisten und Reaktionären mit den einzigen Zielen, die Errichtung des neuen deutschen Volksstaates zu verhindern, das Reich erneut in Ohnmacht und Elend zu stürzen.

Neben uns traf der Haß dieser internationalen Weltverschwörung jene Völker, die ebenso vom Glück übersehen, im härtesten Daseinskampf das tägliche Brot zu verdienen gezwungen waren. Vor allem Italien und Japan wurde der Anteil an den Gütern dieser Welt genau so wie Deutschland bestritten, ja förmlich verboten. Der Zusammenschluß dieser Nationen war daher nur ein Akt des Selbstschutzes gegenüber der sie bedrohenden egoistischen Weltkoalition des Reichtums und der Macht.

Allein schon 1936 erklärte Churchill nach den Aussagen des amerikanischen Generals Wood vor einem Ausschuß des amerikanischen Repräsentantenhauses, daß Deutschland wieder zu mächtig würde und daher vernichtet werden müsse.

Im Sommer 1939 schien England der Zeitpunkt gekommen, die erneut beabsichtigte Vernichtung mit der Wiederholung einer umfassenden Einkreisungspolitik Deutschlands beginnen zu können.

Das System der zu dem Zweck veranstalteten Lügenkampange bestand darin, andere Völker als bedroht zu erklären, sie mit englischen Garantie- und Beistandsversprechen erst einmal einzufangen und dann so wie vor dem Weltkrieg gegen Deutschland marschieren zu lassen.

So gelang es England, vom Mai bis August 1939 in die Welt die Behauptung zu lancieren, daß Litauen, Estland, Lettland, Finnland, Bessarabien sowohl als die Ukraine von Deutschland direkt bedroht seien. Ein Teil der Staaten ließ sich verleiten, das damit verbundene britische Garantieversprechen anzuehmen und ging damit in die Einkreisungsfront Deutschlands über.

Unter diesen Umständen glaubte ich es vor meinem Gewissen und vor der Geschichte des deutschen Volkes verantworten zu können, nicht nur diesen Ländern bzw. ihren Regierungen die Unwahrheit der vorgebrachten britischen Behauptungen versichern zu müssen, sondern darüber hinaus die stärkste Macht des Ostens noch besonders durch feierliche Erklärungen über die Grenzen unserer Interessen zu beruhigen.

Ihr werdet es verstehen, meine Soldaten, daß dieser Schritt für mich ein bitterer und schwerer war. Niemals hat das deutsche Volk gegen die Völkerschaften Rußlands feindselige Gefühle gehegt. Allein seit über zwei Jahrzehnten hat die jüdisch-bolschewistische Machthaberschaft von Moskau aus versucht, nicht nur Deutschland, sondern ganz Europa in Brand zu stecken. Nicht Deutschland hat seine nationalsozialistische Weltanschauung nach Rußland getragen, sondern die jüdisch-bolschewistischen Machthaber in Moskau haben unentwegt versucht, unserem und den anderen europäischen Völkern ihre Herrschaft aufzuoktroyieren, und dies nicht nur geistig, sondern vor allem auch machtmäßig.

Die Folgen dieses Regimes aber waren in allen Ländern nur das Chaos, Elend und Hungersnot. Ich habe mich demgegenüber seit zwei Jahrzehnten bemüht, mit einem Minimum an Eingriffen und ohne jede Zerstörung zu einer neuen sozialistischen Ordnung in Deutschland zu kommen, die nicht nur die Arbeitslosigkeit beseitigt, sondern auch den Gewinn der Arbeit steigend den schaffenden Menschen immer mehr zufließen läßt.

Die Erfolge dieser Politik der wirtschaftlichen und sozialen Neuordnung unseres Volkes, die als letztes Ziel einer wahren Volksgemeinschaft zustrebt, sind in der ganzen Welt einmalige.

Es war daher für mich eine schwere Überwindung, meinen Minister nach Moskau zu schicken, um dort zu versuchen, die britische

18) Hitler's speech to the soldiers of the eastern front. It was from these printed sheets that the commanders of the companies would take their speech to the soldiers, who a few hours later would be called upon to fire the first shots in the war with the USSR.

German *Pz.IVs* of the 4th Company, *36th Panzer Regiment*, *14th Panzer Division* in Western Ukraine, 1941.

A *Pz.III* tank (with a 50mm gun), and a *Pz.IV* tank of the German *11th Panzer Division* identified by the unit's insignia—a ghost with a sword.

Tanks of the *11th Panzer Division* on the battlefield. An officer is observing the battlefield through a stereo-telescope. Careful preparation for a tank attack ensured success for the German tank forces.

The Commander of the *16th Panzer Division* Hans-Valentin Hube. He subsequently became one of the most famous German tank commanders and commanded the *1.Panzerarmee.* This photograph was taken in 1942 when Hube had already been awarded the Knight's Cross with Oak Leaves.

2

The Kiev Special Military District

Before the war the Kiev Special Military District was a kind of talent pool for the upper leadership of the Red Army. The leader of the forces in this district between 1938–1939 S.K. Timoshenko went on to become the People's Commissar for Defence of the USSR, and his successor in this post, G.K. Zhukov, went on to become the Chief of the General Staff. N.F. Vatutin, who was the Chief of Staff in this district between 1938–1940, became the First Deputy to the Chief of the General Staff of the Red Army. Naturally the generals who left on promotion did not forget about their district, and the Kiev Special Military District was an elite district of sorts. At the same time it became an operational centre, and was given pivotal roles in the Soviet battle plans.

Military planning

One important idiosyncrasy of military planning in any country is the fact of the dependence of military decision making on political decisions. In relation to the USSR in 1941 this factor became decisive in the way events unfolded. In developing the plans for the war the General Headquarters deviated from the initial thesis on the timely actuation of the mobilisation mechanism and the deployment of the armed forces under the influence of the political environment. Correspondingly a period of time lasting a few weeks was proposed in which the two countries would 'crawl' to war accompanied by diplomatic notes and ultimata, followed by exchanges of fire on the border. This period would also see transfers of troops, mobilised personnel, and military technology from the interior districts to the border. Following the completion of the deployment of forces both sides would start their first operation. A typical format for the first operation was an offensive with specific objectives. The two sides would plan offensives in asymmetric directions, and the side that was the most successful would be the victor in the initial period of the war.

In a memorandum on the basis for the deployment of forces, dated September 1940, the objectives for the South-Western Front in the first operation were outlined as follows:

> In cooperation with the Army on the left-flank on the western front the forces of the South-Western Front will deliver a decisive blow to the enemy's Lyublin-Sandomir alignment and approach the river Visla. A subsequent strike would be made in the general direction of Kielce, and Krakow, reaching the objective of the river Pilica and the upper reaches of the river Oder.

This plan was detailed in a so-called memorandum of the Chief of Staff of the Kiev Special Military District M.A. Purkayev dated December 1940:

> The most pressing strategic task is to crush, in conjunction with the 4th Army on the Western Front, the German armed forces in the areas around Lyublin, Tomaszov, Kielce, Radom, Rzeszow, Jaslo and Krakow, and on the 30th day of the operation reach the objective of the

> front line along the river Pilica, Piotrkow, Opole and Neustadt, cutting Germany off from its southern allies. At the same time the state borders with Hungary and Romania should be steadfastly secured. The most pressing task is to encircle and destroy, in conjunction with the 4th Army on the Western Front, the enemy east of the river Visla and on the 10th day of the operation reach the objective of the river Visla and develop the offensive in the following directions: towards Kielce, Piotrkow and Krakow.

The realisation of this plan is possible by means of an augmentation of the Kiev Special Military District by redeploying forces from the Odessa, North-Caucasus, Kharkov and Moscow Military Districts and the mobilisation of the Kiev Special Military District by drafting in transport and horses from the wider economy. For the period of the mobilisation and of the concentration of forces the plans for the provision of cover should be in motion, which envisaged the "Stubborn defence of the reinforcements along the state border and the stubborn support of forces from this district that have been mobilised, concentrated and deployed."

It should be noted that in contrast to the plan for the provision of cover for the Western Special Military District, which had deployed the most powerful formation in the district in the shape of the 6th Mechanised Corps in the area around Bialystok with the aim of manoeuvring in various directions radiating out from the Bialystok salient, the headquarters of the Kiev Special Military District approached the preparation of this plan with sufficient formality. Not one of the fully equipped mechanised formations in the district was sent forward to the 5th Army's zone. The 4th, 8th, 15th and 16th Mechanised Corps were congested in the area around Lvov and were separated from the 5th Army's zone by marshy terrain. This subsequently gave rise to specific problems in terms of inflicting counterattacks on the flank of the German tank spearhead, and the commanders of the 8th and 15th Mechanised Corps complained about the unfavourable conditions of the terrain in the directions in which the counterattacks were undertaken to the north of Lvov. Also a catastrophe waiting to happen had been written into the plan in the shape of the 3rd Cavalry Division, which, according to the plan, had been assigned a defence sector at the point where the Rava-Ruska and Strumilov fortified sectors joined. On the third day of mobilisation the division was to be replaced by the 159th Rifle Division, which in reality, and it is easy to see why, did not happen. It was into the 3rd Cavalry Division's zone that the German *XIV Motorised Corps* would break through in the closing stages of the Dubno battles. Put simply the district command were very formal in their approach to the development of a support plan, evidently relying on a sluggish and lacklustre initial period of the war.

In reality however events did not unfold in accordance with the scenario the Red Army had prepared at all. In contrast to the Polish campaign, when in the year leading up to the outbreak of war Poland was given ultimatum demands, no ultimata were proposed to the USSR. The USSR had no intention of breaking away as a European player in the search for a diplomatic solution, and Germany's complete silence in terms of diplomatic channels became a seriously disorientating development for the leadership of the Soviet Union. Forces were concentrated on the Soviet border under the cloak of a wave of disinformation. The intelligence data was contradicted and the realisation of the danger of war came far too late. The political decisions that launched the mobilisation and deployment mechanism were delayed. The measures that were put in place in June were not able to radically alter the environment and the Red Army saw in the war without having mobilised and without having deployed fully. The armies, corps, and divisions that were incorporated into the plans for the first operation were scattered across three echelons without any operational connection between them, each of which were thinly concentrated and poorly mobilised armies of the *Wehrmacht*.

The Mechanised Corps

The principal heroes of the battle that was lost in the first week were the mechanised corps. Before the war the mechanised formations of the Kiev Special Military District had come through all the twists and turns that the organisation of tank forces in the Red Army went through as a whole very well. By the outbreak of the Second World War the brigade represented the principle unit in the tank forces. Soviet tank brigades, as they were in 1939, could not be compared to their namesake formations in the period from 1941–1945. If there were 65 tanks in a brigade during the war the brigade of 1939 was a real monster consisting of 255 BT tanks and 10 chemical T-26s or 267 standard T-26s. Moreover they possessed very weak artillery forces (six 45mm weapons) and just a single motorised infantry battalion. Moreover the need for the latter was cast into doubt, as it was thought that without the special tracked armoured personnel carriers a motorised infantry unit would not be able to cope in a battlefield littered with shell craters. The Red Army mechanised corps in the 1930s were cut from the same cloth: they consisted of a tank brigade operating BT tanks, a tank brigade operating T-26 tanks (a mechanised corps made up solely of brigades operating BT tanks appeared later), a rifle brigade, and auxiliary units including a chemical (flame throwing) battalion. The capability of these mechanised corps to operate in isolation from infantry was very arbitrary.

At the time the Germans entered into the war their tanks forces had much more comprehensively organised structures. The tank divisions of the *Wehrmacht* had extensive artillery and a powerful mechanised infantry with a limited combat strength in terms of their tank fleet. This organisational structure already enabled them to operate independently and far from their infantry. The German *panzer* divisions strived boldly to penetrate the enemy's defences to some depth. When they encountered an organised defensive line, or even if they encountered reserves, they were able to engage them in combat confidently as well as taking and holding the terrain. This was truly a breakthrough in warfare. Now the classic encirclement operation could be conducted on a large scale, and the rapid advancement forwards after breaking through defences made it harder for those defending the front line to rebuild it.

In the Red Army the establishment of the new generation of tank formations began with the former Commander in Chief of the Kiev Special Military District Marshall S.K. Timoshenko taking up his post. At the end of May–beginning of June 1940 the Peoples' Commissariat for Defence and the head of the General Staff presented several variants of their proposals to the Politburo and to the Council of Peoples' Commissars. These variants proposed the formation of principally new mechanised formations—tank divisions. It was proposed that there should be two tank regiments in the line-up of a tank division, as well as a single artillery regiment, one motorised rifle regiment and one anti-aircraft artillery battalion. In the division in total there was to be 11,343 men, 386 tanks (this would consist of 105 heavy tanks, 227 medium tanks, and 54 chemical tanks), 108 armoured fighting vehicles, twelve 152mm howitzers, twelve 122mm howitzers, six 76mm field guns and twelve 37mm anti-aircraft guns. In the final variant of this reorganisation, which was confirmed by the Government, it was proposed that eight mechanised corps be formed, as well as 18 tank and eight motorised divisions. In the Kiev District two of the corps that were written into the programme for the reformation of tank forces were formed—the 4th and 8th. The formation of the 4th Mechanised Corps was delayed by the need to use its units to transport troops to Bukovina in June 1940, but by August 1940 all the mechanised corps had been formed. In the autumn of 1940 a further mechanised corps appeared in the Kiev Special Military District. On 14 October 1940 the Peoples' Commissariat for Defence and the Chief of the General Staff sent these same authorities a report No. org/1/106163ss/ov, which proposed the measures that were necessary for the augmentation of forces in the first half of 1941. Specifically it was proposed that another mechanised corps—the 9th—be formed in the Kiev Special Military District. This idea was implemented in a short space of time.

The formation of the mechanised corps in 1940 was a qualitative jump in the organisation of the tank forces of the Red Army. Now the Red Army had formations that were capable of; travelling dozens of kilometres into the interior from the point at which they broke through; transporting infantry in vehicles behind the tanks, as well as ammunition and fuel; destroying operational and strategic reserves independently; and manoeuvring around and encircling alignments of enemy forces. From the point of view of defence the Red Army received large formations that were capable over dozens of kilometres of eliminating a buckle in the enemy's tank spearheads by employing counterattacks. Moreover, in the Red Army the tank brigades that operated the BT and T-26 tanks, which were capable of being used to support infantry in both defence and attack, had been retained.

Anyone pursuing the leader in this field however, try as they might, would not be able to achieve this result in the space of a year or a year and a half, even if they had started a few years earlier. In relation to the German *panzer* forces the mechanised corps of the Red Army Air Force in 1940 nonetheless represented yesterday's forces. Firstly, on the basis of the experience of the first campaigns, the German *panzer* divisions were balanced and were set out in such a way that they were close to a more or less even number of *panzer* and motorised battalions. The Soviet motorised corps were overloaded with tanks to the detriment of the motorised infantry. Secondly, the technology that was in service, which was commandeered to form the mechanised corps (in the absence of an alternative), was created on the basis of solving simpler problems. The standard M-30 and M-10 howitzers in the mechanised corps were designed to be towed behind STZ-5 tractors. M.I. Potapov, as the commander of the 4th Mechanised Corps, in a speech at a meeting of the commanders of the Red Army in December 1940, said:

> A few words about artillery. The STZ-5 tractor is in service with our artillery, which forms part of the mechanised corps, and this vehicle is not able to keep pace with the tank units so we are not able to achieve cooperation. This tractor must be taken out of service with the mechanised corps and it needs to be replaced with a more powerful, all-terrain example.

M.G. Khatskilevich, the commander of the 6th Mechanised Corps, supported him in his poor assessment of the STZ-5. This tractor-transporter, which had been the dream of the artillerists in the rifle divisions, was poorly suited to mobile formations. The output of the engine in this tractor was just 50 h.p. and it conceded to a great extent to the specially manufactured half-track tractors in the German *panzer* divisions, which were fitted with engines rated at 100–140 h.p. Nevertheless an important step had been made in the building up of the tank forces which had met the requirements of the time.

In the winter of 1941 however, events unfolded that radically changed the face of tank forces in the Kiev Special Military District. Based on the results of the December 1940 meeting of the commanders, and the way the cards were stacked in January 1941, G.K. Zhukov became the new Chief of the General Staff. On 12 February the Peoples' Commissariat for Defence and the General Headquarters presented a new mobilisation plan to the Politburo of the Central Committee of the All-Union Communist Party (of Bolsheviks) and to the Council of Peoples' Commissars of the USSR, known as the MP-41. In accordance with this plan it was proposed that a peacetime army should have two motorised rifle, 60 tank and 30 motorised divisions available, as well as 30 mechanised corps directorates. This in fact entailed the creation of 20 new mechanised corps, which began between February–March 1941. By 8 March 1941 the Politburo had affirmed the appointments of the commanders of the newly formed mechanised corps, as well as the tank and motorised divisions.

Now the overwhelming majority of the tanks in the Red Army were to be amalgamated into mechanised corps with a standard combat strength of 1,031 tanks. This destroyed the diversity in terms of types of tanks in the tank forces of the Red Army. The formations and units designed to support infantry disappeared completely. Theoretically this put a greater number of tanks in the hands of the commanders when undertaking flexible combat operations. Experience in battle however, would not underpin this decision. In 1945, despite the presence of over 20,000 tanks and self-propelled artillery platforms, nobody attempted to create 30 tank armies. They numbered just six and the overwhelming mass of these tanks was distributed between the different types of formations and units, from the equivalents of tank divisions (the tank and mechanised corps) to the brigades and close infantry support regiments.

In the Kiev Special Military District, in addition to the existing formations, the 15th, 16th, 19th, 22nd, and 24th Mechanised Corps were formed. The formation of these new mechanised corps was conducted in an unusual manner, by multiplying the existing formations using simple division. Withdrawing the 15th Tank Division from the line-up of the 8th Mechanised Corps formed the basis for the newly formed 16th Mechanised Corps. Similarly the 10th Tank Division of the 4th Mechanised Corps from the first formation formed the core of the newly created 15th Mechanised Corps under Major-General I.I. Karpezo. The 9th Mechanised Corps, which had just been formed under Major-General K.K. Rokossovskiy did not escape a similar fate. His 19th Tank Division formed the basis for the 22nd Mechanised Corps (which was commanded by Major-General S.M. Kondrusev), which conformed to the standard for 1941. Admittedly to begin with the 9th Mechanised Corps did not stand out in terms of being especially well equipped. Correspondingly, new tank divisions were formed from scratch in the old mechanised corps in place of the divisions that had been withdrawn from their line-up to establish the new formations. In the 4th Mechanised Corps the 32nd Division was formed (which was commanded by Colonel E.G. Pushkin, this division was formed on the basis of the 30th Light Tank Brigade), while in the 8th the 34th Division was formed (commanded by Colonel I.V. Vasilyev, and which was formed on the basis of the 26th Light Tank Brigade operating T-26 tanks). The 35th Division was formed within the 9th (this division was commanded by Colonel N.A. Novikov). Not one of them was able to receive vehicles or tractors in sufficient numbers by the outbreak of war. In addition the 34th Tank Division, which was formed from a tank brigade and operated the slow T-26 tanks, received T-35 tanks, which were not known for their turn of speed, from the 12th Tank Division, which was equipped with T-34s and KV tanks, which meant its marching capacity deteriorated still further. In addition the well-equipped corps such as the 4th and 8th were lumbered with a slow-moving division, which presented specific problems when it came to cooperative manoeuvres. The 10th, 15th, and 19th Tank Divisions that had been withdrawn from the 4th, 8th, and 9th Mechanised Corps sustained another heavy blow in the shape of two poorly equipped formations: the newly formed tank and motorised divisions. Neither the 37th Tank Division, 15th Mechanised Corps (commanded by Colonel F.G. Anikushkin), nor the 39th Tank Division, 16th Mechanised Corps (commanded by Colonel N.V. Starkov), nor the 41st Tank Division, 22nd Mechanised Corps (commanded by Colonel P.P. Pavlov, and which had been formed from the 36th and 38th tank brigades that operated T-26 tanks) had received their required vehicles by the outbreak of war and were only nominally considered mobile formations. The motorised infantry in these regiments advanced on foot, just like standard infantry. They were like legless boxers with strong 'tanks' for fists but with minimal mobility. The situation in the new '200s' (they were all given a number higher than 200), that had been formed from scratch in the spring of 1941, was worse. These were motorised divisions in the newly formed mechanised corps. They did not receive any vehicles as the mechanised units did, but at the same time they lacked horses and wagons that a normal rifle division would be equipped with.

Thus the tank forces in the Kiev district saw in the month of June 1941 in a state of disorder and instability. The close support tanks were withdrawn from the rifle corps, and the corps formed in 1940 had fallen to pieces. If we were to compare the strength, in terms of total weight of the tanks, in the Kiev Special Military District and the *Panzergruppe 1,* and the number of serviceable instruments of war, the tanks together with the motorised divisions, then the picture that emerges is far from one in which the Red Army are overloaded with tanks. In the Kiev Special Military District there were six formations that could operate independently. These were the 8th Tank and the 81st Mechanised Divisions of the 4th Mechanised Corps, the 10th Tank Division of the 15th Mechanised Corps, the 12th Tank and 7th Motorised Divisions of the 8th Mechanised Corps, and the 15th Tank Division of the 16th Mechanised Corps. It was these divisions that were, albeit only in theory, equivalent to the German *panzer* divisions and were capable of conducting manoeuvres that are customary for mobile formations. The rest did not have the prerequisite number of vehicles for this purpose. In total four tank and two motorised divisions. This is wholly comparable with the number of mobile formations in the *SS 'Wiking' Motorised Division*. The motorised division could be considered comparable in a ratio of ½ to the motorised infantry brigade '*Leibstandarte Adolf Hitler*'. If we were to compare not the number of tanks that the opposing sides had but the organisational structures then the number of independent mechanised formations in the Kiev Special Military District and the *Panzergruppe 1* balance completely with one another.

The 4th Mechanised Corps

It makes sense to be on the stronger side in a battle. From the point of view of how well equipped the 4th Mechanised Corps was with new tanks this corps was the clear leader. It was subordinate to the 6th Army under I.N. Muzychenko and served in the Lvov salient, in the area around Lvov. The commander of the corps by the outbreak of war was A.A. Vlasov, who was later taken prisoner and became one of the organisers of the Russian Liberation Army. This fact has left its mark on an illumination of the combat activities of the 4th Mechanised Corps in June 1941. The corps is hardly mentioned although the presence of a large number of new tanks in its ranks was no secret. The degree to which the formations within the corps were equipped with materiel was characterised by the following figures (see table).

It is worth noting that the strength of the tank fleet as a whole is not the sum of the strength of the entire tank fleet in these formations, but also incorporates the corps units. For completeness the information was drawn from a number of sources.

The staffing levels are characterised by the following figures. The 8th Tank Division as of 1 June 1941 comprised 9,456 men; of whom 3,669 were privates in their first year of service; 2,887 were in their second year of service; while 22 were in their third year of service. The 32nd Tank Division as of 1 July 1941 comprised 9,189 men; of whom 6,270 were privates in their first year of service; and 1,367 were in their second year of service. The 81st Mechanised Division as of 1 June 1941 comprised 10,558 men; which included 3,484 privates in their first year of service; 4,483 men in their second year of service; and 28 in their third year of service. In terms of its qualitative composition the division drew men with the rank of private in their second year of service from a series of other divisions in large numbers.

Table 2.1 The availability of combat and auxiliary vehicles in the 4th Mechanised Corps as of 22 June 1941

	8th Tank Division[1]	32nd Tank Division[2]	81st Mechanised Division[3]	Total
KV	52(33 KV-2s)/50	20/49	–	72
T-34	140/140	22/173	–	242
T-28	72/68	–	–	72
BT-7	206/31	0/31	238	355
T-26	12/20	128/70	–	160
T-26 flamethrower	15/16	1/no data	–	18
T-27	35/60	38	–	98
BA-10	57/57	9/27	18	89
BA-20	52/34	10/17	25	81
FAI	5/5	–	–	5
Automobiles	1,205/1,246	52/417	1,094	2,864
Tractors	74/84	5/46	122	291
Motorcycles	136/177	80/94	140	1,050

Notes
1 The numerator is according to documents from the 6th Army and the Principal Automobile and Mechanised Tank Directorate dated 15 April and 1 May 1944, while the denominator is dated 22 June and is according to a report by the commander of the division based on the results of combat activity
2 The numerator is according to documents from the 6th Army and the Principal Automobile and Mechanised Tank Directorate dated 15 April and 1 May 1944, while the denominator is dated 22 June and is according to a report by the commander of the division based on the results of combat activity
3 According to documents from the 6th Army and the Principal Automobile and Mechanised Tank Directorate, dated 15 April and 1 May 1941.

Table 2.2 The availability of combat and auxiliary vehicles in the 8th Mechanised Corps as of 22 June 1941

	12th Tank Division[1]	34th Tank Division[2]	7th Motorised Division[3]	Corps as a whole[4]
KV	57/58	14/7 (+48 T–35s)	–	71 (+48 T–35s)
T-34	100/98	–	–	100
BT-7	128 (4 BT-7A)/83	23/26	85	242
BT-5	15/-	–	12	20
BT-2	6/(ftr).)/-	–	11	15
T-26	41/56	233/	–	290
T-26 flamethrower	20/-	30/	–	50
T-37–38–40	7 T-37/-	4/	19	40
BA-10	56/54	–	18	99
BA-20	28/25	13/ no data	29	75
BA-6	–	–	3	3
FAI	8/-	7/ no data	–	–
Automobiles	1,197/1,188	532/649	1,053	3,385
Tractors	89/70	24/ no data	165	312
Motorcycles	34/49	47/ no data	139	444

Notes
1 The numerator is taken from the Principal Automobile and Mechanised Tank Directorate data as of 1 May 1941, while the denominator is as of 22 June 1941 and is based on a divisional report on battle results.
2 The numerator is taken from the Principal Automobile and Mechanised Tank Directorate data as of 1 May 1941, while the denominator denotes the numbers that went into battle on 22 June 1941, according to a divisional report.
3 According to Principal Automobile and Mechanised Tank Directorate as of 1 May 1941.
4 As of 22 June 1941 according to a regimental report on the results of the air battles.

Table 2.3 The availability of combat and auxiliary vehicles in the 15th Mechanised Corps as of 22 June 1941

	10th Tank Division[1]	37th Tank Division[2]	212th Motorised Division[3]	Corps as a whole[4]
KB	63/63	–/1	–	64/64
T-34	20.37	–/34	–	20/69
BT-7	171/147	–/258	32	360/418
BT-2–5	–	–	–	–
T-28	45/44	–	–	55/44
T-26	15/19	22/22	5	50/45
T-26 Flamethrower	8/8	1/1	–	8/–
T-40	–	–	–	
BA-10	56/53	14/ no data	18	76/106
BA-20	31/19	10/ no data	2	42/46
BA-6	–	–	–	–
FAI	–	–	–	9/ no data
Automobiles	1,166/864	24/ no data	165	1,663/ no data
Tractors	73/ no data	10/ no data	47	155/ no data
Motorcycles	49/ no data	0/ no data	0	0/ no data

Notes

1 The numerator is based on Principal Automobile and Mechanised Tank Directorate data as of 1 May 1941, while the denominator on the divisional commander's report as of 22 June 1941.

2 The numerator is based on Principal Automobile and Mechanised Tank Directorate data as of 1 May 1941, while the denominator on the divisional commander's report as of 22 June 1941.

3 According to information from the Principal Automobile and Mechanised Tank Directorate datad 1 May 1941.

4 The numerator is based on Principal Automobile and Mechanised Tank Directorate data from a period between 25 April–1 May 1941, while the denominator is as of 22 June 1941, according to a corps commander's report on battle results.

The 8th Mechanised Corps was destined to become one of the most important and the most famous participants in the Dubno battles, which was due in no small measure to the widely known memoirs of the commander of the corps N.K. Popel *'At the Most Difficult Time'* a partial screen adaptation produced by N. Ozerov.

The 12th Tank Division on 1 June 1941 comprised 9,488 men; of whom 4,485 were privates in their first year of service; 2,171 were in their second year of service; and 20 men were in their third year of service.

The 34th Tank Division as of 1 June 1941 comprised 9,928 men; however there is no data available on their distribution according to length of service.

The 7th Motorised Division, as of 1 June 1941, comprised 10,511 men; of whom 5,487 were privates in their first year of service; 2,334 were in their second year of service; and 15 were in their third year of service.

The 15th Mechanised Corps, according to pre-war plans, was given the status of the district commander's reserve. In connection with this, from the first day of the war, one could even say from the very first hours of the war, this corps was commanded directly from the headquarters which had been transformed into the South-Western Front.

The 10th Tank Division, as of 1 June 1941, comprised 9,526 men; of whom 3,201 were privates in their first year of service; 3,510 were in their second year; while 20 men were in their third year of service.

The 37th Tank Division, as of 1 June 1941, comprised 9,148 men; of whom 6,329 were privates in their first year of service; 1,128 were in their second year of service; and 36 were in their third year of service.

The 212th Motorised Division, as of 1 June 1941, comprised 10,254 men; of whom 6,031 were privates in their first year of service; 2,284 were in their second year of service; and three were in their third year of service.

The composition of the other mechanised corps was not much different and, as such, the data concerning these corps can be amalgamated into a single table.

On the basis of the data that has been set out it is clear that the degree to which the mechanised corps that were formed in 1941 were equipped with their various vehicles was very low. As a result their manoeuvring characteristics were sufficiently constrained.

Table 2.4 The composition of the 22nd, 9th, and 19th Mechanised Corps in the Kiev Special Military District as of 1 June 1941

Division	Tanks							Artillery				Transport		
	KV	T-34	BT	T-26	Flame-thrower	Floating	Total	76mm guns	37mm guns	152mm howitzers	122mm howitzers	Vehicles	Tractors	M/cycles
Wartime establishments														
Tank Division	63	210	26	22	54	17	375	4	12	12	12	1,360	84	380
Mechanised Division	–	–	258	–	–		275	16	8	12	16	1,587	128	159
22nd Mechanised Corps														
41st TD	31[1]	–	–	342	41	1	415	4	4	4	12	682	15	–
19th TD	–	–	34[2]	122[3]	7		163	4	4	12	12	295	52	10
215th MD	–	–	129	–	–	–	129	8	4	8	24	405	62	–
9th Mechanised Corps														
20th TD	–	–	30	3	3	–	36	4	4	12	12	244	38	10
35th TD	–	–	–	141	1	–	142	–	4	4	6	188	7	–
131st MD	–	–	104	–	–	18	122	16	4	8	16	595	69	17
19th Mechanised Corps														
40th TD	–	–	–	19	–	139	158	–	4	4	8	157	5	–
43rd TD	5	2	–	230	–	–	237	4	4	12	12	630	15	18
213th MD	–	–	–	42	–	13	55	8	4	–	4	140	47	–

Notes
1 All KV-2s.
2 Six BT-7 battle tanks, six BT-7 radio-controlled tanks, 14 TB-5 battle tanks, three BT-5 radio-controlled tanks, five BT-2 tanks with a pair of DA machine guns (Central Archive of the Ministry of Defence, fund 3018, inventory. 1, file 11, p. 189).
3 47 single turret radio-controlled tanks, 75 single turret battle tanks.

Aside from the standard materiel, when thousands of different types were disseminated among the mechanised corps during the last wave, some exotic examples ended up in these formations. As all the available tanks in the Red Army were amalgamated into mechanised corps, so-called 'radio-controlled tanks' found their way into the 22nd Mechanised Corps. These were remote-controlled T-26 tanks. A group of radio-controlled tanks consisted of the 'control tank' and inherently the 'radio-controlled tank,' which was controlled by radio. These tanks were not distributed among the divisions in the 22nd Mechanised Corps, but were subordinated immediately to the corps headquarters as part of the 152nd Separate Tank Battalion. In total as of 22 June the battalion as a whole had: 28 T-26TU tanks, 28 T-26TTs and 17 T-26TS[1] tanks. A further six T-26TS tanks were listed under the corps headquarters. The T-26 was produced as a fuel tanker under this same designation of T-26TS.

Aviation

The Air Forces of the Kiev Special Military District, by the outbreak of war, consisted of 11 mixed aviation divisions which incorporated the following:

Twenty-four fighter aviation regiments, consisting of 1,166 aircraft (159 MiG-3s, 64 Yak-1s, 450 I-16s, and 493 I-153s);

Fifteen bomber aviation regiments consisting of 587 aircraft (68 Pe-2s, 23 Ar-2s, 49 Yak-2 and Yak-4s, 214 SBs, 114 Su-2s and 119 DB-3Fs);

Five ground-attack aviation divisions consisting of 197 aircraft (81 I-153s, 111 I-16bis and five Il-2s).

Apart from that there were two reconnaissance regiments that were subordinated directly to the district air force headquarters, these consisted of 53 aircraft (31 Yak-4s, and 22 SBs).

In total therefore the aviation within the district amounted to 2,003 aircraft. It is self-evident that the aviation fleet was relatively patchy. It included both unreliable and obsolete machines, as well as the newest aircraft designs. Ground-attack aviation consisted of I-153 and I-15bis biplanes that had been written off from fighter regiments. There were very few purpose built ground-attack aircraft and the pilots were just never able to assimilate these aircraft.

The commanders of the aviation divisions and aviation regiments in the Air Forces of the South-Western Front made very poor use of the winter of 1940–1941 to conduct combat training that included flying operations. As a result the vast majority of the young pilots had flown little and had not been trained in combat operations. A sufficiently short period of intense combat training between May–June 1941 did not ensure that they were prepared for armed combat.

During the re-equipping of the Air Force units in the Kiev Special Military District with new aircraft some of the old, better homogenised regiments (the 52nd Short-Range Bomber Aviation Regiment, the 48th Short-Range Bomber Aviation Regiment) did not have the required number of new aircraft types by the time combat operations had begun, while the old materiel had been withdrawn for the new formations. In practice this was expressed as follows: The 48th Bomber Aviation Regiment had 42 aircraft (34 Pe-2s, and eight SBs) and 67 pilots; the 52nd Bomber Aviation Regiment had 36 aircraft (15 Pe-2s and 21 SBs) and 60 pilots; and the 86th Bomber Aviation Regiment had 44 aircraft (nine Pe-2s and 35 SBs) and 66 pilots. Moreover, in the period that immediately preceded the war, the crews had not yet got to grips with the new aircraft. As a result the combat capability of what initially were close-knit regiments was reduced. In turn their old aircraft ended up in the hands of young pilots in the newly formed regiments who did not have sufficient training.

The situation with respect to the system of basing for the district's aviation forces was worse. In connection with the construction that had been rolled-out in 1941 of runways on airfields belonging to the Air Forces of the Kiev Special Military District, the majority of the border airfields were unsuitable for operations on 22 June. The aviation units did not have any reserve

1 State Archive of the Russian Federation, fund 229., Inventory 157, file. 7, volume. 2, p. 453.

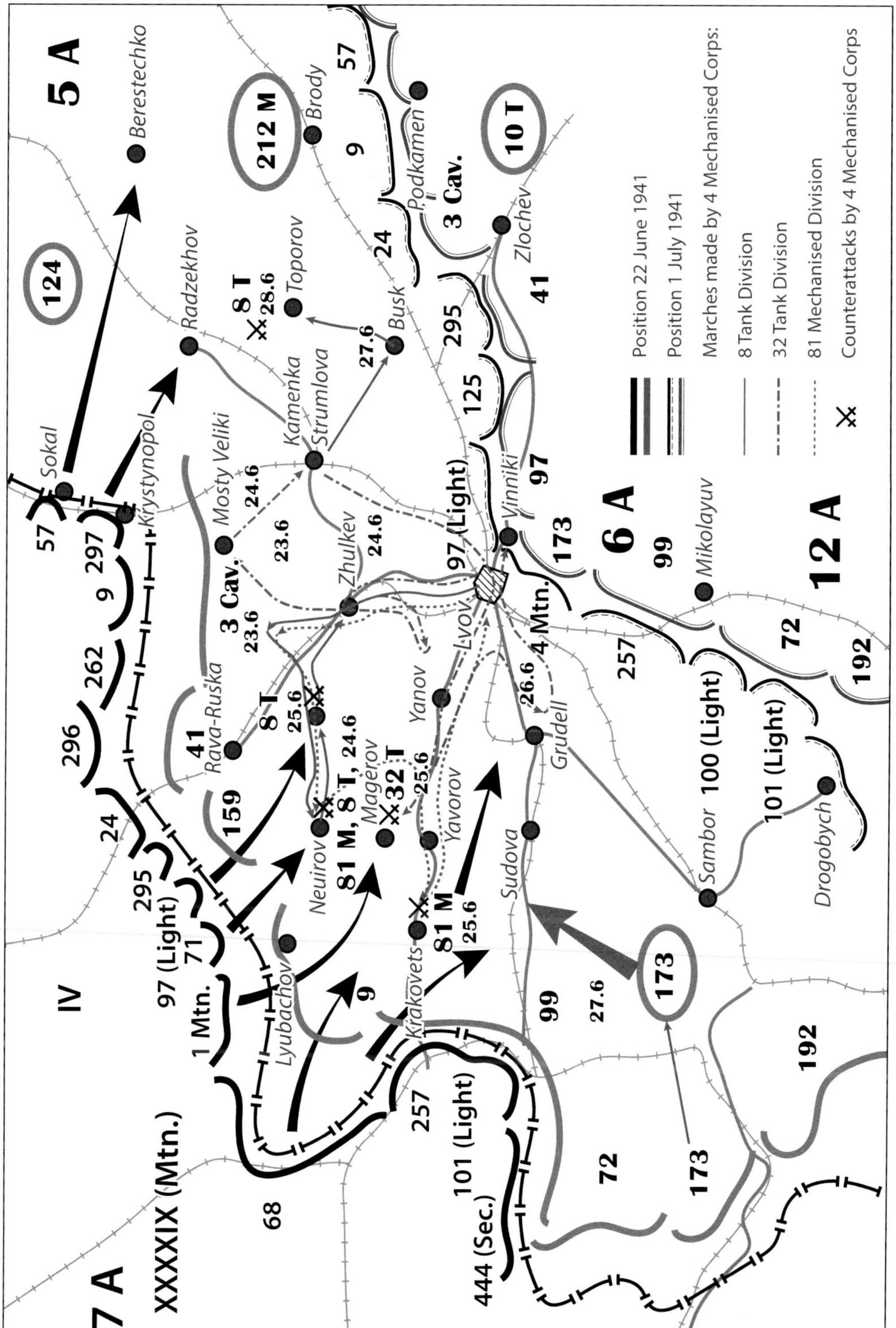

Map 1 The Lvov salient in June 1941.

airfields and were forced to remain at the airfields they had previously occupied even if this meant they were at risk of attack from the enemy.

Fortified sectors

One of the largest military construction projects of the period between 1940–1941 was the construction of fortifications along the new border which had been unofficially dubbed the 'Molotov Line' (see table). In the summer of 1940 the system of fortified sectors was introduced, which in terms of the number of fortifications did not concede to the 'Maginot line'. According to the plan the 'Molotov Line' was to have consisted of 5,807 structures. By way of a comparison the 'Maginot line' consisted of approximately 5,600 structures and the 'Stalin Line' was to consist of 3,187 structures, of which 3,279 were built. Moreover, on the new border more accomplished fortifications were constructed that had Bourge casemates for flanking fire, almost half of which were to have become artillery casemates. The combat characteristics of the structures themselves were incomparably higher. To compare the 'Stalin Line' fortifications with the 'pillboxes' of the 'Molotov Line' was like comparing a T-26 and a T-34. Only some of these ambitious intentions were destined to be realised however. Only around one fourth of these structures were ever built, and those that were built were not fitted with communications and neither were they camouflaged or masked with earth. In comparison with the other sectors of the 'Molotov Line' the fortified sectors in the Kiev Special Military District were at the best state of readiness both in terms of the number of combat capable structures and their overall readiness expressed as a percentage. The majority of the fortified sectors in the Kiev Special Military District ended up in the German invasion zone and had a decisive influence on how events unfolded in the first few days of the war.

Table 2.5 The fortified sectors of the 'Molotov Line' on the territory of the Kiev Special Military District

Name of the fortified sector	Front, km	Depth, km	The No. of defensive centres	The number of pillboxes			The number of Separate Machine-gun and Artillery Battalions[1]	
				In the course of constr.	Built	Combat capable	Depl. As part of the fortified sector	Proposed depl. As part of the fortified sector
Kovel	80	5–6	9	138	None[2]	–	2	–
Volodymyr-Volynskyi	60	5–6	7	141	97	97	4	2
Strumilovsk	45	5–6	5	180	84	84	4	1
Rava-Ruska	90	5–6	13	306	95	95	3	2
Peremyshl	120	4–5	7	186	99	99	2	1

Notes
1 The Russian acronym OPULAB denotes Separate Machine-Gun and Artillery Battalion'.
2 In the Korel fortified sector only the security zone (the forefield), which passed along the state border, was armed and consisted of 14 areas of battalion responsibility and a single separate company position.

The last days of peace

Up until the beginning of June the political environment gave no clues as to the intentions of the Germans. The intelligence at hand did not provide an intelligible answer as to the direction of German aspirations and a deathly silence reigned on the diplomatic arena. On 14 June 1941 the Soviet leadership prepared a foreign policy demarche, a '*TASS*' message was published in the newspaper *'Izvestiya'* in the coded language of the diplomatic service, calling for the Germans to engage in talks.

At the same time measures were taken to enhance the readiness of the army for war. The 'remote' rifle corps moved up towards the border. They were on the march from 18 June onwards and were approaching the following areas: the 31st Rifle Corps (consisting of the 200th, 193rd, and 195th Rifle Divisions) approached Karpilovka, Berezne and Kobylye: the 36th Rifle Corps (consisting of the 228th, 140th and 146th Rifle Divisions) approached Dubrovka, Labun and Staro-Konstantinov; the 37th Rifle Corps (the 141st, 80th and 139th Rifle Divisions) approached Yampil, Volochisk and Yaniv; the 55th Rifle Corps (consisting of the 169th, 130th and 189th Rifle Divisions) approached Nova Ushitsia, Shpykiv and Mohyliv-Podilskyi; the 49th Rifle Corps, consisting of two rifle divisions (the 190th and the 197th), were transported along the railway line to the Husiatyn region and Yarmolyntsi and the 199th Rifle Corps approached the area around Pohrebyshche (on foot). Out of these corps the formations of the 31st and 36th Corps were to participate directly in the Dubno battles. Rifle formations from the covering armies also moved up towards the border. In the course of 16–18 June the 45th and 62nd Rifle Divisions in the 5th Army were withdrawn from the firing ranges along with the 41st Rifle Division of the 6th Army and moved closer to the border. On 18 June a decree was received stating that the 135th Rifle Division of the 5th Army were to advance to Kivertsi camp (close to Lutsk) that had been left vacant following the departure of the 62nd Division. On 19 June an order was received for the creation of a South-Western Front directorate based on the Kiev Special Military District directorate and of its redeployment to Ternopil. On the evening of 20 June a district headquarters train departed for Ternopil, and on the following day a motorised column departed carrying the remaining materiel and personnel. Actually measures were taken that had been written into the plan for the provision of cover. The district's directorates were to have departed for Ternopil on the second day of mobilisation.

All these measures however were delayed. German command had already succeeded in concentrating their invasion forces on the district's borders. The final accord in the developing situation was a sapper from the *75th Infantry Division*, Alfred Liskow, who defected to the Soviet side on the evening of 21 June in the 5th Army zone. He informed us of the planned German attack on the morning of 22 June. M.A. Purkayev immediately informed G.K. Zhukov in Moscow about the defector. This information turned out to be the last straw. Up until this point from 1900 hrs onwards the Politburo had been listening to a sufficiently worrying report by the Military Attache Vorontsov, who had just returned from Berlin. Arriving at the meeting at 2050 hrs G.K. Zhukov added fuel to the fire with the news about Liskow.

The result of the meeting was Directive No. 1, which stated:

"In the course of 22–23 June 1941 a sudden invasion by the Germans is possible on the Leningrad Military District, Baltic Special Military District, the Western Special Military District, Kiev Special Military District, and the Odessa Military District fronts." Troops were ordered to "Be at full combat readiness to counter a possible sudden attack from the Germans or their allies."

This directive reached the districts themselves after midnight and then it began to be relayed to the armies. The need to encode this message delayed its passage out to the troops. The political leadership of the country decided not to put the plan to provide cover fully into action, banning any border crossings by land or by air. Thus, instead of a short order to put the plans into action, a relatively lengthy telegram was sent. In the 5th Army the commander was only informed of the text of the directive at 0230 hrs on the night of 22 June. Just after 0400 hrs M.I. Potapov called the divisional commanders in person and ordered them to alert the troops. There was very little time remaining to bring the troops that were located in the path of the main thrust of the German attack to a state of readiness.

The Commander of the Kiev Special Military District M.P. Kirponos (left) and the Member of the Military Council N.N. Vashutin (centre) attending exercises in the spring of 1941. Although neither of them knew it, they would only have a few months to live. Vashutin was shot and Kirponos was to perish during the withdrawal from the encirclement just outside Kiev in September 1941.

Another photograph of these same exercises in spring 1941.

The Commander of the Kiev Special Military District M.P. Kirponos. He was not an experienced military commander although he became a Hero of the Soviet Union during the course of the war with Finland, where he commanded a rifle division. In June 1941 he was given command of the most powerful formation in the Red Army, the Kiev District.

The Chief of Staff of the Kiev Special Military District M.A. Purkayev. As a sufficiently experienced staff officer he made up to some degree for the district commander's lack of experience.

The Commander of the 5th Army M.I. Potapov. He was a tank crewman by training and was a suitable figure to lead a tank battle. He was taken prisoner just outside Kiev and was released in 1945 (this photograph was taken after the war).

The Commander of the 6th Army I.N. Muzychenko. An energetic, and promising commander, he was taken prisoner just outside Uman in August 1941 (this photograph was taken after the war).

The Commander of the 15th Mechanised Corps I.I. Karpezo.

Two principal guns in the Soviet mechanised formations: the 122mm M-30 howitzer and the 152mm M-10, which were deployed in the area around Knyazhe-Lyatske.

An experimental example of the T-34 tank in 1940 (this photograph is taken from a factory collection). The creation of new tanks shortly before the war was a big step forward for the Red Army.

The BT-7M tank, forward elevation (this photograph is taken from a factory collection). The BT tanks had been the 'calling card' of the Soviet tank forces since the 1930s. Songs were sung about them and cinematic films made about them. By 1941 however their armour no longer met the requirements of the time.

The BT-7M tanks, viewed from above (this photograph is taken from a factory collection). The BT tanks with their diesel engines (such as the BT-7M) began to be produced shortly before the war and externally they could be recognised by a small diameter 'tablet' on the roof of the engine compartment. The two hatches on the turret are also visible, which in the open position made the tank look like the animated character 'Mickey Mouse'.

A BT-7M tank on wheels (this photograph is taken from a factory collection). Tracks have been laid upon the track shoulders. Formally the option to move on tracks was retained for the later series BT tanks, but in practice they were not used owing to the wear in the wheel rims.

The T-35 tanks on parade on 1 May 1941. This tank was produced between February–April 1939 with conical turrets. These five-turret giants personified the might of the Red Army although their practical value by the outbreak of war was sufficiently questionable.

A T-35 tank abandoned on 29 June 1941 in Lvov on *Ulitsa Zheleznodorozhnikov*, next to the Kiev District repair base, with engine failure. This particular tank was subsequently repaired and sent to the Kummersdorf range outside Berlin by the Germans.

A T-34 tank of the 4th Mechanised Corps, which has been abandoned on a street in Lvov. Note the gearbox with the steering clutch plates, which have been attached to the engine compartment hatch—the tank crews carried a repair kit with them.

A flight of MiG-3s from the 15th Aviation Division in flight. Soviet pilots in 1941 still used an obsolete formation of three aircraft. The transfer to pairs of aircraft would take place on the basis of the experience gained after the initial battles.

Another photo of this same T-35 tank in Lvov. This machine was manufactured in 1936 and was overhauled in 1939. The tank's engine access hatch is open.

The Commander of the 41st Tank Division P.P. Pavlov (in a photo taken after the war). He was under investigation on account of the heavy losses his division had incurred, but he returned to his unit. He was taken prisoner in 1943 just outside Kharkov.

3

The Longest Day

At 0330 hrs, along the entire length of the border from the Baltic to the Black Sea, artillery began to thunder and the sky was filled with the rumble of aircraft engines. German artillery and aviation had begun to prepare for the attack. To the accompaniment of this noise German special-forces captured the bridges across the Bug river. All the army groups were assigned separate companies from the 800th '*Brandenburg*' regiment, which it was intended would conduct special operations. Many of these operations were conducted by officers and men who had changed into Soviet uniforms and were armed with Soviet weapons. The advent of such unusual characters was noted in the first report written by the political propaganda directorate of the Kiev Special Military District. They were dubbed "sabotage groups that had changed into our uniforms". The '*Brandenburgers*' captured a road bridge in Ustyluh and a railway bridge in Vygodanka (this was located 13km south-west of Ustyluh). There is nothing extraordinary in the fact of the capture of the bridge by the '*Brandenburgers*' at all. Similar special operations were conducted in 1941 and in 1942. The capture of these border bridges was the first, and unfortunately, far from the last success achieved by the '800th Training Regiment' on the Eastern front. On the first day of the war the success of the '*Brandenburgers*' was brought about by the change from a period of peace to one of war.

Sabotage groups who had changed into Soviet uniforms were not employed to capture the bridge across the Bug river on the central '*Panzerstrasse*'. At least they are not mentioned in a very detailed report written by the *51st Sapper Assault Battalion*. The bridge was captured exclusively by virtue of the suddenness of the attack:

> Following the artillery attack at 0315 hrs an attack group from the 3rd Platoon, commanded by *Feldwebel* Putticher, rapidly broke through the barbed wire fences, reached the far side of the bridge and severed all the cables that were in place. The two Russian customs officials standing at the end of the bridge were shot by individuals who had been specially assigned this task at the very start of the attack.[1]

Evidently by 'customs officials' the author means 'border guards'.

Somehow or other the bridges at the foot of both '*Panzerstrasse*' were captured. Tanks however were not the first to cross them but the assault guns belonging to the infantry divisions. The tanks were only to get going after a significant breach had been made in the Soviet defences. An attack on the forward positions was successful. Oskar Munzel, the author of the book '*Panzer-Taktik*' describes the first few minutes of the war with eloquence:

> The powerful artillery fire from heavy armament was tearing through the patches of mist. At intervals shells would be heard ringing out beyond the Bug River. At 0315 hrs the infantry began their offensive. This came as a complete surprise to the enemy and they put up almost

1 NARA T314R1138 f754.

> no resistance. The important bridge at Sokal has not been destroyed and has ended up in the hands of the advancing units. The fording of the River Bug is progressing flawlessly. The infantry are climbing up the eastern bank of the River Bug and are taking the unfinished enemy positions with ease from an adversary taken completely by surprise. Their artillery is firing intermittently, without inflicting any damage.[2]

The German infantry were to encounter much more serious problems after they had taken the foreshore and moved 2km inland up to the main boundary of the 'Molotov Line'. The pace of the forward advance was suddenly and significantly reduced. Overcoming the fortifications in the path of the *57th Infantry Division*'s attack was only made possible thanks to the assault operations carried out by the *51st Sapper Battalion* that had been attached to the infantry division. The attack weapons turned out not to be very effective. In a report written by a sapper battalion (for the full report see the appendices) it was stated:

> Thanks to the distribution of the fortifications, which to our surprise turned out to be outstandingly skilful, there was a possibility of joint covering fire from the pillboxes which would make an attack much more difficult. The bombardment of the pillboxes and gun ports using assault weaponry had proved almost useless thanks to the high quality concrete and the low positioning of the gun ports with their powerful, spherical screens. Under covering fire from assault weaponry the 1st Strike Platoon was able to approach one of the pillboxes and, first and foremost, to take the armoured canopy out of action using 6kg of explosives. Since the enemy put up a determined resistance, and was supported with effective covering fire from the other fortifications, only after a battle lasting two hours and predominantly by using explosives was it possible to take the gun ports out of action and to suppress the resistance at the entrance to the bunker in a swift attack.[3]

During subsequent attacks, which were undertaken with a high degree of professionalism, the *51st Assault Battalion* succeeded in opening up a road ahead for the infantry. As they had been denied such support the *75th Infantry Division* were held by fire from the pillboxes on the 'Molotov Line' despite the artillery support including up to 21cm mortars. In a report to the headquarters of the *Panzergruppe 1* the *75th Infantry Division*'s losses were assessed as "heavy". Specifically eight officers were lost and the number of men injured reached 170. Moreover, the achievements were more than modest. Correspondingly the *57th Infantry Division*'s losses amounted to 36 killed and 120 injured.[4]

A confident assertion can be made that if it had been any other army, rather than the *Wehrmacht,* on 22 June 1941 the fortifications on the 'Molotov Line' would have proved an impenetrable barrier despite the absence of infantry support. Correspondingly these fortifications also proved to be a 'tough nut to crack' for the Red Army.

Resistance in the border fortifications enabled a certain amount of time to be gained to deploy the rifle formations in the 5th Army to positions along the border. Early in the morning the regiments in the divisions under the 27th and 15th Rifle Corps were alerted and began to move up to the border. Before they had reached them, at a distance of 10–15km, they encountered German forward as well as *aufklärung* units, and between 1100–1130 hrs they engaged in a head-on battle

2 O. Munzel, Panzer-Taktik. Raids gepanzerter Verbaende im Ostfeldzug 1941–1942 (Neckargemuend: Kurt-Vowinckel Verlag. 1959), p.16.
3 NARA T314 R1138 f756.
4 NARA T313 r4 f594.

in several directions in the absence of a continuous front line. The 87th Rifle Division turned out to be in the most successful position in terms of the actual situation at hand. The regiments in this formation moved towards Volodymyr-Volynskyi that had been attacked by the infantry belonging to the German *III Motorised Corps* and engaged them in combat in close formation. In response to an order given by the Commander in Chief of the 5th Army, M.I. Potapov, two tank battalions from the 41st Tank Division were attached to these divisions. This meant that in the first few hours of the war there was in fact a rejection of the pre-war idea of liquidating tanks with the support of infantry—the divisions in the mechanised corps that had been formed in the spring of 1941 began to be torn apart at battalion level so that they could be attached to rifle formations. The T-26 tanks in the 41st Tank Division were tasked with the very same missions that would need to be undertaken as part of the tank brigades, from which correspondingly the divisions were formed. The commander of the 87th Rifle Division, General Alyabushev, decided to perform a counterattack on a German bridgehead at Ustyluh (west of Volodymyr-Volynskyi) and in doing so prevent the capture of the town and the development of the advance along the road. The division attacked using two regiments, leaving a third in reserve to cover the flank, since there was no cover on the formation's left flank. The two T-26 tank battalions were attached to the 96th Rifle Division. The enemy of F.F. Alyabushev's division was the *298th Infantry Division*. As a result of the battle the 87th Rifle Division was able to press the enemy into an area 6–10km to the west of Volodymyr-Volynskyi.

The second Soviet division to find itself in the attack zone of the *XXXXVIII Motorised Corps* also fell into this self-same trap. The 124th Rifle Division, led by F.G. Sushchiy, was alerted and, just like their brethren, they themselves began to move from the Baltic to the Carpathians. By 0900 hrs the division's 622nd Rifle Regiment had engaged spearhead units of the *111th Infantry Division*. A short time later three regiments from this division engaged advancing German infantry divisions in combat, each regiment would take one of them on. The trump card for the 124th Division was the 21st Corps Artillery Regiment in the 27th Corps, which was equipped with twenty 122mm A-19 guns and forty-eight 152mm ML-20 gun-howitzers.

In contrast, however, to the divisions led by F.F. Alyabushev the formation led by F.G. Sushchiy moved towards the border and engaged the enemy in battle some way from a principal transport artery. However, the road that led out of Sokal to the east became an axis for attacks by German *panzers*. Despite the fact that at 0500 hrs the battle for the pillboxes on the 'Molotov Line' was at its height, the commander of the *XXXXVIII Motorised Corps*, Werner Kempf, at this same time raised the question of using the *11th Panzer Division*. Kempf was of the opinion that the time had come to take this division into battle and, taking advantage of the specific confusion among the Soviet forces, to break through to a point deep behind their defences.

The Chief of Staff of the corps immediately turned to the head of the operations department of the *Panzergruppe 1*, informing him of Kempf's intentions to draw the *11th Panzer Division* nearer to the River Bug. He had an unwelcome surprise in store: it turned out that Kleist had reserved the right to take the decision to use the only *panzer* division in the *XXXXVIII Corps*. In his order for the *panzer* group to attack, dated 18 June 1941, this had not been made clear and the corps command only knew of this on the morning of 22 June when the guns were already rumbling. In fact Kempf was told that he was the commander of the motorised corps consisting of two infantry divisions and handsomely reinforced with artillery. Kleist was not just playing it safe. The *panzer* group command were convinced of the existence of a second Russian defensive front line, that is to say the Germans only had a sketchy idea of the Soviet defensive system in the zone of their advance. Correspondingly, according to Kleist, *panzer* divisions should not incur losses during the course of breaking through a second fortified line. In connection with this Kempf was flatly denied the use of the *11th Panzer Division*.

At the same time events in general were developing in a way that did not confirm the presence of a second defensive front. Kempf again asked the headquarters of the *Panzer* group permission to use a motorised corps, albeit just one mobile formation. He was only given the corresponding permission at 1122 hrs. Close to midday the order reached the commander of the *11th Panzer Division*. Kempf had set Crüwell a highly ambitious task—"to take the river crossings across the Styr at Szczurowjce and Berestechko." This entailed an immediate breakthrough deep behind enemy lines. The first problems they would encounter would be predictable and unavoidable despite all the measures that were taken. The combat journal for the *XXXXVIII Corps* records a note as follows: "We are encountering serious delays, since the infantry divisions, despite strict orders, continue to use the highway and are blocking the road." Despite the hard won concept of the '*Panzerstrasse*' freeing up the roads at the appropriate time was turning out to be no trivial matter.

Having received a single *panzer* division, and pushed it forward, Werner Kempf was trying to force another mobile formation to join the battle on a parallel route via Krystynopol in the zone of the neighbouring *XXXXIV Corps*. The bridge across the Bug River at Krystynopol was captured without being damaged and, despite shelling of the road from the pillboxes that remained combat capable, it was still feasible that this bridge could be used. Kempf however received a categorical denial and he was promised that he would be given another *panzer* division "only when the corps has advanced to a sufficient distance."

Kleist's policy surrounding the *panzer* formations joining the battle after the infantry had advanced to a sufficient distance was a universal one in terms of the advance along the northern and central '*Panzerstrasse*'. Almost in synch with the *11th Panzer Division* outside Sokal at 1300 hrs on 22 June the *14th Panzer Division*, belonging to the corps led by E. von Mackensen, crossed the river at Ustyluh. The advent of this division dramatically altered the balance of forces in the battle in Volodymyr-Volynskyi. Apart from that, the overall unfavourable environment surrounding the way the covering army entered the battle developed in its own way. Having concentrated efforts against the axis of the German attack around the highway that runs between Volodymyr-Volynskyi, at the same time the commander of the 87th Division left a more than 20km stretch without protection from their neighbour on their left flank, the 124th Rifle Division. In this period of time the 44th and 299th Infantry Divisions had forded the River Bug and engaged the pillbox installations in combat. If for the 44th Division, that was formed in Austria, the pillboxes were a 'hard nut to crack' (the battles with these pillboxes were described by the formations in the combat journal of Army Group 'South' that evening as "local failures") then the second division had overcome them successfully and, by the evening of 22 June, had advanced a further 10–15km to the south-west of Volodymyr-Volynskyi. In doing so the 87th Rifle Division was considerably outflanked on its left hand side.

The commander of the 6th Army, I.N. Muzychenko, made active use of the aviation that had been subordinated under his control to provide intelligence on the environment. The advent of large-scale enemy forces close to Sokal, and their penetration in an easterly direction, could not fail to be a cause for concern for the commander of the 6th Army. At 1500 hrs the headquarters of the 6th Army ordered the 4th Mechanised Corps to allocate two battalions of medium tanks from the 32nd Tank Division and a single battalion of motorised infantry from the 81st Mechanised Division to destroy the enemy in the area around Radzekhov. In fact this was a signal for heavy-duty reconnaissance with the aim of clarifying the situation on the Army's right flank. The group was led by Lieutenant-Colonel Lysenko (commander of the 323rd Motorised Infantry Regiment, 81st Mechanised Division). A forward detachment of this nature was also sent out on the morning of 22 June from the 15th Mechanised Corps. It consisted of the 3rd Tank Battalion, 20th Tank Regiment, 10th Tank Division, augmented by the 2nd Battalion, 10th Motorised Rifle Regiment from this same division. At 0950 hrs the detachment left Zolochiv with the aim of liquidating the

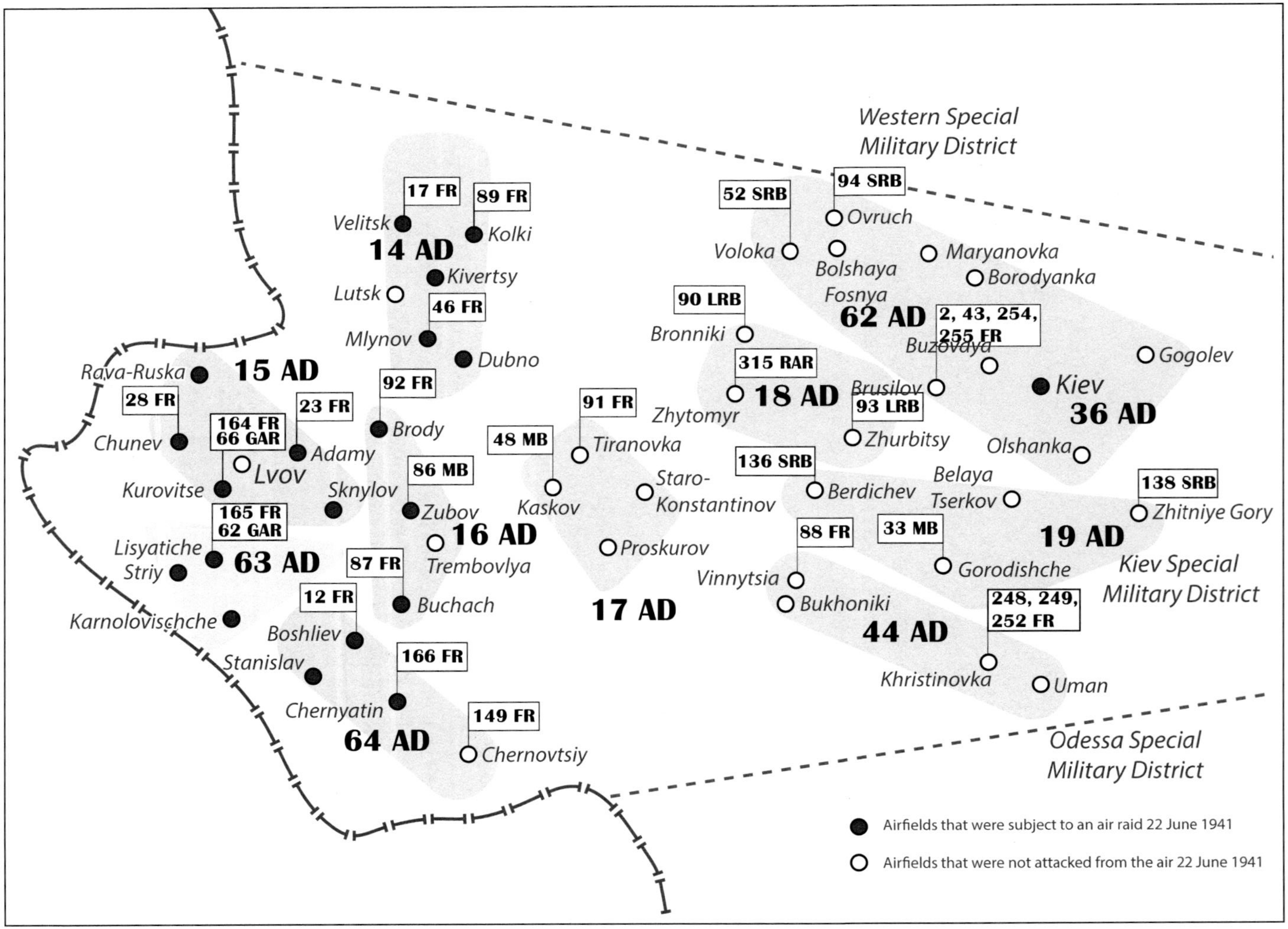

Map 2 The system of bases for the Air Forces of the Kiev Special Military District 22 June 1941.

German airborne paratroopers in the area around Radzekhov (first and foremost at least, the pilots of a downed German bomber that had bailed out by parachute). Thus two detachments that were small, but which were equipped with the latest tanks, were sent to the area around Radzekhov from the mechanised units on the South-Western Front.

As the head of the operations department of the South-Western Front recalled:

> At 1500 hrs we were supposed to send my first report to Moscow. It was me who composed this report. It was probably the most difficult report in my entire career at headquarters. The environment remained unclear as before: the army's true position, where the main thrust of the enemy's strike was likely to fall, and what his plans were—all this could only be guessed at. Our first combat report to Moscow was full of general locations and ambiguities.[5]

Certainly the "Conclusions" to the first intelligence report from the South-Western Front did not appear daunting at all:

1. The enemy has crossed the state border on the front line at Wlodawa, Peremyshl and Lipcani and Vikoverhnya (10km north-west of Radauti), their forces consisted of:
   Four to five infantry divisions and tank divisions in the direction of Lutsk;
   Three to four infantry divisions with tanks in the Rava-Ruska–Lvov directions;
   Two to three infantry divisions in the Peremyshl–Lvov direction;
   Four Romanian infantry divisions in the Chernovitsk directions.[6]

Clearly the German forces had been underestimated. The invading forces advancing in the principal directions—where the 5th and 6th Armies joined—did not differ in the intelligence report from those active in an auxiliary direction.

However, aside from the reporting from the forces themselves, the command of the special military district, which had become the front line, had a powerful tool that was able to enlighten them as to the combat environment in the shape of aerial reconnaissance. Aside from countering the enemy's strikes the aircraft belonging to the aviation divisions also flew reconnaissance flights. Specifically it was the MiG-3s of the 28th Aviation Regiment that flew to the border on reconnaissance missions. High-speed fighters were able to conduct reconnaissance almost without worrying about a response from enemy aviation. Having received the first reports from the troops, together with the data from aerial reconnaissance Kirponos and Purkayev were faced with the question of "What to do next?" Against a backdrop of a dense and dispiriting 'fog of war' decisions had to be taken to ensure that the next question was not "Who is responsible?" The most important tool in the hands of command, which enabled them to have an influence on the situation, was always the reserves. It cannot be said that the front headquarters had a broad choice, the 'remote' rifle divisions, which had begun to advance prior to the outbreak of war, were still some distance from the border. Thus, the 228th Rifle Division, 36th Corps, which was right on the axis of the German advance from the Sokal salient, were at a site close to Shepetovka, that is to say 200km from the border on the morning of 22 June. The resistance however that could be thrown at a cunning enemy, without breaking stride, was already there on the front line. The reserve, which was directly subordinate to South-Western Front command, consisted of the 15th Mechanised Corps led by I.I. Karpezo.

5 I.Kh. Bagramyan, *How the War Started*, p.93.
6 Anon., *A Collection of Combat Documents from the Great Patriotic War* Issue No. 36, pp.9–10.

In the first half of the day the mechanised corps completed the tasks that had been prepared for them prior to the outbreak of war. Early on the morning of 22 June an alert was sounded in the corps. A package containing a directive from the Kiev Special Military District was opened, this was directive No. 0013 dated 31 May 1941. The divisions, in accordance with this directive, began to depart for their assembly areas. The author was not able to find directive No. 0013, however the contents of directive No. 0015, dated 31 May 1941 (which to be precise was a private military order from the headquarters of the Kiev Special Military District bearing this number), to the 37th Tank Division within the corps led by General Karpezo, is known. Put simply this was the so-called 'red package' that was opened by the divisional commander on the morning of the first day of the war. The package, which had been typed by I.Kh. Bagramyan, fitted on just one sheet of paper. In essence the tasks put before the division consisted of the following:

1. In order to cover the mobilisation, concentration and deployment of forces belonging to the Kiev Special Military District, the border units were tasked with stubbornly defending the state border and preventing an enemy incursion onto district territory.
2. The 15th Mechanised Corps, along with the 1st Tank Brigade from the Kiev Special military District's reserves, was to concentrate by 2400 hrs (Moscow time minus one hour) in the area around Sokolivka, Zlochev and Brody.[7]

Clarification was provided subsequently regarding the routes, camouflage and artillery cover for these movements. The departure of the 15th Mechanised Corps to an approximate demarcation line between the 5th and 6th Armies did not preclude its use in any way with the aim of stabilising the front occupied by M.I. Potapov's armies. Correspondingly, at around 1700 hrs in the evening of 22 June, the 15th Mechanised Corps was tasked, along with the 4th Mechanised Corps, to attack enemy tank units around Radzekhov. Since in real terms it was only the 10th Tank Division which possessed a satisfactory degree of mobility that could be concentrated in that area to enact a counterattack at 1800 hrs on 22 June, it was this division that fulfilled I.I. Karpezo's order to attack from the area where they had been concentrated to the north-west and approach the area around Radzekhov.

Aside from their reserve, to which Kirponos had direct access, the commanders of the front could make use of mechanised corps that were subordinate to the army. Front headquarters were not planning to put their 'Hashirajima fleet' (as the Japanese dubbed the super-battleships 'Yamato' and 'Musashi' since they spent almost the entire war at their base) into action and put their trump cards in the shape of the best-equipped mechanised formations on the table without lifting a finger. Correspondingly the 4th Mechanised Corps were given an order via the commander of the 6th Army. In the order, which was signed by M.A. Purkayev, it stated: "The commanders of the front have ordered the commander of the 6th Army, using units from the 4th Mechanised Corps from the Zolkievka region, to launch a major counterattack and destroy the enemy, in conjunction with a detachment from the 15th Mechanised Corps, that had been tasked with destroying enemy paratroopers in Radzekhov."[8]

Furthermore the 8th Mechanised Corps, under D.I. Ryabishev from the 26th Army's line-up, was transferred to Muzychenko, the commander of the 6th Army. The operations report written by the headquarters of the front set out its intentions in plain text: "The group is to move towards the area around Kurovice, Vynnyky, Boryniche, in preparation for a counterattack on the enemy mechanised units discovered in the area around Sokal." In fact Ryabishev received this order at

7 State Archive of the Russian Federation, fund 229, inventory 157, file 7, volume 1, p. 255.
8 A Collection of Combat Documents from the Great Patriotic War, Issue No. 36, p.10.

2040 hrs on 22 June, that is to say a little later than the other commanders in the mechanised corps.

Actually the commanders of the South-Western Front set the objective with a certain pre-emption. If the enemy were to attack in the direction of Radzekhov then by the time the mechanised corps had been concentrated for a counterattack the enemy would already be there. In exactly the same way a gunner firing at a moving target would not attempt to take aim at a constantly moving silhouette, but would aim his weapon at a calculated distance ahead of the target. In general the concise, and very specific, instructions given by the commanders of the front cannot be ignored. The vigorous gathering of mechanised corps that were destined for the enemy alignment around Sokal, long before the arrival of Zhukov, leaves a particularly strong impression. That is to say Kirponos and Purkayev acted without 'prompting' from below. The true authorship of the idea to concentrate three mechanised corps at once against the enemy advancing via Sokal will probably never be known. The signature of Purkayev under the order addressed to the 6th Army (and which was redirected to the 4th Mechanised Corps) does provide an indirect indication. This, however, refers to the instructions from the commander of the front, although this order does have the appearance of having been prepared by Purkayev himself with the tacit approval of M.P. Kirponos.

Unfortunately, the memoirs of I.Kh. Bagramyan, who was the only one who witnessed the actions of the headquarters of the South-Western Front in the first few weeks of the war to write his memoirs, in this case have almost no value as a historical source. He vividly illustrates the discussions in the headquarters on the front line following the receipt of Directive No. 3. However Ivan Khristoforovich does not mention one word about the decisions that were taken between 1500 hrs and 1700 hrs, that is to say long before Directive No. 3. It was these decisions that reached the troops up until the end of the day on 22 June and which were the key to subsequent events. This creates the impression that the commanders of the front sat around all day resting their head on their cheek waiting for the Moscow leadership to give them the fruit of their thinking. Only when the mists had begun to lift did the lifeblood of that fruit finally begin to flow from the Baudot machine as a telegraph roll, the commander and his headquarters had begun their brainstorming. This evidently was not how it happened and there is very visible documentary evidence of this. It is probably the case that what is lacking is the dynamics of the decision-making that remains in the memory of the people and which is rarely reflected in the documents. The memoirs of the head of the operational department of the front line headquarters provide us with only circumstantial data concerning the events of 22 June. If Bagramyan describes the alignment of forces in the front line headquarters correctly, then it was M.A. Purkayev himself who was the most experienced and authoritative figure and it was his opinion that was heeded. Correspondingly a concise assessment of the enemy and a lightning reaction to it would, first and foremost, be a figment of his own imagination.

It is also interesting to note that in an intelligence report from the front line headquarters, which was prepared in the middle of the day on 22 June (at around 1500 hrs), the enemy alignment around Sokal, that is to say the *XXXXVIII Motorised Corps*, had yet to be considered a serious threat. However, the assessment of the enemy changed shortly after and tanks and columns of vehicles belonging to mechanised formations were discovered in the forces advancing in this direction. Tanks and mechanised infantry entailed a strike deep into the interior. Soviet command was as familiar with the condition of the road network as their opponents in the headquarters of Army Group South. The highways leading from Sokal and Krystynopol to Radzekhov and onwards to the east were very suitable as axes for the advance of mechanised formations. In accordance with this thinking three mechanised corps were in the process of being deployed to Sokal. Strictly speaking this brought about a change in the position of the enemy camp. As is evident above, German *panzer* divisions only joined the battle in the middle of the day. Taking into account the delays in the dissemination of data from aerial reconnaissance, as well as reports from forward units, this gives us a time of 1500 hrs as the decisive moment in this decision making process. The topic of Sokal featured heavily in the evening operations report: "The 8th Mechanised Corps (control of which had been transferred from the 26th Army to the 6th Army) was, by the morning of 23 June 1941, moving towards the area around Kurovice, Vynnyky and Boryniche in preparation for a counterattack against the mechanised units discovered in the area around Sokal."[9]

Following an accurate assessment of the environment, and after the correct decisions had been made, these same judgements needed to be quelled. Despite the popular opinion that fear had permeated the Red Army following the repression of 1937–1938, with orders being carried out without question, the actual situation was not so favourable. It was possible that fear was there in certain tactical echelons (which manifested itself on popular public holidays), but in general a direct and unambiguous order from the leadership could simply be ignored. This was exactly how the situation looked in the front line headquarters concerning the counterattack that was to be conducted by the 4th Mechanised Corps.

The commanders of the front line tasked the 4th Mechanised Corps with the counterattack against the enemy's Sokal alignment while the commander of the 6th Army, Muzychenko, considered the situation that was unfolding on his left flank outside Radmyno (close to Peremyshl), at the point where his army met the 26th Army, as very serious. Correspondingly by 1800 hrs on 22 June the commander of the 4th Mechanised Corps, A.A. Vlasov, was steering his division in this direction: "The 4th Mechanised Corps is preparing to attack in the direction of Krakowets and Radymno, with the aim of destroying the enemy which have broken through in the area around Dunkovytsa." This location, Dunkovytsa, was a settlement on the road between Yavorov and Radymno. The order that came from line headquarters was immediately assigned a low priority and in total two tank battalions set off for Radzekhov, under orders from Vlasov, consisting of two battalions of tanks from the 32nd Tank Division and a battalion of mechanised infantry from the 81st Mechanised Division. This detachment had already been despatched prior to this and Muzychenko made no attempt to augment it. As a result of this the plan proposed by front line command, to use the 4th Mechanised Corps solely against the enemy breakthrough in the area around Sokal, was buried before it had been given a chance of getting off the ground. It has to be said that I.N. Muzychenko was actually right in his own way. His rifle divisions were scattered along the front line and the attacks by German infantry divisions caused crises here and there and, in the end, the tanks in the corps led by A.A. Vlasov were deployed as a kind of 'fire brigade'.

Aside from the commanders that were in charge of the armies there was the Supreme Command that were able to take decisions based on the intelligence reports sent in the middle of the day. The decisions taken in Moscow began to be cascaded downwards. The reader should be reminded that the intelligence reports sent to Moscow from the front line headquarters seriously underestimated the enemy. The strength of the attack from the Sokal salient was three times less than it actually was; instead of three infantry divisions only one was mentioned. The advent of the *11th Panzer Division* had gone unnoticed by aerial reconnaissance. Only the advent of the 14th Panzer Division was discovered close to Ustyluh. As a response to such a serene picture of the events that were unfolding in the evening of 22 June Directive No. 3 was issued by Moscow. This Directive was sent from Moscow at 2115 hrs. According to Bagramyan's memoirs it was received at front headquarters after 1000 hrs in the evening. It stated that the "Enemy [...] has inflicted heavy losses and achieved moderate successes" and ordered the launch of a decisive offensive. The tasks that armies of the South-Western Front were set in this document, which was to gain a scandalous notoriety, were formulated as follows:

9 A Collection of Combat Documents from the Great Patriotic War, Issue No. 36, p.12.

c) The armies of the South-Western Front, which were stubbornly holding the line of the state border with Hungary, are to surround and destroy the enemy alignment that is advancing on the front line around Volodymyr-Volynskyi using concentric attacks in the general direction of Lublin employing the forces of the 5th and 6th armies not less than five mechanised corps, and all the front line aviation resources, and are to take the area around Lublin by the end of the day on 26 June. The forces are to ensure their own steadfast protection from the direction of Krakow.[10]

To us today the text of this directive looks absurd. Why refer to Lublin when the German forces, with such a huge numerical advantage, were pulverising the border divisions? If the question is asked: 'Did Directive No. 3 correspond to the situation that was unfolding on the borders?' then the answer would be unanimous—no it did not. If the question is put differently however: 'Did Directive No. 3 correspond to the daily reports issued by the districts?' then the answer would be positive. One cannot fail to agree with the head of the front line operational department I.Kh. Bagramyan: "Involuntarily it crossed my mind that the optimism of the assessments in the document that came from the centre was inspired in many ways by our own relatively bold reports."[11]

A few hours prior to the receipt of Directive No. 3, the commanders of the front line had already assessed the situation and had issued the necessary instructions which were aimed at stabilising it. The last directive to arrive from Moscow on 22 June was only fit for scrunching up and placing in a rubbish bin. Arguably the essence of this message was a requirement to take action against the advancing German alignment of not less than five mechanised corps. Moreover this idea was also buried, again prior to the preparation of Directive No. 3 in Moscow.

Soon after the receipt of Directive No. 3 the Chief of the General Staff, Army General G.K. Zhukov, arrived at front line headquarters together with N.S. Khrushchev, who had been appointed a member of the front line Military Council. Zhukov supported the decisions that had been taken by Kirponos and Purkayev.

The influence of Directive No. 3 cannot be discerned in the orders that were issued after its receipt by the headquarters of the South-Western Front. On the contrary, an understanding of the situation that was unfolding can be traced in these orders as well as a striving to realise the plan for its stabilisation. In Private Battle Order No. 2, addressed to the 6th Army, the front line Military Council sets out precisely the directions that the *Panzergruppe 1* main attacks should take: "By sending mechanised formations in the direction of Ustyluh, Wlodzimierz [Volodymyr-Volynskyi], Krystynopol and Radzekhov the enemy has opened up the possibility of a penetration of the front line held by the defending units on the 5th Army's front."[12] The time on the telegram was 0310 hrs on 23 June. Subsequently, in an order issued to the commander of the 6th Army, the 4th Mechanised Corps were ordered to be sent to attack enemy troops advancing on Radzekhov and the order promised support in the shape of an attack by bombers belonging to the aviation regiment. Muzychenko was also promised that the 8th Mechanised Corps (that were near Rava-Ruska) would be activated to repel attacks on the infantry on his army's front line.

Zhukov, who had arrived from Moscow, understood the problems with orders getting through to the lower levels and promised to take an active role in their realisation. As Bagramyan recalled:

> Zhukov was interested in whether we had any landline communications with Muzychenko. On receiving confirmation the Army General said that he will visit Muzychenko and negotiate with him. Kirponos ordered the commander of the 6th Army to come to the phone at

10 Papers. 1941. Volume 2, p.440.
11 Bagramyan, p.112.
12 The Central Archive of the Ministry of Defence, fund 334, inventory 5397, file 11, p.101.

> once. After hearing the commander's report on the condition of the forces and the enemy, Zhukov emphasised specifically how important it was that 4th Mechanised Corps be redeployed to the army's right flank without delay. A short time later G.K. Zhukov, along with the representatives of front line headquarters, left for the 8th Mechanised Corps, led by Lieutenant-General D.I. Ryabishev, in order to familiarise himself with the state of his forces on the ground and to hasten their movement from the area around Lvov to Brody.[13]

Getting these orders passed down to the lower levels with the help of Zhukov had an effect. Muzychenko, at 0200 hrs on 23 June, wrote a general order for his army which no longer envisaged the use of the 4th Mechanised Corps in the area around Peremyshl and Radymno. The orders that A.A. Vlasov's corps were given no longer referred to the 'Enemy's mechanised alignment at Parkhach', a town to the south of Krystynopol. Time however, had already been lost. If the order to move the 4th Mechanised Corps for action around Radzekhov had been issued a few hours before (at 1800 hrs on 22 June) the chances of this corps engaging the enemy tanks in battle on 23 June would have been so much greater.

An Aerial Pearl Harbor

The first act of the air battle for the skies over Ukraine were the air raids on the Soviet airfields. The task for the 4th Air Fleet was much more complicated than it was for the air fleets in the Moscow direction in the Baltic region. This was not just about a less favourable balance of forces but a whole series of objective and subjective factors. The leadership of the Air Forces of the Kiev Special Military District, under E.S. Ptukhin, paid a great deal of attention to the camouflaging of airfields. Shortly before the invasion the commander of the Air Forces in the district personally conducted a flight over all the airfields with the aim of checking the execution of the decree issued by the Peoples' Commissariat for Defence, dated 19 June, on camouflaging airfields. Therefore the Germans did not manage to discover the system of bases for the aviation of the Kiev Special Military District in its entirety, even though they were very familiar with the border airfields.

In the period between 0400 hrs and 0500 hrs on the morning of 22 June around 300 aircraft from *V Fliegerkorps* attacked 24 airfields where bomber and fighter regiments from the Air Forces of the Kiev Special Military District were based. In the direction of the principal attack by Army Group South was the base for the 14th Aviation Division, under the command of Colonel Zykanov, which was subordinate to the 5th Army. On 22 June three out of four of its airfields (Kolki, Velitsk and Mlynuv) sustained air attacks. Only Fyodorovka airfield, in the area around Novograd-Volynsk, escaped air attack. No precise data is available concerning the losses among the regiments of the aviation divisions on 22 June, however according to the reports on combat strength a calculation can be made of the difference between the numbers of combat capable aircraft on the evening of 21–22 June. Thus the number of combat capable aircraft in the 46th Fighter Aviation Regiment was reduced in the space of a day by seven I-16s and nine I-153s; the number of combat capable aircraft in the 17th Fighter Aviation Regiment was reduced by 18 I-153s; while those of the 89th Fighter Aviation Regiment by six I-16s.[14]

A Senior Lieutenant with the purely Russian name of Ivan Ivanovich Ivanov rammed a German *He-111* bomber, which was heading for the airfield, in an I-153 in a head-on attack. Both aircraft were engulfed in flames and crashed to the ground. I.I. Ivanov was a pilot in the duty flight in the 46th Fighter Aviation Regiment, 14th Aviation Division. Mlynuv airfield, on which the

13 Bagramyan, pp.119–120.

14 The Central Archive of the Ministry of Defence, fund 229, inventory 181, file 33, p. 25.

46th Fighter Aviation Regiment was based, actually became a cemetery for German bombers. *Kampfgeschwader 51 Edelweiss* alone lost seven *Ju-88*s in the area around Mlynuv on 22 June. All of them, according to German information, were shot down by Soviet fighters. A further *Ju-88* from the '*Edelweiss*' squadron was lost in the area around Lutsk, which was also under the jurisdiction of 14th Aviation Division. The reason behind the relatively high losses in the 17th Fighter Aviation Regiment was the human factor. The pilots in the regiment would usually go to visit their families at weekends in Kovel. Saturday 21 June was no exception. When the regiment's airfield came under attack from German bombers they did not encounter any organised resistance: "We were not able to counter the attacks by the bombers; the aircrew were in Kovel visiting their families."[15] Along with this it has to be said that the Germans were not capable of completely destroying the air fleet belonging to the 17th Fighter Aviation Regiment, as less than half of the 50 '*Chaikas*' were lost.

The most dangerous opponent in the battle for air supremacy was the 15th Aviation Division, led by Major-General of Aviation Demidov, based close to Lvov. Two of its fighter aviation regiments (the 23rd and the 28th Fighter Aviation Regiments) underwent conversion onto the newest MiG-3. Adamy airfield, belonging to the 23rd Fighter Aviation Regiment, sustained seven air raids in the space of a day and Chunev airfield, which belonged to the 28th Fighter Aviation Regiment, six air raids. From early in the morning up until 2000 hrs in the evening Soviet pilots countered raids on their airfields, conducted air battles over Lvov and attacked a river crossing on the Bug River close to Sokal. In total the 15th Aviation Division conducted 374 sorties in the course of a day. The *51st 'Edelweiss'* squadron lost at least two aircraft—one in the area around Lvov, and another over Adamy. The pilots in each of the fighter aviation regiments in the division claimed two *He-111*s shot down on this day.

The large-scale enemy air raids forced the command to consider retaining the materiel given the difficulties with airfield manoeuvres. General Demidov decided that from the morning of the 23 June onwards the aviation regiments would be redeployed to Kudrovishche airfield (where the other two regiments in the division were based). It was proposed that they would conduct combat operations from this airfield and would only return to their home airfields after dark. Evidently it was decided that it would be easier to defend a single large airbase with a large number of aircraft.

The heavy losses sustained by the 66th Ground-Attack Aviation Regiment can be explained relatively easily. This was one of the small and quite 'sleepy' airfields in the Red Army Air Force on the first day of the war and was the second on the South-Western Front (the first was the 17th Fighter Aviation Regiment). The crews in this regiment were late in reaching their airfield since they decided that a standard training alert had been sounded. The alert however turned out to be for real and the consequences of them not taking their responsibilities seriously were quick in coming. The first attack led to 34 aircraft being destroyed, or more than half of the squadron's line-up.

The 16th Aviation Division, under Major-General of Aviation Shevchenko, survived air raids on all three of his airfields on the first day of the war. Details of the raid on the airfield at Buchach are set out in the memoirs of the commander of the 87th Fighter Aviation Regiment, which was based on the airfield, Major I.S. Suldin:

> On 22 June at 0430 hrs a telegram arrived from the headquarters of the aviation division, the contents of which was as follows: 'According to information received German aviation is bombing the border cities of Peremyshl, Rava-Ruska and others. The regiment must be brought up to combat readiness." The pilots, engineers, technicians, and junior aviation specialists took their positions next to the fighters in accordance with the battle drill…

15 F.F. Arkhipenko, *A Fighter Pilot's Notes*. M.: (Scientific-Production Enterprise 'Delta', 1999), p.25.

> It would appear that there was full combat readiness, but a sizeable blunder had slipped through, for which many would pay the price. At approximately 0450 hrs a two-engine bomber appeared on the eastern side of the airfield, which could barely be discerned against the rays of the rising sun. Everyone thought the commander of the aviation division had taken off to check on the state of readiness. This however was a *Ju-88*. It attacked the aircraft that had been arranged in a row at low level. On seeing the ominous crosses on the bomber the commanders and the soldiers on the airfield opened fire on it with their rifles. It was too late however. The German aircraft dropped small explosive bombs with precision and strafed the personnel with its machine guns: out of the 10 aircraft that had been lined up seven caught fire and two pilots who were sitting in their cockpits were killed, two junior aircraft specialists were injured. Personnel from the 4th Squadron, who were arranged next to their control point, were injured."[16]

The losses among the regiments in the 16th Aviation Division on the airfields on 22 June 1941 were as follows:

The divisional directorate—one SB and one PVS damaged;
The 86th High-Speed Bomber Aviation Regiment—nine SBs and two Pe-2s destroyed, seven Pe-2s and 21 SBs damaged;
The 87th Fighter Aviation Regiment—nine I-16s destroyed, and 13 damaged;
The 92nd Fighter Aviation Regiment—12 I-153s destroyed, and 20 I-153s damaged;[17]
In the air the losses were one SB, three I-16s, and two I-153s respectively.[18]

By the end of the day the regiments in the division led by Major-General Shevchenko had changed the airfield on which they were based. The 87th Fighter Aviation Regiment flew to Ternopil airfield, the 92nd Fighter Aviation Regiment flew to Ponikovitse and the 86th High-Speed Bomber Aviation Regiment flew to Popovitse airfield.

The air raids were not confined to the border airfields of the 4th Air Fleet "Kiev was bombed and we were told that the war had started," many people know the lyrics of this song. The air defence system around the capital of Soviet Ukraine was in the hands of the 36th Aviation Division. At 0400 on 22 June this division was brought up to combat readiness. At 0715 hrs around two-dozen German aircraft bombed the Kiev airfield from an altitude of 2,000m. The squadron which was scrambled attempted to catch up with the bombers that were fast disappearing towards the west but were unable to do so—it was not easy for an I-16 to catch an *He-111* manufactured in 1941. One of the pilots got distracted chasing the bombers and he was forced to carry out an emergency landing as he ran out of fuel. The 36th Aviation Division did not incur any combat losses in the air and on the airfields on the first day of the war. However pilot Yakovlev of the 2nd Aviation Division entered a spin whilst making a turn after take-off. The aircraft was destroyed and the pilot was killed.

General A. Lohr had carried out the task that had been set of destroying the air fleet on the airfields with an enviable tenacity and consistency. The aircraft with black crosses on them had not only flown as far as Kiev but had even reached the Soviet airfields on the southern face of the Lvov salient. It was here that the aviation regiments of the 63rd and 64th Aviation Divisions were based. They were located at a relative distance from the direction of the main thrust of Army Group South, but from another perspective they were well within range for air raids. The Germans were powerless to prevent the reshuffle of aircraft from the airfields south of Lvov. Therefore the destruction of

16 N.S. Skripko, *On Targets Near and Far* (Moscow: Voenizdat, 1981), pp.124–125.
17 The Central Archive of the Ministry of Defence, fund 229, inventory 181, file 33, p.287.
18 The Central Archive of the Ministry of Defence, fund 229, inventory 181, file 33, p.287.

the airfields was an attractive prospect even in the case of what were clearly secondary Red Army Air Force bases.

Table 3.1 Losses among the aviation regiments of the 15th Aviation Divisions on the ground and in the air on 22 June 1941

	23rd Fighter Aviation Regiment	28th Fighter Aviation Regiment	164th Fighter Aviation Regiment	66th Ground-Attack Aviation Regiment
Shot down in combat	Two MiG-3s	One MiG-3	One I-153	2
Shot down by anti-aircraft artillery	–	One MiG-3[1]	–	–
Failed to return	–	One MiG-3	Four I-16s	–
Destroyed on the airfield	–	Four MiG-3s	15	34 (incl. two Il-2s)
Damaged on the airfield	Nine MiG-3s	Five MiG-3s		
Broke up on landing	Four MiG-3s	Three MiG-3s	–	–
Total	15 MiG-3s	12 MiG-3s	20	36

Note
1 Shot down by friendly fire—The Central Archive of the Ministry of Defence, fund 229, inventory 181, file 47, pp.14–16.

At 0540 hrs the airfield at Chenovtsy was attacked (this was where the 149th Fighter Aviation Regiment, 64th Aviation Division was based) and on which 15 aircraft were destroyed in the hangar. A further two aircraft were shot down in the air. The 166th Fighter Aviation Regiment from that same division lost four aircraft on the airfield, and two in the air. The neighbouring 63rd Aviation Division actually went into combat with one fighter regiment. No accurate data concerning this regiment's losses on the 22 June is available. What is known is that between 22 and 25 June 1941 the aviation division lost between 12 and 20 aircraft on the airfield. It would however be a mistake to think of the *Heinkel* and *Junkers* aircraft as ubiquitous. In the second echelon, and in the direction of the main thrust of the enemy's attack, were the regiments of the 62nd Aviation Division. They were based in the area around Kiev as well as to the east of the city. The division however did not suffer any air raids on 22 June itself. Quite the opposite, the German aircraft just flew past them. A technician in the 94th Aviation Regiment, 62nd Aviation Division, A.D. Buduchev, recalled:

> The war began with an alert at 0330 hrs in the morning. The aircraft were quickly readied for a combat sortie. Time went by and our aircraft had not flown anywhere and there were no aircrew to be seen. We all thought that it was just another exercise (there were a great number of these at that time). When we saw large groups of unfamiliar aircraft however we became concerned—are we really at war? [...] At 1000 hrs an order was read out, that fascist Germany had attacked us, and telling us what our army was to do next, particularly aviation.

It was only in the second half of the day that the 62nd Aviation Division received their combat mission. At 1515 hrs E.S. Ptukhin issued an order, which began with the following words: "On 22 June in the area around Grubeshuv, Korytnitsa, Ustyluh up to 500 enemy tanks gathered and moved towards Volodymyr-Volynskyi and Lutsk." Correspondingly the order was given to attack these tanks. The order was issued to groups of nine SBs from the 52nd and 94th Regiments, which dropped 232 FAB-100 and two FAB-50s. In this first sortie to bomb enemy 'motorised columns' fighters from the 14th Aviation Division (the 17th Fighter Aviation Regiment) accompanied the bombers. On their return from the target the propeller flew off of the aircraft piloted by the commander of the 94th Regiment; Nikolayev's aircraft (it is possible that this was damaged by anti-aircraft fire) and thus he returned to the airfield on one engine.

The 62nd Aviation Division was not the only one in the Kiev Special Military District to have escaped the devastating raids on the airfields. The 22 June was very quiet and matter of fact, despite the outbreak of war, in the 17th, 18th, 19th and 44th Aviation Divisions. They were deployed in the depths of the Kiev Special Military District's formation and moreover away from the air routes that led into Kiev. All three aviation divisions were brought up to combat readiness but their airfields were not attacked and the formations did not incur any losses; not on the ground or in the air. The commanders did not issue any instructions for combat sorties. One aircraft from the 18th Division flew up to the border in the area around Grubeshuv on a reconnaissance mission, although this can almost be put down to private curiosity. The fighters of the 44th Aviation Division took off on intercept and patrol missions but did not encounter the enemy.

One of the problems for aviation in the South-Western Front on the first day of the war was the lack of any intelligible instructions from command. Up until the moment that Germany invaded the USSR the commander of the Air Forces of the Kiev Special Military District, E.S. Ptukhin, and his aviation and political deputies had been in Kiev. They only arrived in Ternopil at 1400 hrs on 22 June. The headquarters director of the Air Forces of the Kiev Special Military District had been in Moscow on 22 June and only returned on 25 June. However, even after the commanders had arrived back, no orders were forthcoming to conduct combat missions. The first order for the scramble of four groups of nine aircraft from the 62nd Aviation Division to Ustyluh came only at 1500 hrs, but the overall Order No. 1 was sent to the aviation units on the front line at 0300 hrs on 23 June. Correspondingly on the first day of the war the aviation divisions acted at their own discretion and in the main were engaged in countering enemy raids on the airfields. Technically, as the example with the 62nd Aviation Division shows, it had been entirely possible to strike the enemy forces on both sides of the border from the evening of 22 June onwards.

The intensiveness of the retaliatory strike made by the Soviet Air Forces can be illustrated using a single figure: on 22 June out of the 587 bombers on the front line only 36 aircraft, or 6 percent of the total number were used. Understandably all these regiments were just not ready on an organisational, or a technical, level to combat the enemy forces on the border. The Su-2 regiments were not combat-capable at all. However an indicator of the intensiveness of their use would always appear low. At the same time it has to be said that the only air strike from the Air Forces of the South-Western Front in the area around Ustyluh was recorded by the enemy. A historiographer in the *14th Panzer Division* wrote: "The advance was accompanied by the enemy dropping their first bombs, which inflicted the first losses." As subsequent events were to demonstrate this was just the beginning.

What then were the results of the first day of the war in the air? The cost that the Germans paid for their successes in attacking the airfields on 22 June to this day remains a subject of lively discussion. In accordance with the calculations carried out by the Russian historian D.B. Khazanov, on the first day of the war *V Fliegerkorps* lost 35 aircraft and 27 crews. In the official history of the 55th Bomber Squadron 13 aircraft are listed in the losses for the first day of the war in the USSR. Seven crews were killed or were missing without trace. The majority of the *Heinkels* in the squadron were shot down by fighters during the attack on the airfield at Mlynuv, becoming victims of the I-16s and I-153s of the 14th Aviation Division, 5th Army. The *Kampfgeschwader 51 'Edelweiss'* incurred even greater losses. The squadron's combat journal paints a far from rosy picture of the end of the longest day of 1941:

After the last aircraft had landed at 2023 hrs Commodore Lieutenant-Colonel Schulzhein took stock of the day in the palace at Polyanka near Krosno: 60 men (15 crews!) had been killed or had disappeared without trace, and in the third group more than 50 percent of the aircraft had either been shot down, or damaged." The *JG3* Fighter Squadron had lost 15 aircraft, including their non-combat losses.

The number of combat aircraft in the Air Forces of the South-Western Front that were destroyed by *Luftwaffe* aircraft on the first day of the war also causes arguments and a clear disparity in the figures cited by different historians. In the Soviet period a figure of 301 aircraft was given.[19] Out of the total figure for the losses, according to this same source, 174 aircraft were destroyed or damaged either in the air or on the ground. The most recent research suggests a slightly larger figure of 277 aircraft destroyed on the ground.[20] The "Memorandum on the losses of materiel in the Air Forces of the South-Western Front between 22–30 June 1941" indicates that on 22 June 135 aircraft were irrevocably lost (that is to say destroyed), with a further 102 being damaged.[21] The difference with the above figure first and foremost lies in the fact that the memorandum does not take into account training aircraft.

Considerable variations are also visible in relation to the losses in the air. The pilots of the *JG3* fighter squadron claimed 25 Soviet aircraft shot down. The combat journal of the Air Forces of the South-Western Front indicate that on 22 June seven bombers and ground-attack aircraft were lost in air combat as well as 16 fighters, two aircraft were shot down by anti-aircraft fire, one aircraft was lost as a result of a crash, 12 aircraft suffered accidents and 19 aircraft failed to return from their sorties.[22] This gives us a figure of 294 aircraft that were knocked out on the first day of the war. Thus on 22 June 1941 the Air Forces of the South-Western Front lost just 14.7 percent of their aircraft. Correspondingly around 12 percent of the air fleet belonging to this front line were lost on the airfields. There was no question of a routing of aviation on "quiet, sleepy airfields." The commanders of the South-Western Front retained sufficient air power in their hands by the end of the day on 22 June to impact on the operational environment.

Deep behind the lines

If the border divisions were engaged in combat, and were correcting their actions in accordance with the environment, then for the rest of the formations on the front line the principal operating document were the plans for the provision of cover. Sometimes following this principle led to ambiguities, if not to absurdities. The 41st Tank Division, which was deployed not far away in a military garrison near Volodymyr-Volynskyi (12km from the border) was to have moved towards the area around Kovel in accordance with the plan to provide cover. Correspondingly the 'red package' was opened as the alert was sounded and the division was formed into marching columns and set off not to meet the enemy that was attacking Volodymyr-Volynskyi but to the north-east, a direction that led away from the battlefield. All that remained outside Volodymyr-Volynskyi was a small proportion of the tank formations, which were subordinate to the commanders of the rifle units.

Since on the first day of the war the enemy was not able to penetrate deep behind the lines the mechanised formations of the South-Western Front avoided being directly involved in the combat operations (with the exception of a small number of tanks from the 41st Tank Division). Their principal operating documents were the plans for the provision of cover, which proposed a move to the second echelon of the army which included them in its line-up. As the main participant in the battle for Dubno, the 8th Mechanised Corps, succeeded in putting around 80km on their tracks on the first day of the war and joined the 26th Army reserves. At this point it is necessary

19 Skripko, p.129.
20 D.B. Khazanov, with reference to The Central Archive of the Ministry of Defence, fund 35, inventory 30802, file 32, pp.1–32.
21 The Central Archive of the Ministry of Defence, fund 229, inventory 181, file 33, pp.21.
22 The Central Archive of the Ministry of Defence, fund 229, inventory 181, file 47, pp.21–22.

to recall, though unkindly, the formal approach of the headquarters of the South-Western Front to the preparation of the plans to provide cover on the border. This envisaged the use of a strong mechanised formation in what was clearly a secondary direction from the point of view of defence. This made the route into battle for D.I. Ryabishev's corps longer and more difficult.

After leaving the permanent peacetime deployment zone the 8th Mechanised Corps incurred the first losses, although they were not yet unrecoverable. The following remained in the fleet, give or take one or two errors, 11 KVs (five were subsequently in need of repair), 10 T-35s, five T-34s, 33 T-26s of various types (including two tractors and two Su-5 Self-Propelled Artillery Systems), 90 BT-7s, 16 BT-5s, 10 BT-2s, 23 T-37s (all of these were listed as belonging to the corps) and 80 T-27s (these were also listed as all belonging to the corps). Crews could not be found at all for certain tanks (such as the T-37s of the 34th Tank Division). The uncomfortable T-27s were used in peacetime for training mechanics and drivers. Their value in combat was virtually nil and their technical condition was disastrous. In total 682 tanks ventured out to meet the unknown: (60 KVs, 38 T-35s, 95 T-34s, 133 T-26 radio-controlled tanks, 131 T-26 battle tanks, one T-26 twin-turret tank, 46 T-26 flamethrower tanks, 152 BT-7s, four BT-5s, five BT-2s and 17 T-40s).[23] Now they had to be taken onto the battlefield. Considering the technical imperfections of the new tanks, and the wear in the old tanks, this was no easy task. On 22 June alone, after an 80–100km march, 12 KV tanks from the 12th Tank Division failed. The exhausting marches and enemy attacks however were still ahead. Commissar Popel recalled: "Vehicle after vehicle, battalion after battalion. Heated tar would not be able to take such a load. Where these vehicles turned, an oily semicircle would appear, scored with dozens of tank tracks. The tanks were rushing to the west, to Peremyshl, leaving behind them symmetrical scar lines."

The manoeuvre, analogous to the movements of the 8th Mechanised Corps, was made by its counterpart in the 6th Army, the 4th Mechanised Corps led by A.A. Vlasov. The only difference being that the individual units within this corps did not move from their starting positions on the approaches to the border. It was the 202nd Motorised Rifle Regiment, 81st Mechanised Division, that remained in Lvov in order to fulfil their garrison duty, as well as the motorised and howitzer regiments in the 32nd Tank Division. Owing to the lack of transport the latter were very late in leaving on the trail of their formation. In accordance with the plan for the provision of cover much weaker units were immediately sent to intercept the German tank spearhead: the 9th Mechanised Corps, led by K.K. Rokossovskiy, and the 19th Mechanised Corps under N.V. Feklenko. Between 1200–1400 hrs on 22 June both corps moved from their bases out to the west. However they had to cover several hundred kilometres until they came into contact with the advancing enemy.

The first corrections in the objectives that had been set in accordance with the plan to provide cover were made in the second half of the day on 22 June. The re-subordination of the 8th Mechanised Corps has already been mentioned above. Several divisions were redeployed to a new area. Thus the 14th Cavalry Division was sent to a location outside Kremenets. In the combat journal this fact was reflected as follows:

> At 1950 hrs the division on the approaches to Iziaslav received a new order from the representative of the Kiev Special Military District headquarters: advance towards Kremenets and organise an anti-tank defence in a mountainous and forested area and do not allow the enemy to break through and advance to the east, south-east or south. The advance to the area around Kremenets is to be completed by the end of the day on 24 June.[24]

23 The Central Archive of the Ministry of Defence, fund 229, inventory 161, file 89, p.90.
24 The Central Archive of the Ministry of Defence, fund 3539, inventory 1, file 36, p.106.

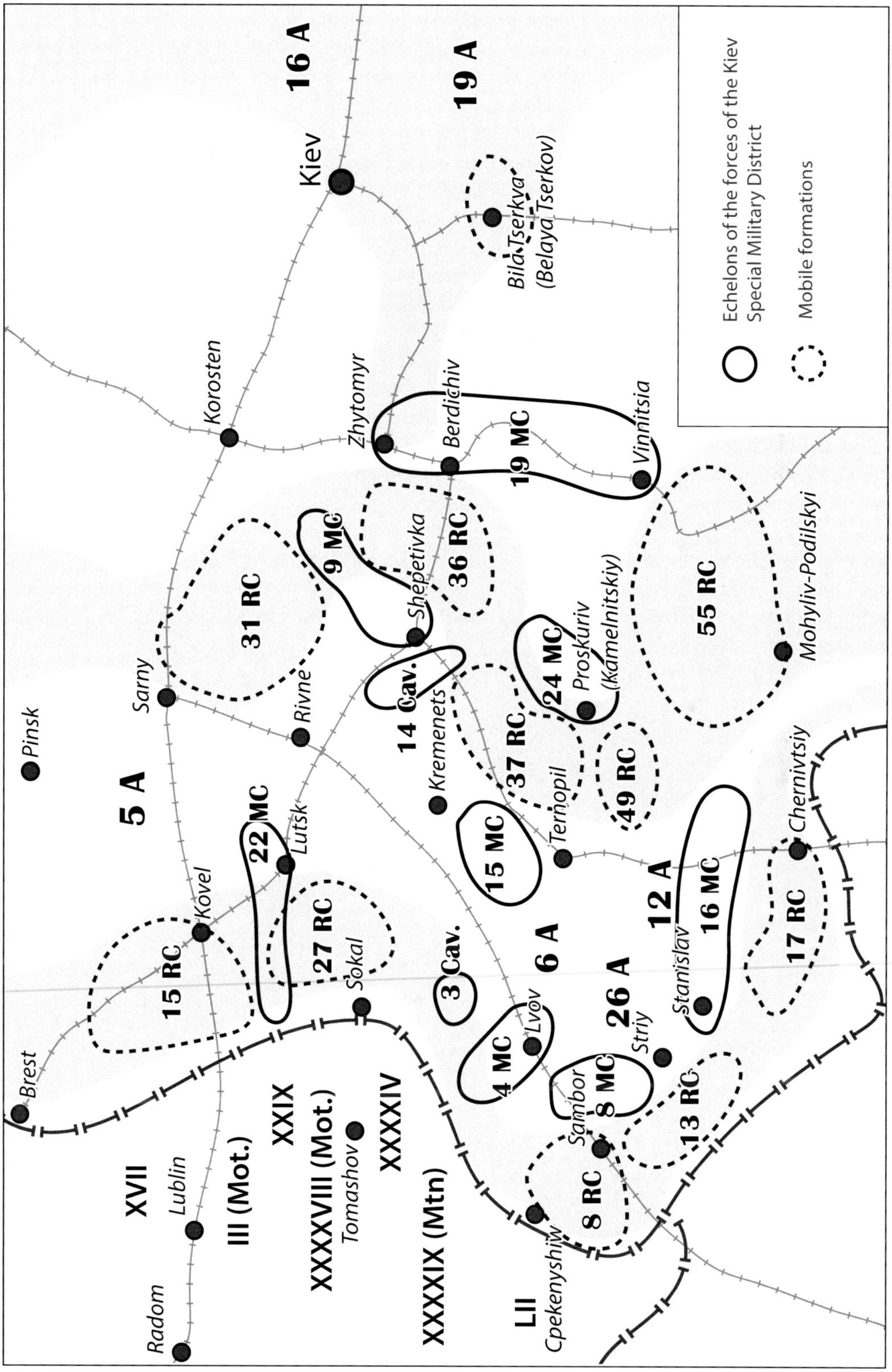

Map 3 The offensive as it unfolded on 22 June 1941.

No explanation was given for the reasons behind the advance to the area around Kremenets specifically, however, in a similar way on the evening of 22 June a proposal began to be drawn up by the front line commanders concerning the enemy's plans to encircle Soviet forces in the Lvov salient. Correspondingly the cavalry division was sent to secure the road along which an attack against the rear of the Lvov salient may be made. Subsequently this proposal weighed on the shoulders of the front line commanders and had a significant impact on decision-making.

Corrections to several of the provisions in the plan to provide cover had already been made by the first half of the day. The 5th Anti-tank Artillery Brigade was to have become the front line commander's reserve unit along with the 15th Mechanised Corps. According to the memoirs of brigade commander K.S. Moskalenko, the commander of the 5th Army, M.I. Potapov, simply bent the brigade to his will. In his account Moskalenko explained the decision he took as commander thus:

> Taking the situation that has emerged into account, I order: the brigade to move, as I have already said, out to Volodymyr-Volynskyi and in conjunction with the 22nd Mechanised Corps, under Major-General Kondrusev, to destroy the enemy that has crossed the border and to restore the status quo. Do not cross the border. I will take full responsibility for any failure of the brigade to fulfil the mission proposed in the mobilisation plan.[25]

With the parting words "do not cross the border" the brigade led by Moskalenko departed at around 1000 hrs on 22 June to their encounter with the *III Motorised Corps*. Subsequent events would force them to recall their commander's instructions "do not cross the border," at best with a bitter irony.

25 Moskalenko, p.27.

The Commander of the 8th Mechanised Corps D.I. Ryabishev. He was a former cavalryman, which was typical of many tank commanders.

T-35 tanks became the real 'star' of the battles in the Ukraine in 1941. They were a little over 50 in number, but every enemy soldier considered it his duty to be photographed standing next to one of these vanquished steel monsters.

A KV-2 tank that had become stuck in the soft ground during the course of an attack. For heavy tanks unsuitable terrain was just as big a danger as shells from enemy guns.

A Soviet T-26 tank that had been disabled in combat. This is an early series machine with two turrets (analogous to the prototype T-26 and the British 'Vickers' tank, weighing six tonnes). Note the armour that has been split open on the left hand turret. The T-26 tanks fitted with twin turrets served in the 19th Tank Division, 22nd Mechanised Corps.

A T-26 tank that has been abandoned in the course of the withdrawal, together with a BA-10 armoured car. The BA-10 armoured car was one of the most widespread examples of an armoured vehicle in the Red Army. By the outbreak of war in the Kiev District there were approximately 700 of these vehicles, only the T-26s and BTs outnumbered them.

Two KV-2 tanks that were abandoned on the streets of Zhovkva (Zhulevka). For the heavy tanks the exhausting marches along the roads of the Lvov salient were often catastrophic, and tanks would fail for technical reasons.

A KV-1 tank from the 8th Tank Division, 4th Mechanised Corps abandoned on a street in Zhovkva on the market square at the gates of the Glinskaya Brama. This is an early series machine, and there is a revolver mounting in place of the front plate of the main body.

German soldiers examine a Soviet T-28E (a shielded tank) that has been abandoned on a street in one of the Ukrainian villages. Additional armoured protection increased the thickness of the frontal armour up to 50–60 mm and that of the side armour to 40 mm. However the weight, which had increased to 32 tonnes, significantly reduced the manoeuvrability of the tank.

A T-28 tank that has been abandoned on the road. The hatch above the engine ventilator has been open either in an attempt to repair the vehicle, or by the curious Germans.

A BA-10 armoured car and artillery armament abandoned somewhere on the roads of the Western Ukraine. The forward axle, along with the wheels, has been removed from this armoured car, more than likely for reasons of 'cannibalism' to repair the vehicles remaining in service.

A T-35 tank that has been left at the disposal of the 68th Tank Regiment, 34th Tank Division in the town of Sudovaya Vishnya. Three of these giants were unserviceable at the very beginning of the war and were abandoned after removal of the sights and machine guns.

Two early series T-34 tanks abandoned on a road. Judging by the position of the cable an attempt was being made to tow the second tank behind the first, which could lead to failure of the engine or the transmission in what was still a raw T-34 tank that was suffering from 'teething troubles'.

German soldiers examine an abandoned T-28 Soviet tank. This is a later series example of a T-28 tank: it is shielded and fitted with a 7.62mm L-10 gun.

Two BT-7M tanks from the 81st Mechanised Division of the 4th Mechanised Corps that were knocked out in Nemirov next to the 'courthouse' at the entrance to the town.

A T-34 tank from the 8th Tank Division that ran into a house during the course of the battles just outside the town of Nemirov. It is possible that the tank became a victim of the driver and mechanic's lack of experience. According to the German version of events however the tank was trying to drive through the house in order to avoid an anti-tank position.

A BT-7M tank of the 81st Mechanised Division, 4th Mechanised Corps knocked out during the course of the battle for the town of Nemirov on the town's market square. The tactical marking—a diamond—can be clearly seen as well as the inscription A2 on the turret.

A T-28 tank of the 15th Tank Regiment, 8th Tank Division disabled during the course of the battle for the town of Nemirov. The tank was disabled on the southern exit to the town, next to the Roman Catholic Church. This example was manufactured in 1937 and is a 'radio-controlled' example (that is to say it was fitted with a radio) and a hand-rail antenna.

German anti-tank guns were of little use against the new Soviet tanks. However they occasionally succeeded in hitting the running gear of the heavy examples. In this photo German soldiers are posing on a KV tank with a broken idling wheel.

A T-35 tank that was abandoned owing to a technical failure in the town of Gorodok (outside Lvov). This is a later series tank with conical turrets. This tank belonged to the 67th Tank Regiment, 34th Tank Division.

A pair of photographs of a T-35 tank abandoned in Gorodok, which was taken by an officer of the *XXXXIX Mountain Corps*. Judging by the towing bar that has been abandoned to the right it is possible to conclude that an attempt was being made to tow this heavy tank (NARA).

Another photograph of this same machine. In the foreground is an abandoned FAI armoured car (NARA).

A German soldier examines ammunition from a T-28E tank. Despite the short length of the 76.2mm barrel the T-28 used ammunition with a long shell casing.

4

The First Test – Radzekhov and Voynitsa

On the morning of the second day of the war the balance of forces for the forthcoming tank battle was finally decided. The concentration of forces, in the shape of mechanised corps appointed by the commanders of the South-Western Front on the evening of 22 June, in the area around Radzekhov, appeared blurred and confused. Despite the decision that had been taken to use the most powerful tank formation in the district in the counterattack—the 4th Mechanised Corps—its participation turned out to be minimal. Firstly, the 8th Tank Division was not able to return to its starting position for the counterattack owing to the fact that the sappers had been very quick in blowing up the bridges over the river Bug, which lay on the route the division was due to take. Secondly, the commander of the 6th Army, I.N. Muzychenko, had made a slight amendment to the corps' mission adding, along with Radzekhov, fighting in support of the 3rd Cavalry Division's front line. The 15th Mechanised Corps even reached the furthest approaches of the battlefield at reduced strength. On the morning of 23 June the principal forces of the 10th Tank Division advanced to the area around the small town of Cholojow, to the south of Radzekhov. Furthermore the 19th Tank Regiment in this division were not able to advance to their appointed position either since they had been delayed by difficult marching conditions. It was in this regiment that the formidable KVs served, which could become the trump card in the forthcoming battle. The 37th Tank Division in the corps, on the morning of 23 June, were still on the march from Kremenets. Even according to the plan it was only to have advanced to the area around Radzekhov by the evening of 23 June. Only a forward detachment of the corps, led by I.I. Karpezo, remained in Radzekhov since there was no suspicion of this detachment being in any danger.

While columns of Soviet tanks and mechanised infantry were rushing towards Radzekhov, which was occupied by this forward detachment, the tip of a German armoured spearhead was heading for the town itself. If the mission put before the Soviet mechanised corps had been communicated as "destroy the enemy" then the aim of the Germans was to bring the junction of the central '*Panzerstrasse*' under their control. The advance of the tank formation in *XXXXVIII Motorised Corps* was to be supplied via Radzekhov. This was not just a point on the map but one of the key points of the entire border battle. The delays with the *11th Panzer Division* entering the battle on 22 June could have cost the Germans a great deal if the Soviet reserves had been able to reach Radzekhov and take up their defensive positions. They had to hurry. Having, on the previous day, advanced 25km from the border the German *Panzer* division had renewed their position by 0330 hrs.

In accordance with the German tactical rules the advance was conducted by *kampfgruppe* in a number of directions at once. The commander of the division, Ludwig Crüwell, divided his formation into two *kampfgruppen*. One of them was to build on the successes of the first day, breaking through some distance into the alignment of Soviet forces, and advance to the eastern sector of the '*Panzerstrasse*', while the second was to capture Radzekhov and secure the advance from the flank. The foundation of the first ('infantry') group was *Schützen-Regiment 110* (110th Motorised Infantry Regiment). Subsequent this alignment of Crüwell's division was retained for the duration of the entire summer campaign. The *Panzergrenadiers* advanced in the first echelon of the division, along with the motorcycles and an *aufklärung* battalion, while in the second echelon, and on the flanks were the tanks. The second *kampfgruppe* (the *Panzer* group), which became the main participant in the battle, was built around the *15th Panzer Regiment*. The importance of the mission decided the arrangement of the reinforcements. Artillery was attached to these forces (in the shape of the 844th Regiment with 150mm howitzers) as well as anti-aircraft armament. As a former cavalryman Crüwell understood the danger of an attack on the flanks in manoeuvre warfare very well and advanced the principal mass of his *Panzer* force to meet it. A mass of *panzers* should have guaranteed success for Kempf's corps in their mission to capture the key points on the '*Panzerstrasse*'.

At 0515 hrs on the morning of 23 June the first tank battle in the Ukraine began. The *Panzerkampfgruppe* in Crüwell's division attacked Radzekhov. After breaking through, with artillery support, to the town itself the German tanks encountered T-34s on its streets. The 'thirty-fours' immediately began to make their presence felt and one of the German tanks had its commander's turret blown off and the tank commander was fatally wounded. The forces however were clearly imbalanced: on the Soviet side was the advanced detachment without artillery support, while on the German side was a reinforced *panzer* regiment with the support of a powerful artillery force. This advantage allowed the Germans to perform an evasion manoeuvre, trapping Radzekhov in a pincer movement. Under threat of encirclement, and having run out of ammunition, the forward detachment of the 10th Tank Division was forced to retreat. According to Soviet records the Germans lost 20 *panzers*, 16 anti-tank weapons and up to a platoon of infantry soldiers in this battle. The losses in the forward detachment were 20 BT tanks, six T-34 tanks, seven men killed, 11 men injured and 32 missing without trace. The destruction of six T-34 tanks should come as no surprise. The attacking tanks were supported by 88mm anti-aircraft guns, which were able to fire on the T-34 tanks on the outskirts of Radzekhov from their stationary positions. The containing manoeuvre forced the Soviet tank crews to counterattack, advancing out from the town's streets to an open area. The Germans described the actions taken by the Soviet tank crews in this battle as "fierce resistance that turned into constant counterattacks, with no accounting for losses."

On taking Radzekhov the Germans began to probe the terrain around the town. At that moment the consolidated detachment from the 4th Mechanised Corps appeared on the scene. Having emerged into the open to the south-west of Radzekhov, our tanks and the German *panzers* clashed face to face. In view of the hummocks the T-34s left to meet the German *panzers* in a line, one after another. A non-commissioned officer in the *11th Panzer Division*, who later became the formation's historiographer, Gustav Schrodek recalled:

> This is hard on our hearts, the fear, horror, but maybe there is joy too since at last we can prove ourselves. Did they see us? Are they mistaking us for their own? Our forces are equal.[...] As soon as they come within around 100m of our guns the 'dance' begins. We send them the first round...Rummm...mm! The first shot hits the turret. A second shot and they are hit again. The command tank, which was the one I ended up in, continues its movement impassively. The same goes for my platoon colleagues as well. Where though is the advantage for our tanks over the Russian ones that was proclaimed for so long? We were always told that all we had to do was simply to 'let it fly' from our guns!

After exchanging several shots the tank crews on both sides moved back.

In the second half of the day the principal forces of the division, led by S.Ya. Ogurtsov, drew near. They were to attempt to win back Radzekhov that had been lost by the forward detachment. At 1500 hrs the 20th Tank, and the 10th Motorised Rifle Regiments went on the attack, although they were devoid of artillery support (the 10th Artillery Regiment was still on its way since at the

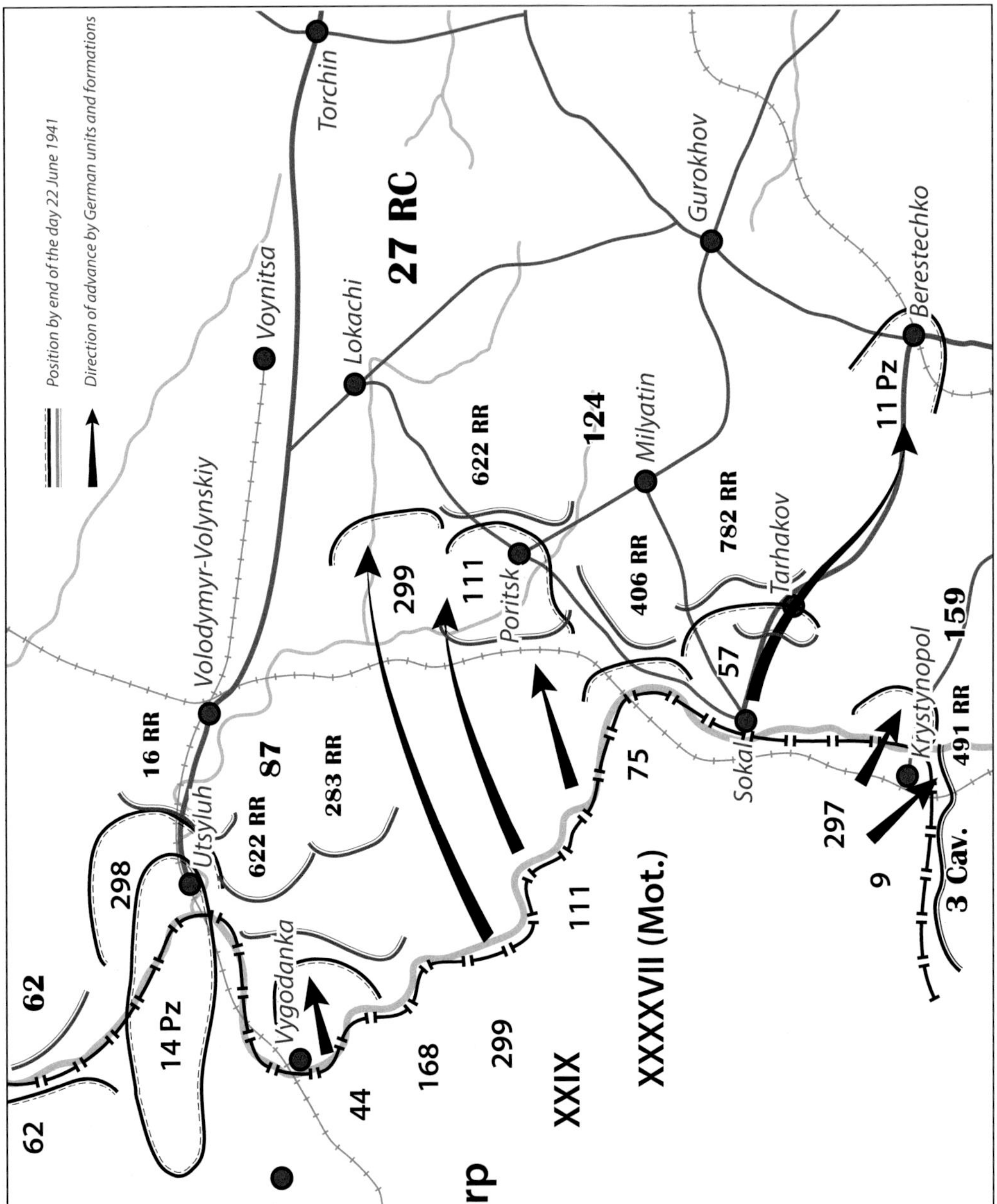

Map 4 The position around Volodymyr-Volynskyi by evening on 22 June 1941.

time the alarm was raised it had been at the military camps in Yanuv). The 19th Tank Regiment took no part in the attack on Radzekhov either since they were not able to get there on time owing to the difficult conditions they had marched through. This attack did not bring success and the 10th Tank Division took up defensive positions on the approaches to the town. This was where the division were to fight for the next few days.

The units in the division led by S.Ya. Ogurtsov were not alone in their attempts to win back the important road junction. This town, from which four columns of smoke from burnt out tanks rose following the next morning's battle, survived several more attacks. A detachment of the 4th Mechanised Corps took an active role in the second half of the battle on 23 June under the leadership of Lieutenant-Colonel Lysenko. This detachment consisted of two battalions of the 32nd Tank Division and a battalion of the 323rd Motorised Rifle Regiment, 81st Mechanised Division. The possible directions from which to attack Radzekhov were limited due to the marshy terrain surrounding the town. To the south-east of the town sprawled an extensive bog. There were favourable conditions for an attack along the highways, as well as the railway line to Lvov from the town of Ganunin to the north-east. Here however the terrain has formed its own natural levees and our tank crews had to overcome the hillocks and, lumbering over the crests of these hillocks, were required to engage the German tanks and their supporting artillery at close quarters.

The aforementioned tank crewmember of the *11th Panzer Division*, Gustav Schrodek, described this phase of the battle as a close quarters 'dogfight':

> The first shells whistle all around us. Nevertheless they are still falling way short of the target. Since our own guns are much more efficient at a distance of 400m we had to hold our nerve and wait for the Russian tanks to get closer. The small folds in the terrain shield us from the first wave of attacking tanks. When they do appear we will be in the best position to open fire with all we have got. Everything is engulfed in tank fire [...] new targets are appearing all the time. They are taking aim and being destroyed. The Russians are overwhelmed. They are sending more and more tanks over the tops of the hillocks but they just cannot break through our formations.

Subsequently on the pages of memoirs, as well as research, the Germans announced that between 40 (under Oskar Munzel) and 68 (under Gustav Schrodek) Soviet tanks were destroyed in this battle. Munzel also wrote: "The German tank crews sustained inconsequential losses." This assessment however does not correspond with the opinion of the commander in the immediate aftermath of the battle. The commander of the *11th Panzer Division* on the evening of 23 June reported to Kempf:

> The tank battle near Radzekhov finished on the whole at 1230 hrs. The enemy has certainly lost 33 of their 50–60 tanks, including their super-heavy tanks. Our own losses are as follows:
> Seven tanks sustained unrecoverable losses;
> Three officers have been killed, as well as 10 men of lower rank;
> Fifty of the men with lower rank have been killed (including in the formations that are subordinate to the tank regiment).
> Losses in the *5th 'General Goering' Panzer Battalion* are relatively high. A battery commander has been killed.
> The enemy fought very skilfully, and stubbornly.[1]

1 NARA T314 R1138 f 847.

The number of tanks damaged from the *11th Panzer Division* was not communicated. Based on the overall statistics for combat activity as a whole their number should be one and a half to two times higher than the figure for the unrecoverable losses among the combat vehicles. The battlefield remained in German hands and the figure cited by Crüwell for the Soviet losses should match our documents precisely. A detachment of the 32nd Tank Division lost 11 tanks, and claimed 18 enemy tanks destroyed, a battalion of the 323rd Motorised Rifle Regiment lost 13 men killed, and 18 injured. The losses in the detachment of the 10th Tank Division, as has already been mentioned above, was 20 BT tanks, six T-34s, seven men killed, 11 injured and 32 that were missing without a trace.

In the combat journal of the *XXXXVIII Corps* the experience gained outside Radzekhov was summarised as follows:

1. What we did not anticipate in this battle was the fanatical fighting spirit of the Russian tank crews. Despite our obvious advantage in terms of strength of numbers and in anti-tank weapons the enemy light tanks continued to attack, despite their losses. Even when they were in a hopeless situation, with their engines smashed and their caterpillar tracks ripped they would fire until they had no ammunition left or would start fighting afresh once our tanks had passed them. Almost all the crews were found dead, or burned in their tanks.
2. Some very fast, heavy enemy tanks appeared with 76.2mm armament that are capable of firing very accurately over a long range. Our tanks clearly concede to them. The 37mm anti-tank armament is hopeless against them, they can only be hit at close range, with an 88mm anti-aircraft gun at higher than average range.
3. The value of the anti-aircraft formations in land battles is confirmed.[2]

The 'thirtyfours' proved themselves to be a powerful adversary in the first tank battle. It still remained for them to encounter the German *Panzers* at the right place and the right time. For this they would have to endure laborious marches.

The reasons for lingering for a while on the roads during the course of endless marches emerged at the same time as the battles outside Radzekhov. At the same time that the first tank battle in Ukraine was underway the *kampfgruppe* from the *Schützen-Regiment 110, 11th Panzer Division* had advanced 15km further east by 1700 hrs on 23 June and reached Lopatina, while the *61st Motorcycle Battalion* had reached the river crossings at Berestechko, some 30km to the east of the place where the division spent the night. The bridge over the River Styr, close to Lopatina (Scurowisce), was blown up and the continuation of the advance of the *11th Panzer Division* was halted until the beginning of the following day. The crossings at Mervy (in the area around Berestechko), which the motorcycle battalion in Crüwell's division approached, was defended by large numbers of Soviet forces and the motorcyclists had been ordered to map the activity in this direction. Munzel confirms that the crossings were captured, although this in all probability was a mistake.

This breakthrough by the German mechanised units deep into the alignments of front line troops was discovered and was a logical cause for concern. A reconnaissance report from the front line, written at 2200 hrs on 23 June, noted: "According to aerial reconnaissance information from the area around Radzekhov, in the direction of Berestechko and Brody, at 1600 hrs a large number of tanks were on the move, and at 1620 hrs Berestechko, and Gorokhov were occupied by enemy mechanised units." What is interesting is that the information on the breakthrough did not come from the specialised 315th and 316th Reconnaissance Aviation Regiments but from the crews of

2 NARA T314 R1138, ff.490—491.

the 15th and 16th Aviation Divisions, part of the 6th Army, that had taken off to bomb and carry out reconnaissance on the enemy in the area around Sokal.

The reaction to this aerial reconnaissance information was immediate, if not premature. Let us not forget that command had to work 'in anticipation', sending the mechanised corps to locations on a proposed route that the enemy advance might take. In view of the fact that the 5th Army's front line had collapsed nothing good could come of a breach in the right flank of the 6th Army. By 1520 hrs on 23 June the commander of the 6th Army had sent the 8th Mechanised Corps in the direction of Brody. A short while later, in response to disheartening reports from pilots, order No. 23 dated 23 June 1941, also came through from the Chief of Staff of the South-Western Front for the 15th Mechanised Corps, which was directly subordinate to front line headquarters. The corps was given the following order:

> In view of the advent of enemy tanks in the region around Berestechko, and the forests to the west, the region around Brody must be held stubbornly by a motorised division, having protected itself from the direction of Radzekhov and Krystynopol. Enemy tanks and tankettes need to be attacked and destroyed in the direction around Berestechko in conjunction with the 8th Mechanised Corps, which will be approaching the area around Brody by the morning of 24 June 1941.

The 212th Motorised Division of the 15th Mechanised Corps had always made a defensive stand from the first day of the war to the north of Brody. Its presence provided some hope that the breakthrough by the enemy will not be so lightning fast and so crushing.

Carrying out this order the commander of the corps, I.I. Karpezo, sent the 10th Tank Division to Brody at 0700 hrs on 24 June and the 37th Tank Division defended the 10th Division from the rear. The latter was then sent from to the forests to the west of Brody to carry out an attack on Leshnev. Strictly speaking this manoeuvre bordered on blatant adventurism. In the name of what was still a tenuous threat of an attack via Brody the 15th Mechanised Corps was taken away from their position outside Radzekhov, which opened a 'window' in the direction of Lvov. Between the right flank of the 6th Army and the front line units outside Brody a breach of generous proportions opened up. The Germans could attack Busk unopposed and then retake the roads from Lvov to the east. Therefore shortly after the error had come to light, amid the suggestions of a breakthrough via Brody, an order came through for the formations to return to their starting positions. At 1700 hrs on 24 June I.I. Karpezo ordered the 10th Tank Division to return via Radzekhov. The division, led by S.Ya. Ogurtsov, completed a 45km march from which it returned, reaching its initial deployment only by dawn on 25 June. The 19th Tank Regiment in this division only received the order to return when it was in the forest to the south-west of Brody. As a result this regiment only returned to the positions that it had occupied back in the evening of 23 June by 2000 hrs on 25 June 1941, having covered 105km in a march between 24–25 June 1941, without taking part in any fighting. The 37th Tank Division was also turned around through 180 degrees and by 0600 hrs on 25 June had returned to its defensive positions on the front line to the north along the river Radostavka. Thus a bold attempt to launch the 15th Mechanised Corps into battle had to be abandoned. In essence the formation led by General I.I. Karpezo conducted defensive missions for the majority of the Border battle, and was an extension of the crooked flank of the 6th Army.

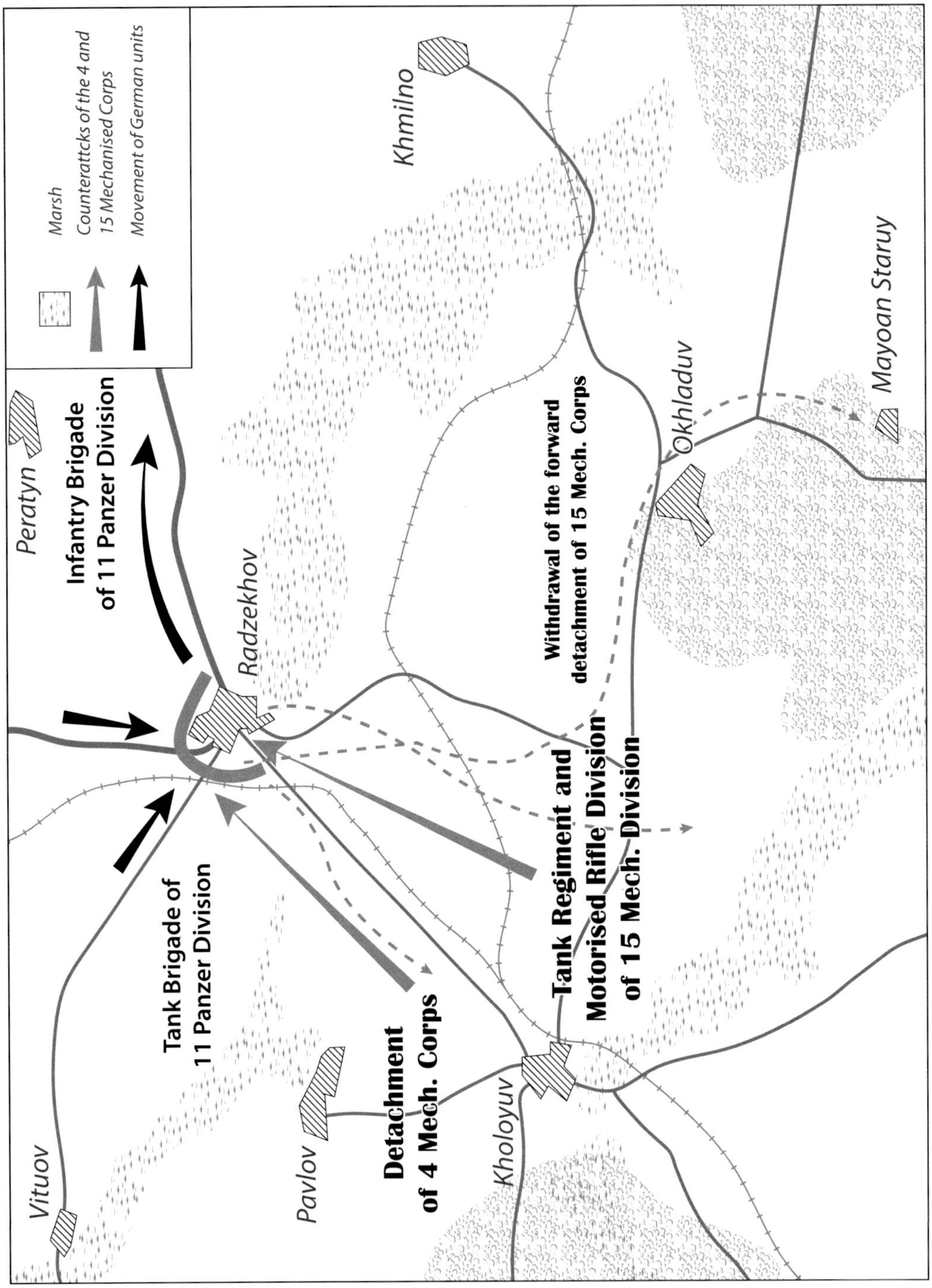

Map 5 The tank battle near Radzekhov 23 June 1941.

The command of the South-Western Front reacted very nervously to the information that spoke of the German *panzer* spearhead turning south behind the lines of the forces in the Lvov salient. Actually, after turning off the central '*Panzerstrasse*' to the south, the German *panzer* divisions could recapture the escape routes for the 6th and 26th Armies as well as units within the forces of the 12th Army. Considering there was no clearly defined front line at this point the German mechanised corps units could reach behind the lines in the Lvov salient very quickly. The next time around a characteristic idiosyncrasy of the way a defensive operation is conducted would emerge—namely the uncertainty of the enemy's plans. The German units did indeed break through to Berestechko and Scurowisce (Leshnev). From the river crossings at Scurowisce it was only 30km to Brody. In itself a turn to Brody towards the Lvov salient would appear logical. East of Berestechko and Brody the River Ikva runs in a north-south direction with a very marshy floodplain. It would have been very sensible not to try and cross this border but to turn south. This variant of the course of events could not be excluded from the possible actions taken by the enemy.

Incidentally aerial reconnaissance reports also had an effect on the enemy's activities on 24 June. The ambivalence of the 15th Mechanised Corps made them nervous since the tanks and vehicles of the Soviet tank units broke cover onto the roads where they were then discovered from the air. On the morning of 24 June an entry appeared in the combat journal of the *XXXXVIII Corps*: "At around 0700 hrs our aerial reconnaissance first reported large-scale concentrations of enemy tanks to the south of the highway." Pay particular attention to the word 'first.' The movements of the 15th Mechanised Corps in the first two days of the war went seemingly unnoticed. The capabilities of the apparently ubiquitous German aircraft were not limitless.

Messages from aerial reconnaissance forced the German command to slow the pace of the advance to the west somewhat. The *57th Infantry Division* received an order at 1500 hrs that no units were to cross the River Styr except *aufklärung* units. The intentions of the divisional commander for at least one regiment to cross to the eastern bank of the Styr were broadcast to Kempf by radio. The division was to have been at full readiness to counter attacks by Soviet tanks on the corps' flanks. Within the confines of this strategy for the defence of the *11th Panzer Division*'s flank the order came through to blow up the bridge near Leshnev.

However, apart from the perceived and the simply imagined threats on the second day the dangers of a very palpable and unpleasant threat arose. On the 6th Army's front line the events occurred that Muzychenko had warned about. G.K. Zhukov wrote:

> ...By the end of the day [23 June] German forces had found a weak link: they dealt a heavy blow at the point where the Rava-Ruska and Peremyshl fortified sectors joined, which was defended by the 97th and the 159th Rifle Divisions. The latter was in the process of being formed and the line-up of the division included a significant number of untrained reserve soldiers. They were not able to withstand enemy attacks and went on the retreat, creating serious problems for the neighbouring units. The countermeasures adopted by the commander of the 6th Army, General I.N. Muzychenko, did nothing to rectify the situation and by the end of 24 June the breach in the defence had reached 40km at this point.[3]

In the previous few days the 4th Mechanised Corps, instead of participating in the counterattack on the front, was engaged in solving the crisis that had arisen as a result of the *17. Armee*'s infantry formations in the direction of Lvov.

3 Zhukov, p.273.

The War in the Air

Although according to the impressions of German tank crews close to Radzekhov they faced waves of Soviet T-34 tanks, as well as 'Stalin's falcons' in the shape of BT bombers, there was no such close cooperation between the Air Forces of the South-Western Front and the mechanised corps. The aviation divisions received their mission instructions from front line Air Force command on how they were to attack the enemy troops and conducted them according to their available forces and capabilities. Moreover the order that was received from Ptukhin was relatively complex (see the appendices).

The air raid on enemy troops (the first one was near Ustyluh on 22 June) encountered a relatively fierce enemy resistance. The 86th High-Speed Bomber Regiment, 16th Aviation Division, took off towards the target in two groups: a group of nine aircraft under the command of Lieutenant-Colonel Sorokin and a group of six aircraft under the command of the deputy regimental commander Captain Beliy. The first took off at 0530 hrs and the second at 0540 hrs. It was proposed that the fighter cover would be provided by the aircraft of the 92nd Fighter Aviation Regiment. In view of the lack of communications on the fighter airfield in Brody the SBs were sent into battle at 0440 hrs. The fighters however completely failed to materialise. It later emerged that the airfield on which the 92nd Fighter Aviation Regiment were based was subject to an air attack. As a result seven I-153s were damaged in the raid (which were repaired the following day). In the end the SBs in Sorokin's group flew to the target without fighter cover. Over Brody Sorokin's group encountered one and a half-dozen '*Messerschmitts*' that more than likely were from the same group of aircraft that bombed the fighter airfield. Out of the nine Soviet bombers three were shot down and a further two were damaged and landed on their 'bellies'. The group under Captain Beliy encountered the '*Messerschmitts*' but managed to escape and successfully bombed the concentrations of tanks and artillery 4km to the west of Krystynopol. On their return to their airfield these same SBs that had evaded an encounter with *Me-109*s were attacked in error by our own I-16s. One bomber was damaged and ground looped on landing. The aircraft was completely destroyed but luckily the crew escaped injury. The fighters in the aviation division covered Ternopil (front line headquarters) and conducted reconnaissance around Sokal and Krystynopol. The German advance could clearly be seen and the villages that were burning in the enemy occupied zone could be seen from a distance. It is interesting to note that the 87th Fighter Aviation Regiment had now moved to a new base and operated from Ternopil airfield, which reduced the time for reconnaissance reports to be delivered to front line headquarters. The '*ishachki*' of the 87th Regiment along with the '*MiGs*' of the 15th Aviation Division became the 'eyes' of the South-Western Front headquarters. In total the 16th Aviation Division flew 173 combat sorties, dropping 120 FAB-100 bombs on the enemy.

The aircraft of the 62nd Aviation Division received no less a rebuff when they attacked Ustyluh and Grubeshuv since the river crossings over the Bug were afforded intensive protection from the '*Luftwaffe*'. The 94th and 52nd Regiments of SB bombers flew 91 combat sorties, dropping 500 FAB-100 and 84 FAB-50 bombs, for the loss of 14 aircraft and 42 aircrew. However it has to be noted that not one regiment dropped this number of bombs in the space of one day over the entire Border battle. The other aviation formations that took off to attack these same targets also sustained heavy losses. Thirty-three crews, after having bombed Ustyluh and Grubeshuv from an altitude of 1,900m in DB-3s belonging to the 18th Aviation Division, lost nine aircraft to escorting enemy fighters. In total the DB-3s flew 42 sorties in a day, dropping 298 FAB-100 bombs. The crossings at Ustyluh were defended by the *I* and *II Grouppen* of *JG3* Fighter Squadron. The first of these reported 19 aircraft shot down on 23 June, and the second 15 aircraft shot down. The majority of the aircraft shot down were SBs and DB-3s.

Following the specific confusion of the first day of the war the Soviet aviation formations gradually participated in the combat operations. Aside from the missions that were set by front line command, aviation also operated in the interests of the Army. The *'MiGs'* of the 15th Aviation Division, over the course of a day on 23 June, covered the advance of the units in the 4th Mechanised Corps from the air. Over 10 air battles and a total of 91 combat sorties the pilots of the 23rd Fighter Aviation Regiment lost four *'MiGs'* and claimed six enemy aircraft shot down. Out of the six enemy fighters that had been shot down four were for some reason identified as Polish PZLs. It is possible that this referred to the German *'Heinkel-129'* reconnaissance aircraft, which were far from reminiscent of the Polish aircraft in terms of their aerodynamic configuration—a parasol-monoplane. The 28th Fighter Aviation Regiment conducted 29 air battles, over the course of 140 combat sorties. The regiment claimed four enemy aircraft shot down for the loss of three crews and the failure of eight aircraft. In total the 15th Aviation Division conducted 345 combat sorties on 23 June, dropping 45 FAB-50s and 58 AO-10 bombs (from both fighters, and bombers).

Ptukhin's clear instruction dated 23 June made reference to the strongest regiment in the 17th Aviation Division: "The 48th High-Speed Bomber Aviation Regiment (which were equipped with Pe-2 aircraft) are to be re-dispersed to operational airfields along with the withdrawal of airfields across the border and are to be carefully camouflaged." Evidently the commander of the Air Forces of the South-Western Front was attempting to preserve the regiment from air raids and to use the newest bombers as his trump card. On 23 June *'peshki'* did not depart on any combat missions and neither did they incur any losses in the air or on the ground. The fighters of the 17th Aviation Division covered the railway junctions.

From the components of the 19th Aviation Division on 23 June it was only the 33rd High-Speed Bomber Aviation Regiment that was active (the other two regiments were not mentioned in the order issued by Ptukhin). This regiment bombed Parkhach and Krystynopol, completing 36 combat sorties and dropping 156 FAB-100 bombs. One SB was shot down by a fighter, while another was damaged.

Overall it could be said that the Air Forces of the South-Western Front increased their activity level significantly on the second day of the war. Some 183 combat sorties were used to strike the enemy, or 31.2 percent of the total.

24 June

Gradually the ideas of Kirponos and Purkayev, concerning ways of stabilising the front line that had been fractured on the first day of the war, began to look more and more positive. South-Western Front command decided to use 'remote' rifle divisions, that had encountered the war half way on their journey to the border, to construct a new defensive front line. Their mission was as follows: "With the support of the anti-tank sectors, not to allow the enemy's mechanised units to breakthrough to the east." Correspondingly in a position at right angles to the central *'Panzerstrasse'* three divisions of the 36th Rifle Corps advanced along the frontier of the River Ikva on a broad front, while divisions from the 31st Rifle Corps advanced at right angles to the northern *'Panzerstrasse'*. This shield was not able to withstand the enormous enemy forces, however the counterattacks by the mechanised corps were designed to reduce the enemy's forces that remained at the cutting edge of the main thrust.

However all these measures merely promised a change in the situation for the better. Considering the tactics employed by Crüwell with his 'infantry' and *'panzer' kampfgruppen* no counterattack would be able to halt the advance of the *XXXXVIII Motorised Corps*. While the *'panzer' kampfgruppe* would stray from the Soviet tanks, the 'infantry' group, in accordance with the principle of 'Listen to advice but do your own thing' would have covered another several dozen kilometres. Therefore the information received from aerial reconnaissance and the alignment of a shield in the shape of a front line to the south did not have any decisive influence on the advance of the *11th Panzer Division* towards Dubno. Any direct influence on the 'infantry' *kampfgruppe* was lacking on 24 June. They did not encounter defensive lines busy with infantry and artillery or any attacks from tank units.

Early in the morning units of the *11th Panzer Division* crossed the River Styr and prepared to advance to the east. Crüwell's division was due to push forward in two groups: the motorcycle battalion from the bridgehead that had been captured that morning near Ostrov, and an 'infantry' *kampfgruppe* from a bridgehead near Scurowisce. An unexpected opponent however stood in the way of a decisive forward thrust.

> At around midday the commander of the corps verbally, along with the corps' headquarters, which broadcast it by radio, gave the target for the advance—Dubno. At 1000 hrs the motorcycle battalion left from the bridgehead near Ostrov, and the *110th Schützen-Regiment* departed from the bridgehead at Scurowisce at the same time, although in view of constant air raids the forward advance was slow.[4]

Prior to this in the early hours of the morning the 'Stalin's falcons' had attacked the river crossing at Scurowisce disturbing the build-up of forces at the bridgehead. The issue of the air raids by the aviation divisions of the Air Forces of the South-Western Front will be examined in a little more detail later on, but it makes sense at this point just to mention the outcome: Dubno was not captured on 24 June. By 1800 hrs the 'infantry' *kampfgruppe* in the division had advanced as far as Werba on the outer approaches to Dubno. Crüwell's division moved in a vacuum, and it was only small, individual subdivisions that happened to find themselves on the '*Panzerstrasse*' that put up any resistance to them at best. Despite this the *11th Panzer Division* were not able to carry out Kempf's order due to the impact of powerful air attacks. The Dubno storm was postponed until the following day. The sheer humiliation of this fact is recorded in an entry in the combat journal of *Army Group South* dated 24 June. "Overall our air forces have secured air superiority." If they had secured it then they secured it, but they had forgotten to let 'Stalin's falcons' know.

The delay in moving the *11th Panzer Division* forward on 24 June also influenced the long-term plans of German command. They envisaged a further mobile formation joining the battle on the central '*Panzerstrasse*' in the shape of the *16th Panzer Division* led by Hans-Valentin Hube. After stretching along the road the 60km 'hose' made up of subdivisions of the *11th Panzer Division* finally stretched all the way to the territory of the USSR. Correspondingly a decision was taken in the middle of the day to commit Hube's division to battle along the road itself via Krystynopol. A further delaying factor were the border fortifications of the 'Molotov Line'. The pillboxes in the area around Krystynopol continued to growl with gunfire and the command of the *XXXXVIII Army Corps* had promised to beat a path for the *16th Panzer Division* by the middle of the day on 24 June. By evening the units in Hube's division had begun to reach the territory of the USSR and advanced towards Radzekhov. The rearward units of the *11th Panzer Division* that had concentrated along the '*Panzerstrasse*' hindered any further movement forward. As follows from the *XXXXVIII Corps*' notes Kempf himself took the decision to stop pushing Hube's division along a dead highway: "The orders issued by the corps' headquarters of the *11th Panzer Division* to free up the road for the passage of the *16th Panzer Division* by 2000 hrs are not to be realised, since the Corps' Commander, based on his personal observations of this location, has given a verbal order that this deadline be extended until 2400 hrs. Therefore the main body of the *16th Panzer Division* can use this evening as an opportunity to rest."[5]

4 NARA T314 R1138, f491.
5 NARA T314 R1138, f492.

Aleksandrovka

The main event of the 24 June was, naturally, the tank battle that unfolded half way between Volodymyr-Volynskyi and Lutsk. Sometimes this is linked to the name of the village of Voynitsa, although the actual battlefield was to the east, close to the village of Aleksandrovka. The fact that there are a relatively large number of villages named 'Aleksandrovka' is another matter, and it would be more accurate to link this to the less widely used name of 'Voynitsa'. The precursors to the clash of Soviet and German tanks near Aleksandrovka happened on 23 June. Meanwhile the front line command was feverishly gathering its mechanised corps for a counterattack, the 5th Army command were also planning to send their reserves into battle with the aim of stabilising the situation. Among these was the 135th Rifle Division, which was part of the 22nd Mechanised Corps and the 1st Anti-Tank Artillery Brigade. The commander of the 5th Army, M.I. Potapov, formulated the objectives for the troops subordinate to him as follows: "The army is to continue to stubbornly defend the front line that is in our hands, without letting the enemy break through: the reserves are to destroy the Volodymyr-Volynskyi enemy alignment and restore the state border."

The initial time for the counterattack was set for 2200 hrs on 23 June, however considering the dangers of concluding a march in daylight for the 135th Rifle Division and the 22nd Mechanised Corps, it was postponed until the morning of 24 June. It was envisaged that they would take up their starting positions by 0400 hrs on 24 June. The 135th Rifle Division, under General F.N. Smekhotvorov, by the morning of 24 June had taken up its initial position for an attack on the boundary between Aleksandrovka (3km east of Voynitsa), Krukhenichki and Lokachi. In doing so the division used its right flank to block the northern '*Panzerstrasse*'. Further north was an enormous marshy forest and it would not have made much sense to seal this off. Behind the 135th Rifle Division, to the east of Aleksandrovka and in the glades to the south, the 1st Anti-Tank Artillery Brigade was taking up its position, as well as the 460th Artillery Regiment, 27th Rifle Corps, and the artillery of the 135th Rifle Division. They had been unified into a common artillery group led by the head of 5th Army artillery Major-General V.N. Sotensk. It should be noted that in accordance with a report by the commander of the 5th Army, Potapov, the lack of artillery rounds for the 37mm and 85mm anti-aircraft guns was keenly felt, and in connection with this two batteries from the 1st Anti-Tank Artillery Brigade, which were equipped with this armament, did not take part in the battle. The main armament for the anti-tank crews under Moskalenko was to have been the 76mm guns. The 19th Tank Division by the morning of 24 June had still not arrived at the starting point and as such the counterattack, set for 0400 hrs on 24 June, was postponed to a later time—to await the arrival of the 19th Tank Division.

However the alignment that had been put together by Potapov never succeeded in going on the offensive. At 0800 hrs on 24 June the tanks and motorised infantry that belonged to the *14th Panzer Division* and which had advanced along the '*Panzerstrasse*', supported by air strikes and forestalling the Soviet troops, themselves attacked the 135th Rifle Division from out of the forest to the north of Voynitsa, driving them back five or six kilometres to the east.

Shortly after midday and to the sound of rumbling gunfire the 19th Tank Division, 22nd Mechanised Corps approached the battlefield. Moreover 'approached' is a big word. The build-up of the division had not yet been completed and only part of the force would be able to participate in the battle. The starting positions for the offensive, which had been pre-determined, had already been taken by the enemy. Without waiting for the formation to build-up the corps commander of the 22nd Mechanised Corps, Kondrusev, ordered the attack at 1330 hrs. Thirty minutes later, at 1400 hrs, just 45 T-26 tanks and 12 BA-10 armoured cars, which had been unified into a single tank regiment under the command of Lieutenant-Colonel B.G. Bibik, moved forward into battle. The German infantry that had come under attack began to retreat, however a short time later

German tanks came out of the woods to meet the consolidated regiment of T-26 tanks, these German vehicles were recognised as 'medium' tanks. The battle continued for two and a half hours. The outcome of the clash of the light T-26s with the German *panzer*s was predictable. The T-26s did not have an upper hand, not in terms of speed, visibility for the crew, or in terms of armour. According to a report written by the head of the 19th Tank Division "Following the loss of more than half of our tanks the retreat began."[6]

The German side characterised the events as "A protracted battle of tank against tank" in which, according to the first report, 21 Soviet tanks were destroyed. This coincides relatively accurately with the Soviet assessment of the loss of half of the vehicles that took part in the attack (45 T-26s). Moreover the Germans listed nine "20–30 tonne" heavy tanks among their losses. Considering that neither the T-34 nor the T-28s were in service with the 19th Tank Division, this claim does seem strange to say the least. Overall the attack on the T-26s was assessed with a degree of respect. In the history of the *14th Panzer Division* it is described as follows: "In the second half of the day on 24 June a powerful enemy tank attack was repelled by the infantry and the *36th Panzer Regiment* close to Aleksandrovka." It is hard to imagine a 'powerful attack' in terms of the T-26s, nevertheless this is how it appeared to the enemy.

Enemy losses in this tank battle were assessed by the Soviet side as eight medium, and two heavy tanks. According to a daily report written by the *14th Panzer Division* to the headquarters of the *III Motorised Corps* our own losses in the battle near Aleksandrovka amounted to six tanks. Furthermore the number of Soviet tanks destroyed was raised to 87. The next morning this claim had risen to 158 tanks, 40 anti-tank guns, and eight artillery batteries.[7] Subsequently the number of tanks destroyed had jumped to 176 units, with 40 anti-tank guns, and 12 artillery batteries. Aside from this wholesale increase on the initial figure a realistic explanation for what happened to these figures could be the fact that the tank duel continued as the 19th Tank Division approached. Photographic material confirms the participation of radio-controlled tanks belonging to the 22nd Mechanised Corps outside Voynitsa. Clearly then the battle was not solely confined to the attack on 45 T-26s given the mechanised corps' involvement in the fighting with the *14th Panzer Division*.

In the history of the *14th Panzer Division* the battle continued into the next day: "The tank battle near Aleksandrovka developed in such a way that up to 25 June 156 enemy tanks had been destroyed."[8] Considering that as of 0600 hrs on 26 June the 19th Tank Division had just four tanks, 14 guns and two battalions of motorised infantry the German figures on the battle look, at the very least, plausible. Of the 163 tanks and the fact that field artillery was 100 percent complete in this formation, almost nothing remained. In the battle outside Voynitsa the commander of the 22nd Mechanised Corps, Major-General S.M. Kondrusev, was killed and the commander of the 19th Tank Division, Major-General K.A. Semenchekno, was injured. After taking the T-26 tanks of the division into a tank battle the commander of the 37th Tank Regiment, Lieutenant-Colonel B.G. Bibik, was captured, the commander of the 38th Tank Regiment, I.F. Samsonov, was killed and the commander of the motorised rifle regiment, Lieutenant-Colonel V.V. Sokolin, was wounded and later succumbed to his injuries.

The fuel for the increasing German claims concerning the numbers of Soviet tanks that were destroyed could be the steady harvest by the Germans of immobilised tanks on the way to Lutsk.

The combat vehicles in the 22nd Mechanised Corps undoubtedly remained on the roads as a result of a lack of fuel, as well as technical problems. During the retreat these tanks became trophies for the Germans. Somehow or other though the tank battle outside Aleksandrovka forced

6 The Central Archive of the Ministry of Defence, fund 3456, inventory 1, file 11, p.13.
7 T313 R4 f 830.
8 Grams, *Die 14.Panzer-Division 1940—1945* (Bad Nauheim: Verlag Hans-Henning Podzun, 1957), p.24.

the Germans to stop their rush towards Lutsk at some point. A daily report written by the *14th Panzer Division* for 24 June indicates: "It is doubtful that we will be able to reach Torchin today." Torchin was located around half way between Voynitsa and Lutsk, a '*Panzerstrasse*' passed through the town. Along which Mackensen's corps would proceed.

The events of 24 June were not limited to the tank battle with the *14th Panzer Division* outside Aleksandrovka. Between 1700–1800 hrs on 24 June the German *13th Panzer Division* reached the 135th Rifle Division's position. The *13th Panzer Division* was moving more slowly than its neighbour to the south of the '*Panzerstrasse*' along rural roads. Correspondingly the attack hit the left flank of the 135th Rifle Division. After a two-hour battle, and after losing the majority of its personnel and its artillery materiel, the 135th Rifle Division and the 1st Anti-Tank Brigade were pushed back in the direction of Lutsk.

Losses however for the *13th Panzer Division* also seemed relatively grievous. The famous western researcher Thomas Yentz provides very eloquent information concerning the condition of the tank fleet in the *1st Battalion, 4th Panzer Regiment*, in the *13th Panzer Division* (see table).

Table 4.1 The number of combat-ready tanks in the *1st* and *4th Tank Regiments, 13th Panzer Division*

	Pz.II	*Pz.III*	*Pz.IV*	Commanders' tanks
On the morning of 24 June	19	34	10	2
In the evening of 24 June	18	12	8	2

As we can see the number of combat capable tanks in the formation has fallen sharply and moreover to a large extent this concerned *Pz.III* medium tanks. Subsequently the number of combat capable *Pz.III* tanks in this battalion never reached 30 examples. What were for 1941 relatively heavy losses can be explained first and foremost by the clash with the 1st Anti-Tank Artillery Brigade. Taking stock of the battle outside Aleksandrovka (Voynitsa) it can be said that the units of the 5th Army did win time to organise defences outside Lutsk. Without the tank battle the *III Motorised Corps* would undoubtedly have reached Lutsk on the evening of 24 June. However only while both *panzer* divisions in Mackensen's corps were halted at the furthest approaches to the town.

The War in the Air

In the history of the *11th Panzer Division* the following lines are dedicated to the air raids carried out by Soviet aviation on 24 June:

> The Russian air raids, which were favourable in the continuing clear weather turned out to be an obstacle to our subsequent offensive. The engineering troops rebuilt the bridge over the Styr once again and at a location near Scurowisce we crossed the river and advanced on in the direction of Dubno. With the onset of darkness the *15th Panzer Regiment* had surpassed the daily marching objective of 50km, despite their participation in the fiercest combat.[9]

After finally coming round following the thunderous blow of 22 June the Air Forces of the South-Western Front attacked the enemy's mechanised and motorised columns that were advancing into the interior. High-speed bomber regiments of the 16th Aviation Division

9 Schrodek, *Ihr Glaube galt dem Vaterland. Geschichte des Panzer-Regiments 15 (11.Panzer-Division)* (München: Schild Verlag, 1976), p.130.

(consisting of 18 SBs, and Pe-2s) attacked enemy columns advancing via Berestechko, some 90 FAB-100 bombs were dropped without incurring losses. The aviation division only lost two I-153s that failed to return from a reconnaissance sortie. The bombers of the 17th Aviation Division (made up of 59 SBs and Pe-2s) also participated in the attacks on the columns in the area around Brody. Some 170 combat sorties were flown and 316 FAB-100 bombs were dropped as well as six FAB-50s. Two Pe-2s were shot down over the target by anti-aircraft fire, including the aircraft flown by the commander of the regiment Major Tsarikov, all the crew were killed. It is not clear what the targets were exactly that were attacked in the area around Brody since the enemy had yet to reach there as of 24 June. First and foremost the crews employed a relatively broad definition of the 'Brody area', as the central '*Panzerstrasse*' ran to the north of the town, not far from Leshnev. The 19th Aviation Division (made up of 71 SBs and Yak-2s) worked the columns in the area around Berestechko, Scurowisce and Radzekhov. Some 300 FAB bombs were dropped at the cost of one SB shot down by anti-aircraft fire. The crews observed direct hits and the pilots of the 136th Regiment attacked a column of tanks from an altitude of 800m in Yak-2s near Scurowisce and even claimed three enemy aircraft shot down. The 62nd Aviation Division (consisting of 93 SBs, and Pe-2s) also went into action, predominantly against targets on the central '*Panzerstrasse*' in the area around Leshnev and Scurowisce. The targets on the highway between Brest and Kovel were bombed using whatever was left. In total the bombers serving in the aviation divisions dropped 246 FAB-100 and 256 FAB-50 bombs. Losses amounted to six aircraft. A further two SBs were destroyed and five damaged as a result of an enemy attack on the airfield at Kremne. Overall one cannot fail to notice that the map of combat activity involving the bombers of the South-Western Front on 24 June was a far cry from traditional patterns. The air raids on the motorised and mechanised columns on that day bear no resemblance to the suicide attacks that are well documented in historical literature in which the majority of the unescorted SBs, and DB-3s were destroyed. This illustration would have been more typical of the Western Front. On the South-Western Front the losses among the bomber aviation regiments could be described as moderate.

The unceasing attack on the airfields forced the air forces of the front to examine the potential for an airfield manoeuvre. The newest '*MiGs*' in the 15th Aviation Division, 6th Army on 24 June were redeployed to Zubov airfield belonging to the neighbouring 16th Aviation Division. It is worth noting that as a result of this, up until 2200 hrs, the 28th Fighter Aviation Regiment was grounded due to a lack of fuel following their redeployment. Cover was only provided for the 86th High-Speed Bomber Aviation Regiment between 2000–2100 hrs. The 23rd Fighter Aviation Regiment in turn provided cover for Zubov airfield, that is to say strictly speaking the division actually covered itself. This airfield manoeuvring was a double edged sword, the new locations did not have fuel, ammunition, or spare parts. Overall the redeployment had a negative impact on the operations of the 15th Aviation Division, as only 24 combat sorties were flown on 24 June.

On that same day there was a change in the command of the front line air forces. E.S. Ptukhin was again relieved of his service duties and was replaced by Lieutenant-General of Aviation F.A. Astakhov (who commanded the front line air forces up until the spring of 1941). Back on 20 June 1941 Ptukhin was removed from the post on account of "a high accident rate in the district's aviation divisions." However the outbreak of war forced an end to this staff reshuffle. Ptukhin's subsequent fate was tragic. On 3 July 1941 Yevgeniy Savvich was arrested and later shot. However one cannot fail to notice that the return of the former commander of the air rorces improved the management of the Air Force. Bagramyan wrote:

> Astakhov knew how to get the hang of things quickly. He knew the front line aviation units and the people within them well; and the pilots had respect for him, and loved him. The results of Fyodor Alekseyevich's efforts were quick in coming. Specifically he

> succeeded in making a drastic improvement in aerial reconnaissance. The results they achieved bore this out.[10]

Excluding Voynitsa on 24 June the front line air forces were the most active participant in the battle as it was flaring up. Aviation was perhaps the only way of slowing the advance of the leading formation of the *XXXXVIII Corps*. In the end the commander of the *11th Panzer Division* lashed out in a report to Kempf, which could even be called a complaint. General Crüwell wrote to his commander:

> There is a well-founded conjecture that the division will complete the tasks it has been set for today. Nevertheless this was in doubt for some time although the resistance offered by the enemy's ground forces could be described as not exceptionally heavy.
>
> The air raids however that the enemy has inflicted on us since early this morning on the sub-divisions packed onto one highway are the reason behind the delays, as well as the heavy losses in terms of both personnel and materiel. As its stands the division has lost 16 men killed and 50 injured, for the most part seriously. Furthermore on the basis of incomplete information the division lost 16 items of materiel, including the most valuable ones such as the heavy tractors.
>
> One look at the map is enough to be convinced that the disposition of the *11th Panzer Division* is attracting enemy air attacks and as such tomorrow, and over the next few days, we can expect them to continue and possibly to intensify.
>
> Therefore I strongly urge you to instil in the upper echelons an understanding of the fact that we urgently require fighter cover. With this aim in mind I have requested the attachment of one additional anti-aircraft battery on a self-propelled chassis, specifically the 16th Battery from the *'Herman Goering' Regiment.*
>
> I understand that the resources that can be spared to support the division are limited and that there are other locations in which they are also in short supply.[11]

Soviet aviation of course was in no position to stop the advance of Crüwell's division. However there is no doubt that were it not for the air raids the pace of the *11th Panzer Division*'s offensive would have been much faster. As the *4th Panzergruppe* 's offensive in the Baltics showed the pace of the advance of the mechanised formations can exceed 50km per day. It should be noted that the weak fighter cover was due to organisational, rather than technical problems. The combat journal of the *XXXXVIII Corps* notes: "The many requests for fighter cover sent to the *panzer* group from the corps can only be realised to a small degree, in as much as the fighters are not yet at the disposal of ground forces."[12] The actions of *JG3* on 24 June could hardly be called successful. If on 23 June *JG3* claimed 37 enemy aircraft destroyed then on 24 June the pilots in this squadron claimed just eight Soviet aircraft shot down.

As the enemy moved forward new factors emerged that impacted on the course of the air war. The non-combat losses in the Soviet aviation regiments began to rise. First and foremost it was the 14th Aviation Division that suffered the most from this and their airfields lay in the path of *Panzergruppe 1*. By 24 June the regiments in this division that were based on airfields at Mlynuv,

10 Bagramyan, p.139.
11 NARA T313 R1138 f 915–916.
12 NARA T313 R1138 f 491.

Kolki and Velitsk were forced to redeploy to Fyodorovka airfield near Volodymyr-Volynskyi. During the course of 22–24 June 1941 the division led by Colonel Zykanov lost:[13]

Ten aircraft, shot down in air combat;
Two aircraft shot down by enemy anti-aircraft artillery;
Eight aircraft that failed to return from their combat sorties;
Fifty-three aircraft destroyed on the airfield;
Five aircraft destroyed during withdrawal;
Forty-two aircraft that remained on territory captured by the enemy;
Nine aircraft were lost in accidents.

In total the 14th Aviation Division lost 129 machines in this way, including 26 training aircraft. As is evident from the above statistics 100 aircraft were lost somehow or other on the airfields themselves. The reader is to be reminded that by the outbreak of war there were 182 combat aircraft listed in this formation. The routing of the formation was not the result of a single attack on a 'sleeping' airfield. The division was systematically destroyed over the course of several days. The 17th Fighter Aviation Regiment, which was based on Velitsk airfield, was only destroyed on the third day of the war.

> On the morning of the third day a dozen *Me-109* fighters arrived. They split into two groups: six aircraft banked left, and six aircraft banked right, and then attacked us as if they were on a firing range. The strafing runs were accurate, confident, as if they were firing at targets towed behind an aircraft. As a result there were only 10 serviceable I-153s and one single MiG-1 left on the airfield, all the other aircraft, which amounted to around 150, were damaged.[14]

The fate of the 14th Aviation Division in the first few days of the war, reflected, just like a mirror, a catastrophe that had befallen the Air Forces of the Red Army. The enemy's rapid advance in the directions taken by the principal thrust of their attack forced the Soviet forces to abandon materiel, even if it had only been slightly damaged, or that had simply ran out of fuel. At the same time the lack of airfield manoeuvring led to large-scale losses on the airfields.

Naturally not all the aviation divisions on the South-Western Front ended up under the steamroller in the path of the main attack. The fate of the 14th Aviation Division was nevertheless an exceptional case. The situation as a whole however did not inspire optimism. Thus the 16th Aviation Division had 63 serviceable combat aircraft remaining by 24 June out of the 182 aircraft that they had at the outbreak of war. Correspondingly 13 aircraft were shot down in air combat, two failed to return from their combat mission, 31 were destroyed on the ground, and 47 were listed as being out of service for a period of time.[15] A further nine I-153s were sent to Lutsk (that is to say to the notorious 14th Aviation Division). In the 86th Bomber Aviation Regiment in this division on 24 June five SB-2s and four Pe-2s were listed as combat capable. Twenty-two SBs, and four Pe-2s were listed as unserviceable. The force of 35 SBs, and nine Pe-2s that were on hand as of 22 June was but a memory. The pace at which the materiel was taken out of course varied from formation to formation. For example the 15th Aviation Division on the third day of the war retained more than half of their aircraft. The distribution of the aircraft that the formation lost to technical failures was as follows (see table).

13 The Central Archive of the Ministry of Defence, fund 229, inventory 181, file 47, p.17.
14 Arkhipenko, p.25.
15 The Central Archive of the Ministry of Defence, fund 229, inventory 181, file 33, p.287.

It is clear that on the third day of the war losses on the airfield equalled the losses in the air (with the exception of all the Ground-Attack aircraft that the regiment lost on the morning of 22 June).

Table 4.2 The losses in the 15th Aviation Division between 22–24 June 1941[16]

	MiG-3	I-16	I-153	I-15	Il-2
Shot down in air combat	4	3	2	2	–
Shot down by flak	5	–	1	–	–
Failed to return	13	8	–	4	–
Destroyed on the airfield	23	11	–	27	3
Destroyed (abandoned) on the airfield	2	–	4	–	–
Accidents	1	–	1	2	–
Total	48	22	8	35	3

In total in the first three days of the war the aviation division lost 116 aircraft out of the 236 they had at the outbreak of war. However after three days of intense fighting not much was left of this former might in the shape of the fully-fledged MiG-3 regiments. By the end of the day on 24 June the 23rd Fighter Aviation Regiment listed six MiG-3s at combat readiness and four I-153s; while the 28th Fighter Aviation Regiment listed 21 MiG-3s; the 164th Fighter Aviation Regiment had 13 I-16s, 15 I-153s and one I-15; the 66th Ground-Attack Aviation Regiment had 19 I-15s and three Il-2s.

Given these statistics it is clear the losses inflicted in the air and on the ground significantly reduced the combat capabilities of the aviation division. However by the start of the decisive battle on the ground their combat capability had been retained.

25 June

As discussed above, the concept of a battle with the enemy's forces that had broken through at the point where the 5th and 6th Armies joined, which had been developed by front line command, envisaged not only a counterattack using the mechanised units along the flanks, and aerial attacks, but also keeping an advancing enemy back from the front line. For this to happen the so-called 'remote' rifle formations were activated, which had begun their march to the front line back in the middle of June. A look at the map shows that the choice that front line headquarters made in terms of using the River Ikva as a delaying boundary was very successful. This small river flowed from the north-west to the south-east, intersecting the path of the German advance between Volodymyr-Volynskyi–Zhitomir, and between Sokal–Berdichev. The river, with its marshy floodplain, could present a serious obstacle for the German *panzer* divisions even if the defensive positions along its banks were taken by the formations stretched along the front line. The main task was to reach this objective and at the very least to consolidate it. Against the backdrop of battles on the border and the columns of black smoke that were thrown up by tank battles, columns of these 'remote' corps were approaching the Ikva from the east. From the west came the tanks, vehicles and motorcycles of the German *panzer* divisions throwing up clouds of dust.

The overall disposition of the *11th Panzer Division* on 25 June remained unchanged. The 'infantry' *kampfgruppe* led its forward advance. The *panzer* regiment (or more accurately the

16 The Central Archive of the Ministry of Defence, fund 229, inventory 181, file 47, p.31 (on the back of the page).

'panzer' kampfgruppe) became stuck due to problems encountered on the way and on the morning of 25 June remained outside Ostrov, but Crüwell did not stop this advance. He stubbornly moved forward, bearing in mind that 'Time is blood.' By 0730 hrs the 'infantry' *kampfgruppe* in the division was taking the heights to the south-west of Dubno. At the same time the *aufklärung* battalion in the formation was nearing the end of a wide evasive manoeuvre via Manylov (a town, which was upstream of Dubno). The divisional command, as before, did not take a gamble on a successful seizure of just one river crossing. Both of them were attacked simultaneously. If it had been destroyed it would have been possible to regroup the forces that had recovered next to the ruined bridge for the next sector and not lose the momentum.

From the Soviet perspective the first dramatis personae in the wild drama that unfolded on the banks of the Ikva were the forward detachment of the 40th Tank Division, 19th Mechanised Corps. The division sent a tank company forward under the command of Senior Lieutenant Ivashkovskiy (this company consisted of 16 T-26 and T-38 tanks). At 1400 hrs on 24 June this company was ordered to take the river crossings in the area around Mlynuv and Dubno. Ivashkovskiy's detachment arrived in Mlynuv on time in order to fight the *aufklärung* battalion in Crüwell's division head on. Having lost two tanks the detachment of the 40th Tank Division departed from the river crossing.

Soviet commanders assessed the German forces in this battle as "An infantry regiment that was well equipped with anti-tank weaponry." This was clearly an exaggeration. The standard line-up for an *aufklärung* detachment in a German tank division was 407 men, which was approximately equivalent to a battalion. Its armament consisted of 25 armoured cars, three 37mm anti-tank guns, 11 other armour-piercing guns and two 75mm infantry guns. According to the mobilisation document *KStN* dated 1 February 1941 the armoured cars were distributed as follows: one *SdKfz 247* (an unarmed commander's armoured vehicle), one *SdKfz 263* (an eight-wheeled armoured car with one 7.92mm machine gun and a powerful radio set), four *SdKfz 223*s (a four-wheeled armoured car with a 7.92mm machine gun and a medium range radio set), three *SdKfz 232*s (an eight-wheeled armoured car with a 20mm gun), four *SdKfz 222*s (a four-wheeled armoured car with a 20mm gun) and 10 *SdKfz 221*s (a four-wheeled armoured car with a 7.92mm machine gun). By all accounts the impression of large anti-tank capabilities may have been created by the numerous 20mm automatic guns on the armoured cars in the *aufklärung* detachments in Crüwell's division. It is important to note at this point that the battles near Mlynuv provide an example of how to use an *aufklärung* battalion as an independent unit, not strictly for reconnaissance, but for conducting combat operations of their own. This approach was employed by German command sufficiently often.

If the 228th Rifle Division under Colonel A.M. Ilyina, which had been tasked with the defensive line running from Mlynuv to Dubno, was able to entrench itself successfully, then the 25 June could have become the blackest day for the *11th Panzer Division*. This however did not happen. On the morning of 25 June the Soviet rifle division was only just approaching Dubno and Mlynuv from the east. One of its rifle regiments, along with a howitzer artillery regiment (the 767th Rifle Regiment and the 366th Howitzer Artillery Regiment), advanced towards Mlynuv; while the second regiment along with light artillery regiments (the 799th and the 669th Light Artillery Regiments), an anti-tank battalion and a reconnaissance battalion advanced towards Dubno. The third regiment was in the second echelon. Everything was decided by a time discrepancy of literally a few hours in reaching the objective of the River Ikva. At 1100 hrs the *Schützen-Regiment 110, 11th Panzer Division* attacked Dubno from the south, while at the same time an *aufklärung* battalion, that had broken through near Mlynuv attacked from the north. At 1410 hrs on 25 June Dubno was captured. In his report Crüwell wrote that the town was occupied "in force" by Soviet troops. However up until the moment of the attack by the Germans the 529th Super-Heavy

Howitzer Regiment, as well as separate Red Army units, and possibly the soldiers from the airfield servicing battalion, were already there.

According to German information the trophies they captured in Dubno were as follows:

42 new 21cm guns;
62 machine guns;
95 Trucks;
50 Tractors;
Large reserves of petrol, oil, and flour;
Ammunition stores;
2,500 prisoners of war.[17]

According to Soviet information the 529th Super-Heavy Howitzer Regiment had twenty-seven 203mm B-4 howitzers, which were abandoned owing to a lack of tractors. There is every likelihood that this is the reason behind the overlap in the data for the captured B-4 and other weapons. That is to say the initial report concerning the capture of 42 weapons, including the 21cm examples, was interpreted subsequently as the capture of forty-two 21cm weapons.

After the enemy had forestalled the 228th Division in their advance to the boundary of the River Ikva their position could confidently be described as catastrophic. Aside from the defence along the marshy river they had to either recover these positions, or engage the enemy on open ground. Considering that on 1 June 1941 there were 8,210 men serving in the 228th Rifle Division, the majority of whom were in their first year of service, the chances of beating the enemy back from the positions they occupied following the disastrous delay on the morning of 25 June were practically non-existent. However since the opposing German units were considered assault troops (since they were a very long way from the border) an attempt was nevertheless made to win back Dubno and Mlynuv. A reconnaissance battalion even stormed into the centre of Dubno. However both forward regiments in the 228th Division were pushed back to their original positions. There were few tanks in the 'Angern *kampfgruppe*' but artillery was an advantage for the German tank divisions over the entire course of the war. Another attempt was made on the night of 25–26 June when one reinforced battalion each tried to recapture the towns of Mlynuv and Dubno in a night-time attack. The attack on Dubno was repelled, but Mlynuv was successfully captured and held. The *aufklärung* battalion of the *11th Panzer Division* passed through it in the course of an evasive manoeuvre and it turned out that the German battalion in the town was relatively small.

As the report by the Commander of the 40th Tank Division states:

> From 24 June to 25 June 1941 the tank company, operating in conjunction with the 228th R[ifle] D[ivision] attacked the en[emy] in fierce fighting killing troops and destroying weaponry. By the end of the day on 25 June 1941 the tank company had lost 11 T-26 tanks, two T-38 tanks and had three T-26 tanks in its line-up that required repair.

This battle saw an episode in which very peculiar use was made of a T-26 as a flamethrower tank by Lieutenant Oskin. Since his tank was not loaded with the mixture he used his tank as a flamethrower tank, destroying the Germans by firing his DT machine gun, as well as using the tank tracks themselves. In the combat journal of the *XXXXVIII Corps* the actions of the Soviet forward detachment are described in a laconic phrase: "The offensive is developing well, the attacks on our flanks from enemy tanks are being repelled."

17 NARA T313 R4 f1079.

Lutsk

The events that took place on 25 June on the approaches to Lutsk are in sharp contrast to the combat activity outside Dubno, which was clearly unsuccessful for the Soviet forces. The combat journal of *Army Group South* notes: "The *6. Armee*, which was subordinate to the *Panzergruppe 1* along with the *XXXXVIII Motorised Corps*, was able to capture Dubno, while the *III Motorised Corps*, which successfully conducted a tank battle in the course of its advance on 24 June, reduced the pace of the offensive considerably, only reaching Lutsk in the evening of 25 June."

In contrast to the approaches to Dubno, where Red Army units were practically absent, the 135th Rifle Division, which nevertheless retained their combat capability, had been pushed back to the approaches to Lutsk along with the 1st Anti-Tank Brigade. In the course of the day on 25 June the *14th Panzer Division* pushed through their defences and advanced along the northern '*Panzerstrasse*' via Torchin after losing 17 tanks.[18] That is to say the losses turned out to be officially higher than on the previous day in the course of the battle outside Voynitsa (Aleksandrovka). Infantry support would have proved very useful in these conditions. However despite the reduced pace of the advance of the *III Motorised Corps* they did not enjoy the support of the *298th Infantry Division*. This division was being pinned down by an attack from the 215th Motorised Division, 22nd Mechanised Corps. In accordance with the plan it was due to participate in the counterattack on 24 June but in view of its poor mobility in respect of an advance to the designated area the division was delayed. The division, under Colonel P.A. Barabanov, having completed a 120km march had only set off for the area around Werba by 2000 hrs on 24 June (this location is 8km north of Volodymyr-Volynskyi). Correspondingly the *298th Infantry Division* was forced to liquidate the threat to the flank of the *III Motorised Corps* and to counterattack. In the course of the pre-emptive attack the Germans succeeded in pushing units of the 215th Motorised Division back from the near approaches to Volodymyr-Volynskyi. What were successes in a tactical sense however had little effect on the advance.

This success, although it was limited, was unexpectedly achieved by the *13th Panzer Division* which had advanced using the rural roads. In view of this the division succeeded in avoiding Soviet defences that had been prepared on the highway that was being used as a '*Panzerstrasse*'. Having unexpectedly become a forward division, under General Duwert, they advanced towards Lutsk in the afternoon of 25 June, capturing the western part of the town as well as the bridge over the River Styr in this same area. However if the 228th Rifle Division had been pushed back in their march towards the boundary of the river Ikva then the 131st Motorised Division succeeded in taking up positions outside of Lutsk that bordered on the River Styr. On 22 June there were 123 tanks in the 131st Motorised Division (28 BT-7s, 59 BT-5s, and 36 BT-2s).[19] Of these vehicles 83 departed on the march on the evening of 22 June. The remaining 40 were unserviceable owing to wear on the tracks and on the track pins. By 25 June five of these tanks had been repaired and had been sent on to Lutsk in pursuit of their counterparts. After a 120km march only 35 tanks had reached the assembly area in Bronniki (to the west of Rivne) of the 83 that had set off. It was these same tanks, in the form of a single composite battalion and two reconnaissance companies, that took up a defence in the area around Lutsk on the morning of 25 June along with the motorised rifle regiments of the 131st Motorised Division. Despite the obvious weakness in this detachment the Germans managed to ford the River Styr whilst under fire in the evening of 25 June. There was no lightning fast attack in the middle of the day as there had been in Dubno however.

On 27 June the mission for the 27th Rifle Corps on the left bank of the River Styr, if not yet completed, had at least halted. Since the *13th Panzer Division* was located close to Lutsk the only

18 18 NARA T313 R4 f935.

19 19 The Central Archive of the Ministry of Defence, fund 229, inventory 157, file 7, volume 1, p.113.

way to pull away and over the river was via the river crossings to the north of the town. The bridge that was designed for road and horse-drawn traffic had already been blown up. In this uncertain environment, when an enemy breakthrough is to be expected at any minute, it is always difficult to anticipate the moment when the breakthrough will happen. They were either early or late. This was true of the entire war and on both sides of the front line.

The railway bridge across the River Styr at Rozhishche provided hope of an organised river crossing that would allow the materiel to cross unscathed. An enormous number of people had gathered next to this bridge. On many occasions in the course of the war river crossings served as the last hope for the salvation of people who were covered in gunpowder residue and were also dead tired. The bridge was fired upon by artillery and aircraft strafed and bombed it, yet this did not stop those intent on escaping a mousetrap.

As the Commander of the 1st Anti-Tank Artillery Brigade, K.S. Moskalenko, recalled:

> Suddenly the logistics sub-divisions rushed onto the bridge together with the horse-drawn artillery from the line-up of the 27th Rifle and 22nd Mechanised Corps. Yielding to the panic, several hundred people, jostling with one another, attempted to break through to the other side. Their horses broke their legs between the railway sleepers, the wagons and armament were all bunched together forming a traffic jam. An unimaginable frenzy started. People were unharnessing the horses, trying to rush back to the bank or fell straight into the water. After several enemy shells had exploded nobody was left on the bridge apart from overturned carts and vehicles. It would take several hours to clear the bridge. There was no time to think again as the lives of many thousands of people were at stake. I sent two KV tanks from the 41st Tank Division that were at my disposal onto the bridge. These powerful combat vehicles cleared the bridge using their own weight and we had restored this river crossing.[20]

The use of at least one KV-2 on the river crossing at Rozhishche is confirmed in archive documents. The 41st Tank Division was unavoidably taken apart to plug the gaps. Its KV-2s were no exception. According to a report written by the divisional commander P.P. Pavlov, a single KV was stopped by Moskalenko and sent into battle to cover the bridge, it was true that its main armament was a machine gun (with a rate of fire for the 152mm gun, with which it was also equipped, of one shell every three and a half minutes this is not surprising). An attempt by German *panzers* to break through to the bridge was unsuccessful owing to the presence of the KV, it was "Attacked by two enemy tanks armed with 20mm guns [evidently these were *Pz.II*s – author] and these enemy tanks had come straight from the battlefield."[21] The Germans noticed the arrival of the KV tanks, the *14th Panzer Division*'s daily report stated: "The enemy's heaviest tanks appeared on the *aufklärung* battalion's front line for the first time."[22]

Over the course of the night of 26 June the 135th Rifle and 19th Tank Divisions and 1st Anti-Tank Brigade crossed to the right flank of the Styr on the railway bridge, getting away from the forward German units that had been pressing. A broad front from Rozhishche to Ostrozhets (15km south-east of Lutsk) was defended by the motorcycle regiment of the 22nd Mechanised Corps and the 131st Motorised Division of the 9th Mechanised Corps. Now the defensive capabilities of the Soviet forces on the boundary of the River Styr in the area around Lutsk had increased significantly.

20 Moskalenko, pp.39–40.
21 The Central Archive of the Ministry of Defence, fund 3456, inventory 1, file 11, p. 93.
22 NARA T313 r183 f152.

Aufklärung and motorcycle battalions in the *14th Panzer Division,* that had followed the departing Soviet forces, nevertheless managed to secure a fragile bridgehead at Rozhishche. In essence this served as a 'suitcase without a handle,' which it would be a shame to throw away, but which could not be carried easily. The main forces within the division replaced their neighbour, the *13th Panzer Division*, on the bridgehead near Lutsk. They were to have attempted to break through onto the '*Panzerstrasse*' heading east. In turn the *13th Panzer Division* were to have launched an attack by-passing Lutsk from the south. In this situation this fragile bridgehead that was located to the side of the '*Panzerstrasse*' was not absolutely necessary and only served to disperse the forces. Furthermore, for the Germans, it became a headache in view of the need to reinforce it. According to the daily report from the *14th Panzer Division* dated 26 June:

> In accordance with the report from 1800 hrs the enemy attempted to crush the bridgehead with considerable artillery support. In order to offer their assistance to the motorcycle battalion a rifle battalion and one heavy battery with one artillery reconnaissance battery have been sent there immediately. At present the battle continues. A radiogram received from the motorised battalion gives a figure for the losses of around 15 percent.[23]

Details concerning the actions of the 9th Mechanised Corps between 26–28 June have not survived. In their memoirs M.E. Katukov and K.K. Rokossovskiy dismiss in broad terms the inaccuracies with which these events are linked together in time. The fact that not everything went smoothly was recorded on an operational intelligence report from 5th Army headquarters dated 28 June, which states: "The 20th Tank Division, which was encircled in the course of a battle with motorised and mechanised enemy units, has escaped this encirclement in the area around Lutsk." The reports from the *13th Panzer Division* however spoke of fierce enemy resistance and that the formation was moving forward at a slow pace. As a whole the tank battle outside Voynitsa (Aleksandrovka) and the battle with the mechanised corps under K.K. Rokossovskiy cost the Germans dear. Thus on 2 July 1941 some 120 combat capable tanks were listed as in service with the *14th Panzer Division*, while the *13th Panzer Division* listed 78 tanks.[24] Some eight and 60 tanks respectively were in for repair at the time, and 14 and eight tanks respectively had been subject to irrevocable losses. Therefore the *13th Panzer Division*, which had forced its way around the units of the 9th Mechanised Corps, did suffer quite severely for 1941 standards.

The War in the Air

If the most powerful mechanised corps in the South-Western Front were not able to gather in their initial positions for a counterattack then the Air Forces of the South-Western Front were operating with sufficient energy as before. A description of 25 June, written by Schrodek, begins with the words: "Soviet aircraft again took to the skies with the first rays of the sun." Columns of tanks from the *11th Panzer Division*, and the units attached to them, were opposed by the majority of the bomber formations of the Air Forces of the South-Western Front. The 17th Aviation Division conducted 113 combat sorties in which 360 FAB-100 bombs were dropped. Our own losses for our aviation divisions were one Pe-2 shot down by a fighter and one SB shot down by anti-aircraft artillery. The 19th Aviation Division conducted 64 combat sorties on columns in the area around Scurowisce and Berestechko and 277 FAB-100 bombs were dropped. Losses amounted to three SBs. The 18th Aviation Division dropped 20 tonnes of bombs over 13 combat sorties in the area

23 NARA T313 r183 f152.
24 NARA T313 R4 f1477.

around Krystynopol and Berestechko; a single DB-3 was shot down by enemy anti-aircraft fire. Fighters from the 15th Aviation Division also attacked columns that were moving along the road between Berestechko and Radzekhov.

The majority of the air formations flew two sorties each: one in the morning and the other in the afternoon. The 62nd Aviation Division was probably the only division to spend much of the day unoccupied. It was focused on air raids north of Kovel carrying out 54 combat sorties with no losses. As we now know however the German mechanised corps were not active in this direction and in general the area around Kovel was on the periphery of the offensive by *Army Group South.*

German fighter-pilots claimed 30 Soviet aircraft destroyed on 25 June. The majority of these aircraft shot down were claimed by pilots from *II Group JG3* Fighter Squadron, some 16 aircraft, mostly in the area around Berestechko. The new Pe-2s were initially recorded as French Potez-63 aircraft. The designation 'Pe-2' only appeared in claims submitted by pilots two or three days later. The activity in which the *Luftwaffe*, and 'Stalin's falcons' were engaged is assessed in the combat journal of the *XXXXVIII Corps* as follows: "As anticipated at Corps' headquarters Russian aviation, having assessed the situation, has been conducting constant attacks on the corps' units that has advanced some distance ahead. Although this slows down the offensive our fighter aircraft are already beginning to demonstrate their effectiveness."[25]

It would be pertinent at this point to remind the reader that on 25 June the corps received its next orders for Ostrog and Kremenets. Neither of these points was reached. Overall however a mission to cover columns of tanks and vehicles was not a first priority one for the *Luftwaffe.* In this period the *V Fliegerkorps* continued their operations aimed at destroying Soviet aviation on the airfields. The Germans did achieve some success in this field, despite the fact that the airfields were far from 'sleepy'. Thus on Gogolev airfield seven TB-3s from the 14th Heavy Bomber Aviation Regiment were destroyed. On Zubov airfield five I-16s, and one I-153 were damaged in a sudden attack at 0720 hrs in the morning. On Popovitse airfield one SB and five I-15s became victims of an air raid.

On the Periphery of the Battle

Having advanced in the direction of the breakthrough by the 1st Tank Division from the south face of the Lvov salient, and having been transferred initially to come under the 6th Army, the 8th Mechanised Corps remained on the periphery of the battle for a considerable time. Its first manoeuvre was to advance to the area around Kurovice, Vynnyky and Boryniche, to the west of Lvov. The corps received the order from front line headquarters at 2040 hrs on 22 June 1941. It was issued within the confines of the general assembly for forces to prepare for a counterattack against the enemy that had broken through from the Sokal salient. Between 2300–2400 hrs on 22 June the mechanised corps began to march to a new area along two routes and in the afternoon of 23 June the leading units in the corps had reached their designated area. At around 1520 hrs on 23 June the commander of the 6th Army sent the 8th Mechanised Corps to the area around Yavorov. The first to move to the new assembly area between 0330–0400 hrs on 24 June was the 34th Tank Division. The manoeuvres began to take their toll on the materiel in the formation: at the time of the departure to the area around Yavorov 29 T-26s, 17 T-35s, six BTs and 45 vehicles were listed as remaining. At around 0600 hrs the remainder of the units in the 8th Mechanised Corps joined the 34th Tank Division. This was as a result of I.N. Muzychenko's wish to use the mechanised corps, led by Ryabishev, for a counterattack in the area around Rava-Ruska. The 8th Mechanised Corps

25 NARA T314 R1138 f494.

was only withdrawn from Muzychenko's authority on the morning of 24 June and again returned to use in front line counterattacks.

One peculiarity of the tank battle in the triangle formed of Lutsk—Brody—Dubno is the fighting on the 6th Army's front line, in which the most powerful corps in the Kiev Special Military District—namely the 4th Mechanised Corps—participated. While the 22nd Mechanised Corps engaged the enemy tanks in battle outside Voynitsa on the northern face of the Lvov salient units of the 4th Mechanised Corps clashed with enemy infantry. As the commander of the 6th Army had anticipated the Germans began to probe the defences of the 6th Rifle Corps. On the evening of 22 June a so-called Lubachuv 'corridor', 15km wide, began to form in the army alignment. Into this corridor came the *295th* and *71st Infantry Divisions*, and the *IV Army Corps* of the *17. Armee*. In the evening of 23 June this 'corridor' turned into a 24km wide breach along the front line. The next participant in this spearhead was Nemiruv. I.N. Muzychenko found himself in a very difficult position. He had already been forced to give away the 8th Mechanised Corps, which had only just marched to Yavorov, for counterattacks against the points where the Germans had broken through. G.K. Zhukov insisted that he give away the 8th Tank Division for a counterattack on the front line. This division was forced to mobilise en route, having withdrawn the 15th Tank Regiment, 8th Tank Division from the march, which had advanced towards Yazuv Stary. Even units in the 81st Mechanised Division participated in the counterattack. Two battalions from the 53rd Tank Regiment in the 81st Mechanised Division saw action in the battle, as well as one company from the 323rd Motorised Regiment, without artillery support. Detachments from the line-up of the two formations in the 4th Mechanised Corps attacked Nemiruv at different times. In the morning the *71st Infantry Division*, having passed through the town, survived an attack by tanks from the 81st Mechanised Division. This attack came as a complete surprise for the Germans and heavy losses were inflicted on the marching infantry columns. Eloquent lines can be found in the combat journal of the 81st Division for this day: "The town burned, the streets were strewn with fascists corpses."[26] However without significant support from motorised infantry the BT tanks were not able to secure a foothold in the town. A regiment of the *71st Infantry Division*, which had transferred to the defence of Nemiruv, weathered the next attack from the 8th Tank Division better, despite the fact that T-34 and T-28 medium tanks had participated in the attack. By 1700 hrs the battle was over, it had cost the 8th Tank Division 19 T-34 tanks and the 81st Mechanised Division 36 BT-7 tanks. The units from the 4th Mechanised Corps were not able to capture and hold the town, although the German offensive had been halted for some time.

The eradication of the threat however of a German breakthrough towards Lvov was not even envisaged and the 4th Mechanised Corps, instead of turning against *Panzergruppe 1*, was forced to perform the role of a 'fire brigade' for the 6th Army. In the area around Krakovets (to the east of Yavorov) the Germans overturned the defence of the 97th Rifle Division on 25 June and by 1600 hrs the division had commenced a disorganised retreat. Up until this point an attempt was made to stabilise the situation in a counterattack along the highway towards Yavorov by units in the 81st Mechanised Division. However these counterattacks were unsuccessful and by 1730 hrs both the 97th and the 81st Divisions were stripped of their artillery following attacks by German artillery that were directed by an aircraft. Units in both divisions began their retreat along the highway to the east, abandoning their heavy weaponry. The situation was exacerbated by the fact that the materiel that had been wrecked was blocking the highway and the marshy terrain did not enable them to get around the burning tractors under fire from the enemy. By the evening the 323rd Motorised Rifle Regiment; part of the 125th Artillery Regiment; and an operations group from the 81st Division were surrounded. In the course of the 26–27 June individual

26 The Central Archive of the Ministry of Defence, fund 81sd, inventory 1, file 23, p.7.

groups of soldiers and commanders were able to break through to the south from this encirclement by swimming across the River Shklo. In the encirclement the divisional commander Colonel Varypayev, the chief of staff Colonel Spesivtsev, the commander of the 323rd Motorised Rifle Regiment Lieutenant-Colonel Lysenko, the chief of staff of the regiment Captain Ivanushkin, the commander of the 125th Artillery Regiment Major Kobya and other commanders of the units in the division had disappeared without trace. In total the 323rd Regiment lost 80 percent of its personnel in this encirclement; the 125th Artillery Regiment lost 30 percent of its personnel and 80 percent of its materiel. The 53rd Tank Regiment lost up to 50 tanks in a battle near Krakovets. A characteristic detail is that if on the evening of 24 June there were 86 STZ-5 tractors (which was the main means of towing the artillery) listed as serving in the division then on 25 June this figure had sunk to 25 units. At a cost of significant losses the 81st Mechanised Division prevented a German breakthrough towards Yavorov. The opponent for our forces in this battle was the *257th Infantry Division* and this episode is described as follows in the history of this regiment: "Heavy fighting with Russian motorised and tank sub divisions."

The 32nd Tank Division, 4th Mechanised Corps was also thrown into the battle against a breakthrough by the German *XXXXVIII Corps*, which included the *257th Infantry Division*. By 1400 hrs on 25 June this regiment had gathered at its initial positions and at 1820 hrs the division attacked units in the *1st Gebirgsjäger Division* in the *Mountain Corps,* under Kubler, in the direction of Basyaka, Varenitsy and Semeruvka. The division did not receive support from the retreating infantry of the 6th Rifle Corps and it actually attacked with individual tanks. As a result of the battle 16 tanks, four 75mm guns and eight anti-tank weapons, as well as 14 trailers along with their armament, were claimed as lost. There were no tanks in the formations of the *XXXXIX Mountain Corps*, they can theoretically be substituted by '*Sturmgeschütz*' Self-Propelled Artillery Systems, 5–7 examples of which were attached to the *1st Gebirgsjäger Division* under Hubert Lanz. Our own losses in E.G. Pushkin's division were 15 tanks. In the history of the *1st Gebirgsjäger Division* the battles at the settlement of Yazuv Stary are described as follows:

> Our positions are located on the uplands and the enemy tanks can be easily discerned. Our 3.7cm anti-tank gun waits patiently while the tanks come within a suitable firing range. When the distance gets to 600m the gun opens fire. Almost every shot hits the target. The tracers from the shells are clearly visible. Then however we couldn't believe our eyes: our anti-tank shells were just bouncing off the tanks. The enemy tanks kept advancing towards us without stopping and were firing at us with all their weapons. Then something unexpected happened: after recovering from the fright of seeing these steel giants, our infantry began to attack, throwing hand grenades at the tanks.[27]

Hand grenades turned out to be sufficiently effective against the attackers without the support of infantry and artillery. One cannot fail to agree with Yefim Pushkin, who when summing up the results of this combat activity, wrote in a report:

> The order for the division to attack a location heavy with enemy anti-tank armament (6km to the east of Yavorov) could be considered the next instance of inappropriate use of the division, and what is more in unfavourable conditions (in the area around the river Yaksha and the marshy valleys close to Yazuv Stary) without the **support of artillery and without the cooperation of the infantry**. [author's use of bold].

27 Lanz, *Gebirgsjäger: Der 1. Gebrigsdivision 1935–1945* (Bad Nauheim, Podzun, 1954), p.137.

Moreover attacks from Soviet tanks left their mark. In the course of two days the *68th Infantry* were attacked in a miscellaneous order by all three divisions of the 4th Mechanised Corps. The division suffered serious losses but its condition was characterised in the combat journal of *Army Group South* as "completely out of action." In the end, as of the evening of 25 June, the command of the *17. Armee* sent a request to the *Oberkommando des Heeres* to replace the *68th Infantry Division* with the *4th Gebirgsjäger Division* from the *Oberkommando des Heeres* reserves. This request was satisfied and, from the morning of 26 June onwards, the division was relegated to the reserves.

The third division in the corps under A.A. Vlasov, which had formally been excluded from the order for the counterattack, attacked units serving in the neighbour to the left of the *Mountain Corps*, the units of the *IV Corps* in Mageruv, using 54 tanks from the 15th Tank Regiment on the evening of 25 June. In the history of the *97th Light Infantry Division* this episode is described as follows:

> The enemy infantry sat on the combat vehicles that had gone on the attack in the light of headlights and spotlights. While the infantry sub-divisions were attempting to go on the defensive several tanks did nevertheless manage to get through and, sewing chaos and destruction, they destroyed everything in their path. The devastated sub-divisions however again mounted a circular defence and specifically, thanks to the tenacity and steadfastness of the infantry troops, they succeeded in avoiding a panic. At 0500 hrs the division sent a radiogram to everyone: "The enemy has broken through the defences in Mageruv. The division is withdrawing; the forward edge of the defensive line is; Shezhets and the forest west of Kreymonka—the eastern extremity of the forest is further south." Soviet forces however were not able to make use of their victory. Their attacks were not coordinated. Therefore with the help of artillery and anti-tank crews a large number of tanks were destroyed. Those that escaped withdrew one by one. In Mageruv and its suburbs Soviet tanks were ablaze, illuminating the battlefield with their flames and with the glow of their headlamps that remained switched on.[28]

The scenario was, evidently, a standard one: since they did not have the option of capturing and holding the locality, Soviet tank forces nevertheless forced German infantry units to stop and go onto the defensive. Overall I.N. Muzychenko succeeded in holding the army's front line using counterattacks by the 4th Mechanised Corps and at *Army Group South* headquarters the question of a an attack on the rear of the 6th Army using the *XIV Motorised Corps* (the *9th Panzer Division* and the *SS Motorised Infantry Brigade 'Leibstandarte Adolf Hitler'*) from the area around Radzekhov to the south was examined. This plan however was cancelled. This was precisely how the initial plan by *Army Group South* command to introduce the *XIV Motorised Corps* into the area around Rava-Ruska on the second or third day of the operation developed. Holding the 6th Army's front line provided a secure base for counterattacks by the mechanised corps from the area around Brody to the north, on the flank of the *Panzergruppe 1.*

An assessment of the environment by German command is characterised by an entry in the Combat Journal of *Army Group South* dated 25 June: "The enemy has put up, as before, fierce resistance in close combat ahead of a decisive outcome, and has been very active in conducting defensive operations by carrying out powerful counterattacks, drafting in a large number of tanks."

28 Ott, *Jaeger am Feind: Geschichte und Opfergang der 97. Jaeger-Division 1940–1945* (Verlag der Kameradschaft der Spielhahnjäger, 1966), pp.36–37.

A T-28 tank abandoned somewhere in the Western Ukraine. These tanks with three turrets (one with a 76.2mm gun, and two with machine guns) were created based on an impression of the British 'Independent' tank. The T-28 was manufactured in comparatively large numbers, more than 400 examples, and was actively deployed in battles in 1941. For a tank that operated in 1941 its armour was very thin and was easily penetrated by German guns.

German artillerymen inspect a Soviet KV-1 tank that was disabled outside Radzekhov. This was a 1941 built machine, with a 76mm F-32 gun.

Another Soviet KV-1 tank that was knocked out in combat outside Radzkehov. Note the damaged track rollers on this vehicle—the Germans fired with intensity at the flanks with the aim of breaking through the thinner side armour.

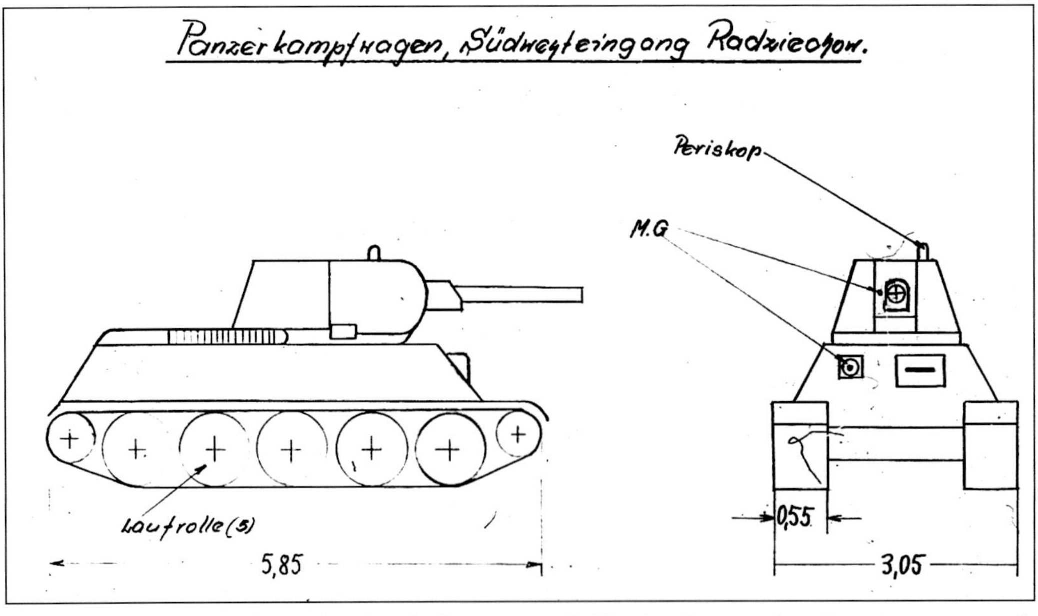

A schematic diagram of a T-34 tank, which was compiled by the Germans based on the outcome of the battles outside Radzekhov (NARA).

A T-26 tank knocked out in the 'killing field' outside Voynitsa. Light Soviet tanks were an easy target for all the anti-tank armament at the *Wehrmacht's* disposal, including tank guns.

The Commander of the 22nd Mechanised Corps S.M. Kondrusev. He was killed in combat just outside Voynitsa.

A burning BA-10 armoured car. Many Soviet armoured cars, including those armed with 45mm guns, were extremely vulnerable in combat due to their thin armour.

A T-34 tank from the 32nd Tank Division, 4th Mechanised Corps knocked out in the area around Yazuv Stariy. The later series tanks, fitted with a 7.62mm F-34 gun, entered series production shortly before the war.

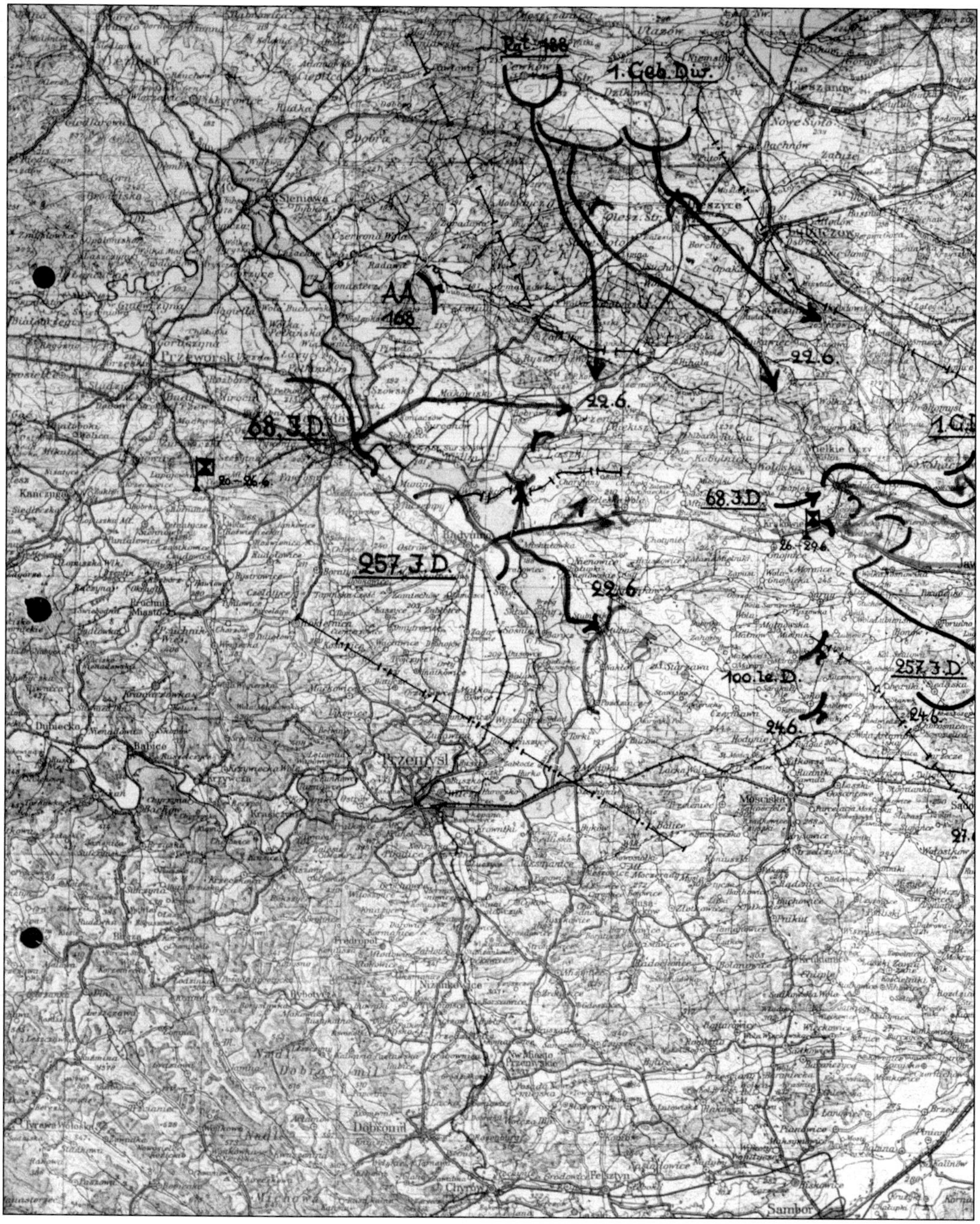

A map of the combat activities of the *XXXXIX Mountain Corps* in June 1941. Evidently the town of Yavorov had become a 'breakwater' of sorts in the path of the corps owing to Soviet counterattacks.

22.-30.6.
Rawa Ruska
Mosty Wielkie
27.6.
71. J.D.
24.6.
27.6.
1. Geb. D.
4. Geb. D.
257. J.D.
29.6.
71. J.D.
1. G.D.
LEMBERG
(LWOW)
30.6.
Gródek Jagiellonski
257. J.D.
29.6.
30.6.
Komarno

This same group of T-34 tanks in Yazuv Stariy. As can be seen in the photograph another T-34 is standing some distance away. This photograph was taken without delay by a staff officer of the *XXXXIX Mountain Corps* (NARA).

Staff officers of the *XXXXIX Mountain Corps*. In the centre is the Corps Commander and Cavalier of the Knight's Cross Infantry General Ludwig Kubler (NARA)

The crew of a T-28 tank check their orders. Their combat vehicle is visible in the background, a T-28 fitted with an L-10 gun.

A T-28 tank that has been destroyed and burnt out. The small machine gun turrets have been blown off by an internal explosion.

A.M. Ilyin, the Commander of the 228th Rifle Division (in the photo he holds the rank of General).

A Soviet T-26 tank that has been disabled. The white stripes on the turret have been applied for the benefit of identification from the air.

Soviet 152mm ML-20 howitzers abandoned in a field. In the course of mobile warfare heavy artillery would often fall victim to tanks whilst on the march.

A later series T-26 tank (manufactured in 1939) that has been knocked out in combat. The white triangle was the Red Army's insignia for identification by aviation.

A KV-1 tank fitted with a 76.2mm F-32 gun that has been abandoned on the battlefield. A hit by a shell can clearly be seen on the turret that did not penetrate the armour.

The crew of a Pe-2 prepares for a combat sortie. In 1941 the Pe-2 aircraft was the most modern Soviet bomber. Subsequently these aircraft were employed widely in the Air Forces of the Worker's and Peasant's Red Army.

German soldiers and members of the local population examine abandoned military pontoon vehicles. The pontoons are covered with tarpaulin. A pre-war Soviet tank division was generously equipped with engineering equipment.

The Commander of the 40th Tank Division M.V. Shirobokov. A post-war photograph when he held the rank of a Major General of Tank Forces.

A T-35 tank abandoned due to an accident with the engine on 2 July 1941 close to the village of Ozhidov, just outside Lvov. This tank bore the serial number No. 744-67 and was the last T-35 manufactured in the Soviet Union. After the manufacture of this machine production of Soviet five-turret giants was brought to an end.

A T-35 tank abandoned owing to a technical problem, from the 67th Tank Regiment's fleet, 34th Tank Division, in the town of Gorodok (Grudek-Yagedonskiy). This tank was manufactured in 1939 and has conical turrets. The nose of another T-35 is visible to the left of this tank, on which the leading wheel has been ripped off. In total three T-35 tanks were abandoned in this location at once.

A truck belonging to the *SS 'Wiking' Division* passes a KV-1 abandoned in Zhovkva next to the Glinskaya Brama.

A damaged *Pz.III* tank belonging to the *9th Panzer Division* in the Western Ukraine.

The remains of a KV-2 tank somewhere outside Kovel. This machine belonged to the 41st Tank Division, and was most likely blown up by the crew.

5

Leshnev and Brody – "Striking with Fire and shining with a glint of Steel"

The onward march of time at the start of the general counterattack by the mechanised corps of the South-Western Front had both positive and negative aspects. On the one hand German *panzers* in the division advanced forward and were only held back by air attacks and periodic attacks from different directions. On the other hand reserves were drawn from the interior but it was technically impossible for them to be put into operation up until 25 June. This enabled M.P. Kirponos to gather attack forces from the 8th and 15th Mechanised Corps, from the Lvov salient, and the 9th and 19th Mechanised Corps drawn up from the interior. If the previous plan (order No. 0015) was just a heavy blow 'in the gut' from the south on the enemy as they advanced eastwards, then this new decision by front line command for a counterattack looked like a 'pincer movement'. That is to say an attack was now proposed against the enemy alignments that were converging from the north and the south, with the aim of surrounding the forces that had broken through the front line to some depth. The objective of the northern element of the 'pincer' offensive, in accordance with the new order No. 0016 issued by the forces of the North-Western Front, was formulated as follows:

> The 5th Army Command under General Potapov are to bring the 9th and 19th Mechanised Corps together under his command and they are to occupy a starting point for an attack on the front line at Grudek and Rymno (both of these points are 8km to the south-west of Lutsk) with the aim of assisting the 8th and 15th Mechanised Corps in the routing of the Radzekhov alignment in an attack along the railway line (from Lutsk to Brody). This starting point is to be occupied by 0430 hrs on 26 June 1941. The attack is to commence at 0900 hrs on 26 June 1941.

Therefore this counterattack was aimed at the German units that were advancing along the central '*Panzerstrasse*'.

However the environment on the front line was not changing by the day, but by the hour. An order written in the late evening of 25 June would be obsolete by the next morning. In the evening of 25 June the terrain to the south-east of Lutsk was already in enemy hands. Moreover German infantry and tank divisions were spread out across this entire terrain from the border up to the rivers Styr and Ikva including the towns of Lutsk and Dubno. It should be pointed out at this point that the capture of the initial position for the counterattack was a sufficiently widespread phenomenon in defensive battles and not only in 1941. A line that was designated as the starting point for the 5th Guards Tank Army for a counterattack outside Prokhorovka, in July 1943, was occupied by the enemy until P.A. Rotmistrov's tank crews advanced towards their starting point. This led to two of the tank corps in the 5th Army advancing along a section of terrain that was not suitable from a tactical perspective. In 1941 a widespread basis for designated locations, such as starting points for counterattacks, rapidly passing into the hands of the enemy was an underestimation of the breadth of the zone of the German advance. The result of this was the emergence of a classic attack on the flank in a bloody, head-on battle. For example the clash between the 2nd Tank Division, 3rd Mechanised Corps and the German *6th Panzer Division* in Raseiniai, in the Baltic Region, developed in accordance with this scenario.

The border battle in the Ukraine was no exception and the episode in which the initial boundaries were captured was played out. It cannot be said however that this head-on battle occurred completely naturally. The German advance up to the boundary formed by the River Ikva forced command to change the objectives for their mechanised corps on the move. First and foremost this involved the formations that were subordinate to the 5th Army. In as much as the news of the loss of Dubno broke before the corps under Feklenko and Rokossovskiy had gone on the offensive, M.I. Potapov succeeded in preparing a new order, which stated specifically:

9. The 9th Mechanised Corps (excluding the 131st Motorised Division) is to go onto the offensive at 1600 hrs from the boundary formed of the River Putilovka in the direction of Dubno with the aim, in conjunction with the 19th Mechanised Corps, of destroying the enemy in the area around Dubno.
10. The 19th Mechanised Corps is to have taken the area around Dubno by the end of the day on 26 June 1941.[1]

From the idea that Kirponos first formulated of attacking from the north towards the mechanised corps from the Lvov salient, the mission for the formations that were subordinate to Potapov changed again. Now they were to strike the enemy units that had broken through beyond the Ikva. In the end the 19th Mechanised Corps was forced to conduct a head-on battle in what were ever worsening conditions.

In turn the Germans were not planning to rest on their laurels. The mission for the *XXXXVIII Corps' 11th Panzer Division*, that had advanced at the cutting edge of the main attack, was to extend the offensive from Dubno onwards towards the east to Ostrog and Shepetovka. The divisional commander, General Crüwell, adopted the approach in battle on 26 June that he had adopted near Radzekhov on the first day of the war. The motorised infantry *kampfgruppe*, the so-called *'Angern Gruppe'* after the Commander of the *11th Schützen-Brigade* (11th Motorised Infantry Brigade) Gunther Von Angern, received the order to commence the forward offensive, together with the motorcycle crews, while the flank of the offensive was secured by the *'panzer' kampfgruppe*. This time it was not a defence of the southern flank that was required but a defence of the northern flank. This same method was adopted that was employed near Radzekhov—capturing and holding the road junctions on the flank of the formation. This point was Mlodava (10km to the north-east of Dubno). On this occasion the enemy for the Germans was the 43rd Motorised and Mechanised Rifle Regiment, 43rd Tank Division (two battalions using vehicles) with a platoon of tanks and a battery of regimental artillery. It was a forward detachment of the division that captured Mlodava in the evening of the previous day. In the morning of 26 June the regiment's positions were attacked by the Germans. Thanks to the high concentration of the infantry in the forward detachment of the 43rd Division the battle was more vigorous than chasing the detachment of the 10th Tank Division out of Radzekhov. Using the tanks as a weapon against similar vehicles, the tank crews of the I.G. Tsibin's division were able to knock out two vehicles in the *'panzer' kampfgruppe* from Crüwell's division out of action. These losses are confirmed by

1 *Collection of Combat Documents from the Great Patriotic War* Issue No. 36, p.133.

German data: "At 0630 hrs following a ferocious battle with enemy infantry and artillery forces Mlodava was taken, although we had to come to terms with the loss of three tanks."[2] Schrodek was playing down the details of the battle for Mlodava. This settlement was not taken in a head-on attack. The Germans only succeeded in driving out the forward detachment from the settlement by outflanking them from the side and putting them in danger of an encirclement. This same approach was applied in the battle for Radzekhov on 23 June. To a certain extent Crüwell's actions could be described as a highly polished template.

Meanwhile the main force of the 43rd Tank Division began to draw up towards the outer approaches to Dubno. The artillery in the division (the 43rd Howitzer Artillery Regiment) that had moved from the area around Taikury under tow from tractors, at a speed of 6km per hour, was still on the move and was not able to open fire until the start of the attack. The presence however of the retreating infantry and artillery from the 228th Rifle Division, 36th Rifle Corps in this area, made the objective of the formation much easier. After having halted the infantry that were pushing back from Dubno the commander of the 43rd Tank Division, Colonel I.G. Tsibin, used the infantry and the artillery in the 228th Division in his offensive. The tanks in the 43rd Division that had reached the objective of the offensive were amalgamated into the 86th Tank Regiment for ease of command. The regiment commenced the attack comprising of two KV tanks, two T-34s and 75 T-26s. Thus, a German *kampfgruppe* that was part of a *panzer* division and a Soviet tank division, that was not at full complement, clashed in a battle to the east of Dubno. The tank division led by Colonel Tsibin did, it was true, have the support of the infantry in the rifle division. With respect to the number of tanks and infantry the enemy forces were more or less equal, but the German side had a significant advantage in terms of heavy artillery on account of their own corps units, as well as those that had been attached to them.

The 43rd Tank Division's offensive on Dubno began at 1400 hrs instead of the 0900 hrs that had been set by front line command. The new tank types—the T-34s and KVs were liquidated in the attack. The battle lasted until the onset of dawn. Light T-26 tanks came up behind them. According to a report written by Tsibin, the outcome of the battle was as follows:

> As they followed the enemy's tanks on their retreat the units in the division approached the eastern outskirts of Dubno, to the objective of Pantaliya, near Rachin. The enemy blew up all the bridges behind them as they withdrew towards Dubno, thus stripping the division of the [capability] of breaking through to Dubno on the shoulders of its retreating infantry.[3]

This episode became well known and the withdrawal of Tsibin's forces towards Dubno is considered just about the most successful counterattack by a Soviet tank formation in the Border battle. However this version of the battle is not confirmed in German documents. The blowing up of bridges on the central '*Panzerstrasse*' would have been an extraordinary event, which would most likely have been reflected in all manner of reports. The Germans even recorded the fact of the preparation of the bridges for blowing in their combat journals, let alone them actually being blown up as such. Nothing of the kind however can be found in the documents. According to the combat journal of the *XXXXVIII Corps*, over the course of the day, the *panzer kampfgruppe* in the *11th Panzer Division* was engaged in combat close to the river crossing over the River Stubla near Varkovichi until the evening. This location is to the east of Mlodava, which had been captured in the morning.

2 Schrodek, p.131.
3 *Collection of Combat Documents from the Great Patriotic War* Issue No. 36, pp. 237–238.

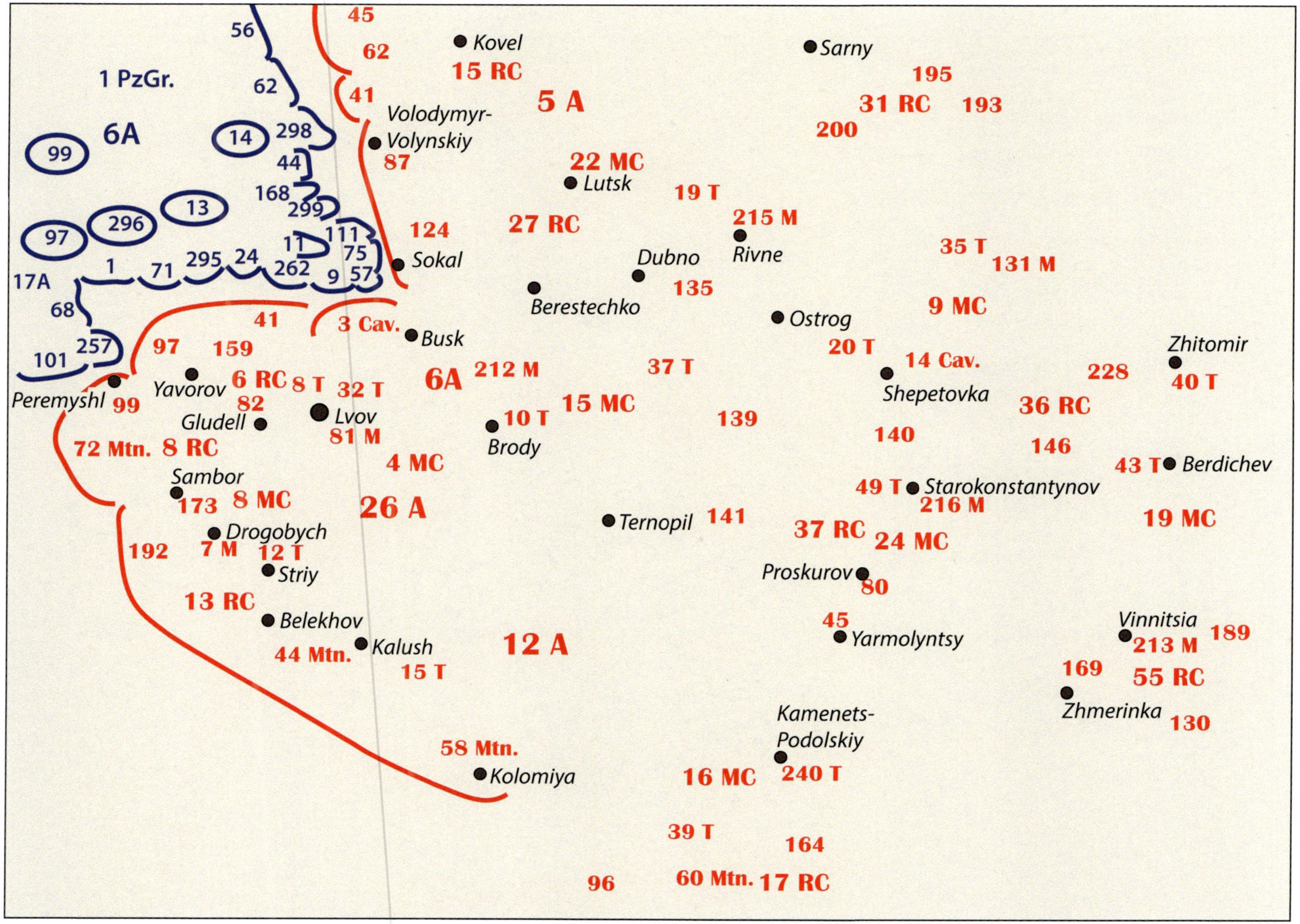

Map 1 The position of the Army Group South and Kiev Special Military District formations as of the evening of 21 June 1941.

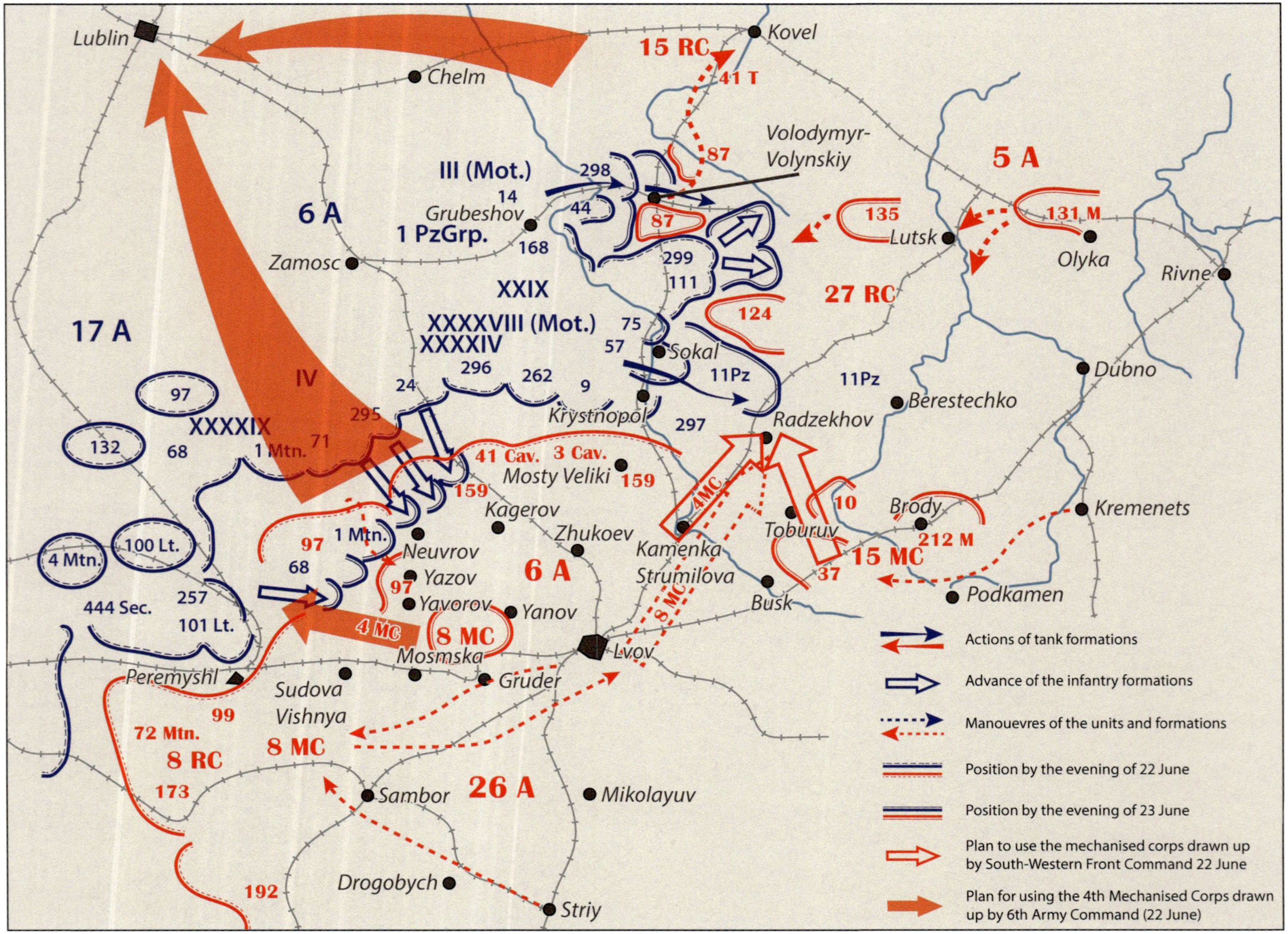

Map 2 Combat activity on 22–23 June 1941.

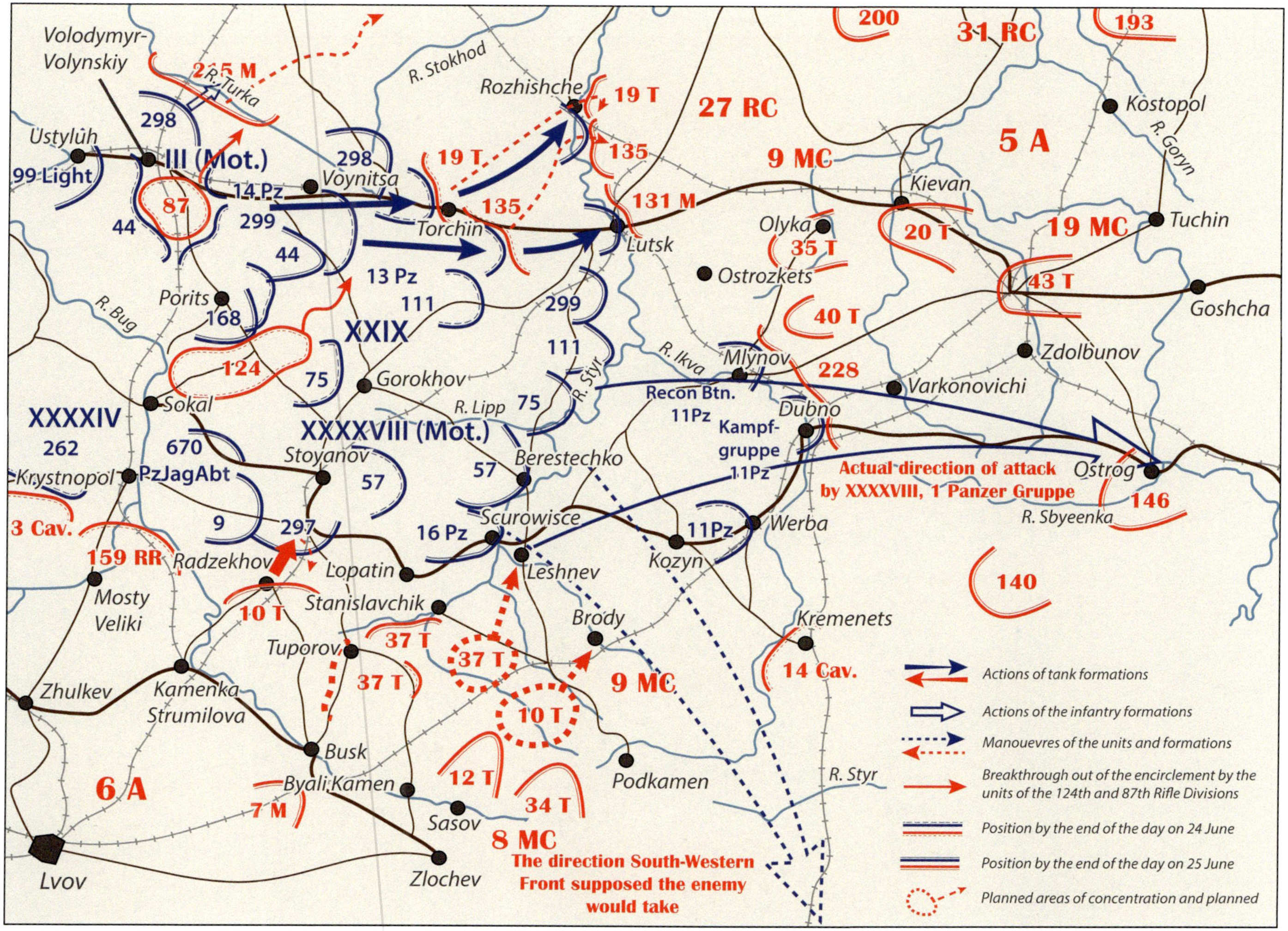

Map 3 Combat activity on 24–25 June 1941.

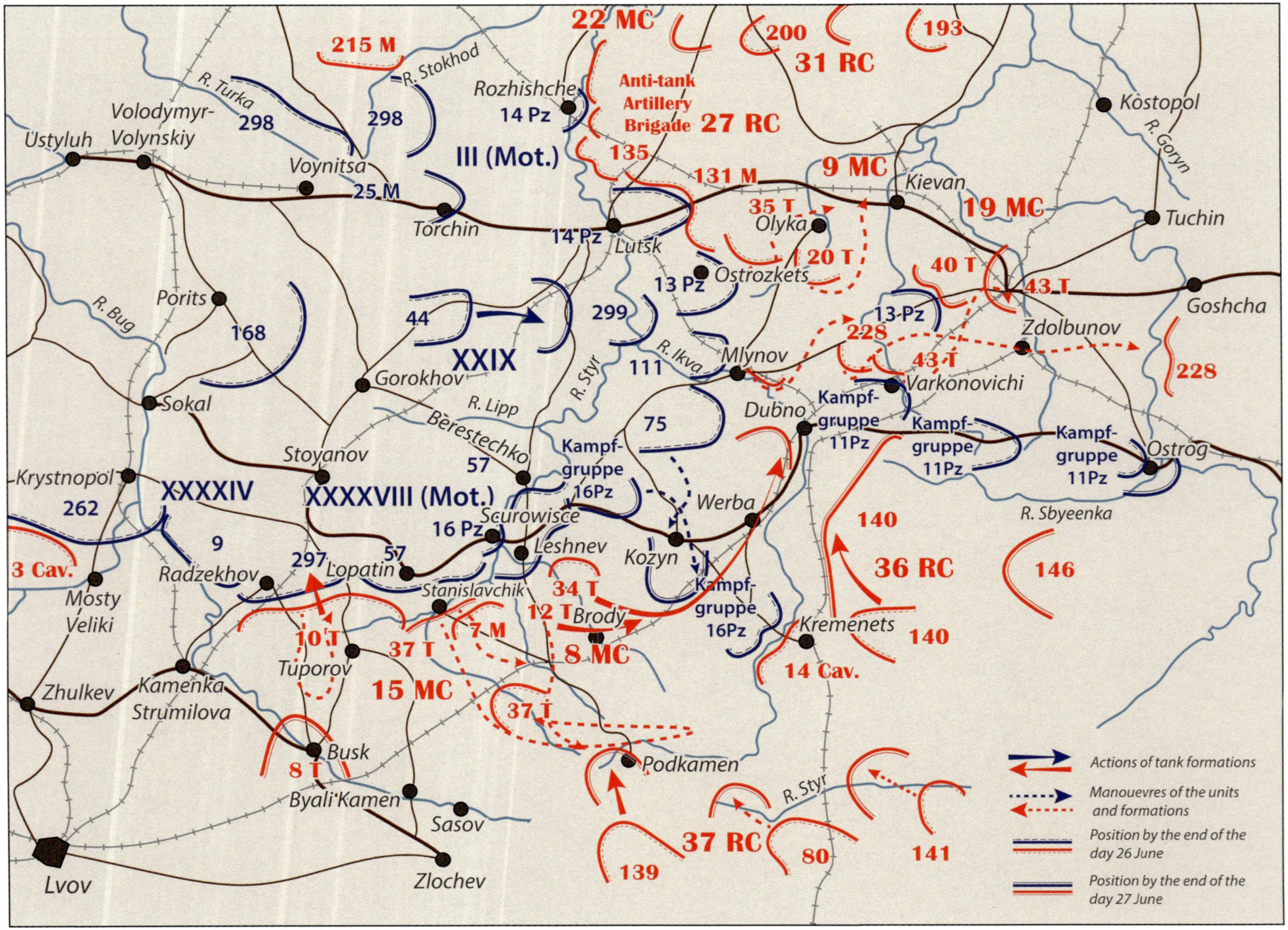

Map 4 Combat activity on 26–27 June 1941.

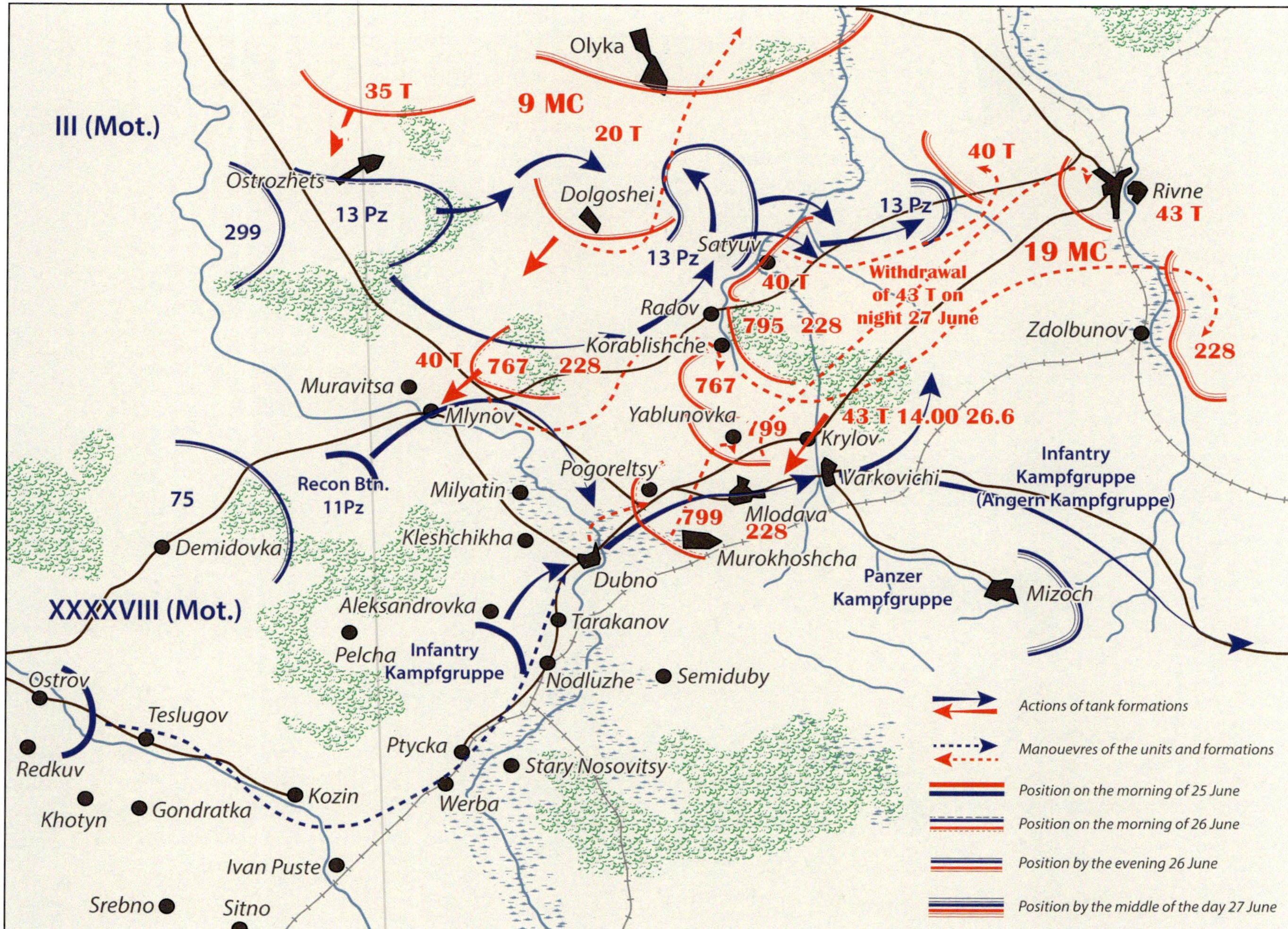

Map 5 Combat activity in the area around Dubno on 25–27 June 1941.

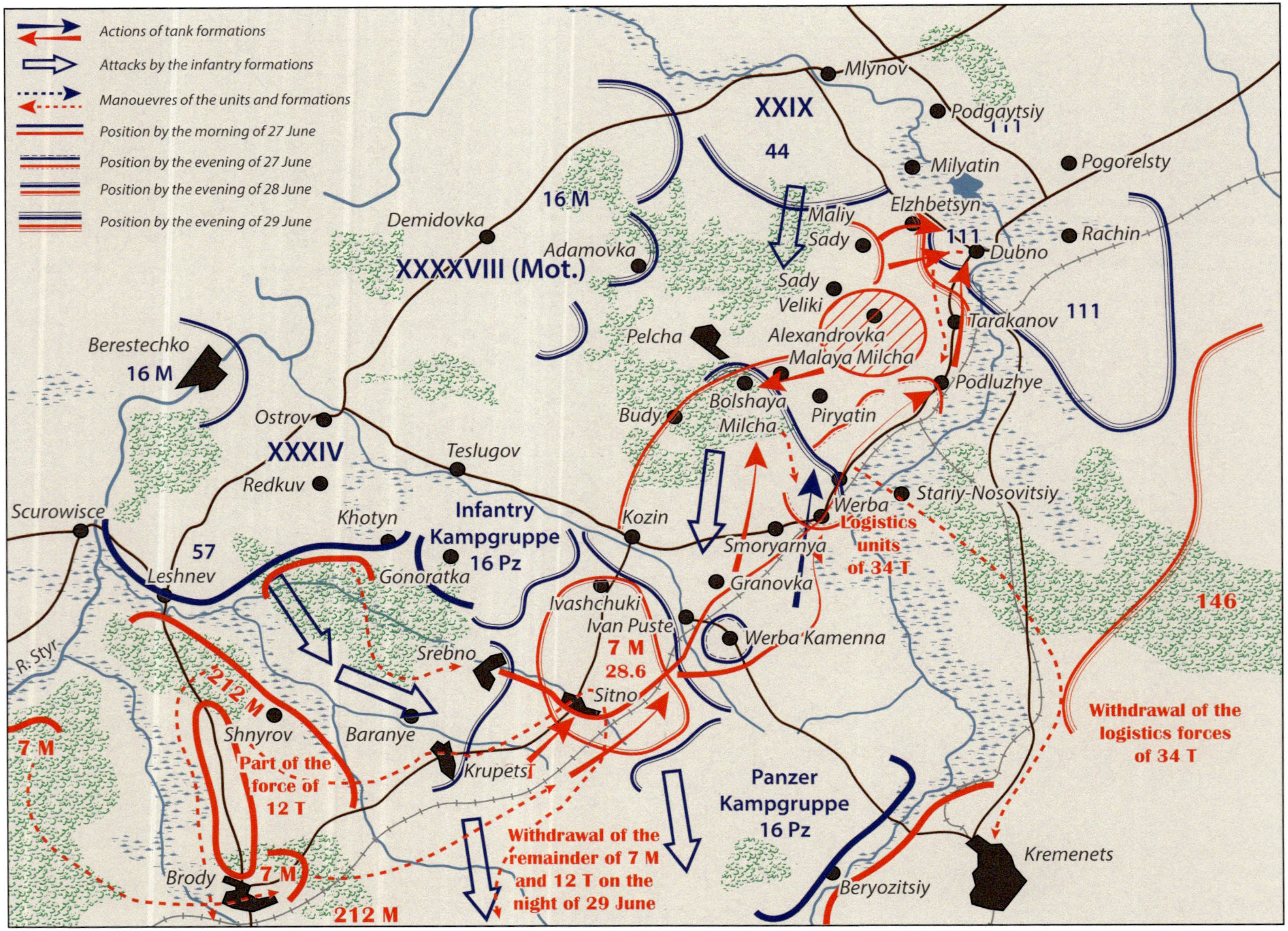

Map 6 Combat activity in the area around Dubno. 27–29 June 1941.

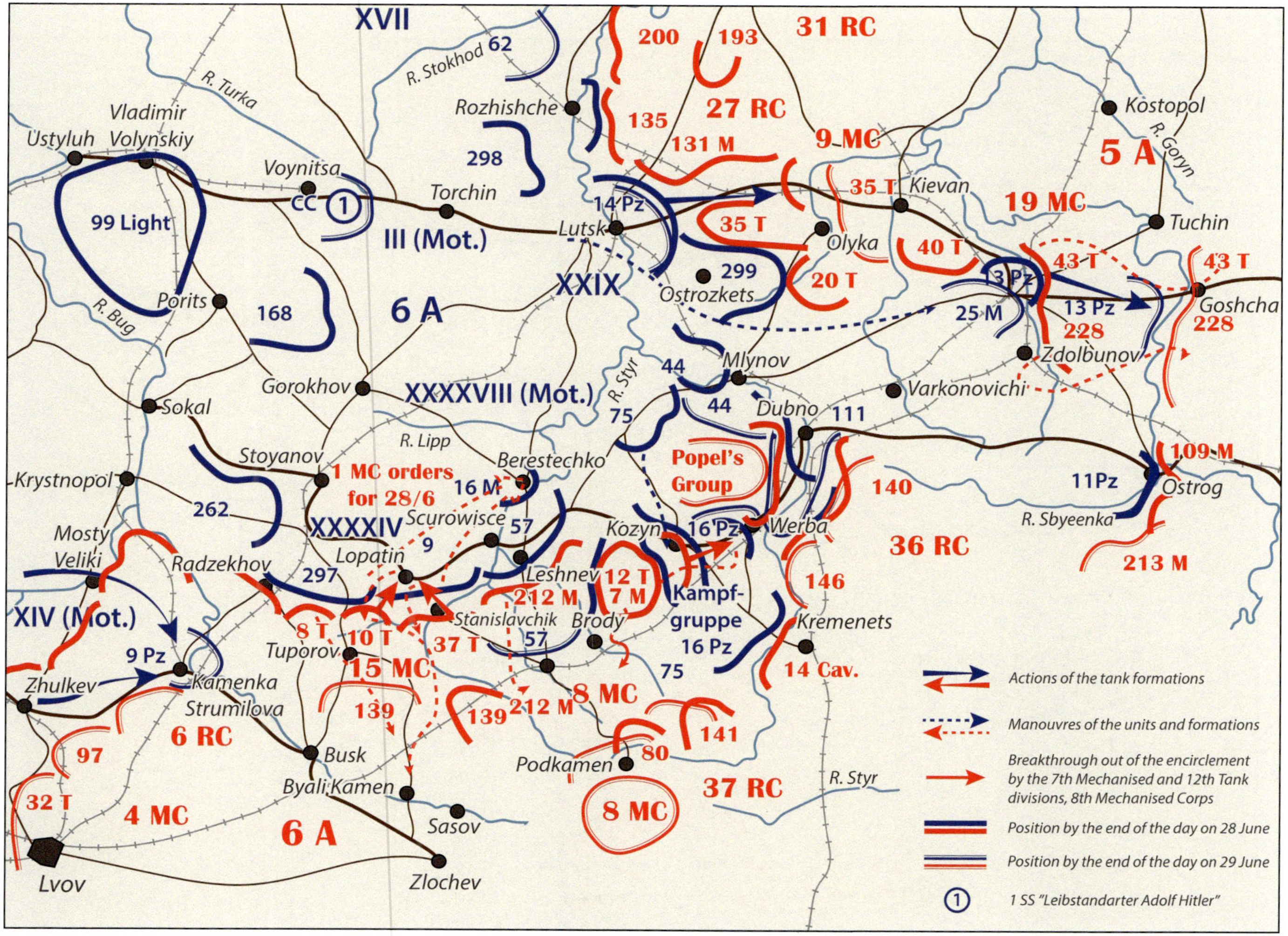

Map 7 Combat activity on 28–29 June 1941.

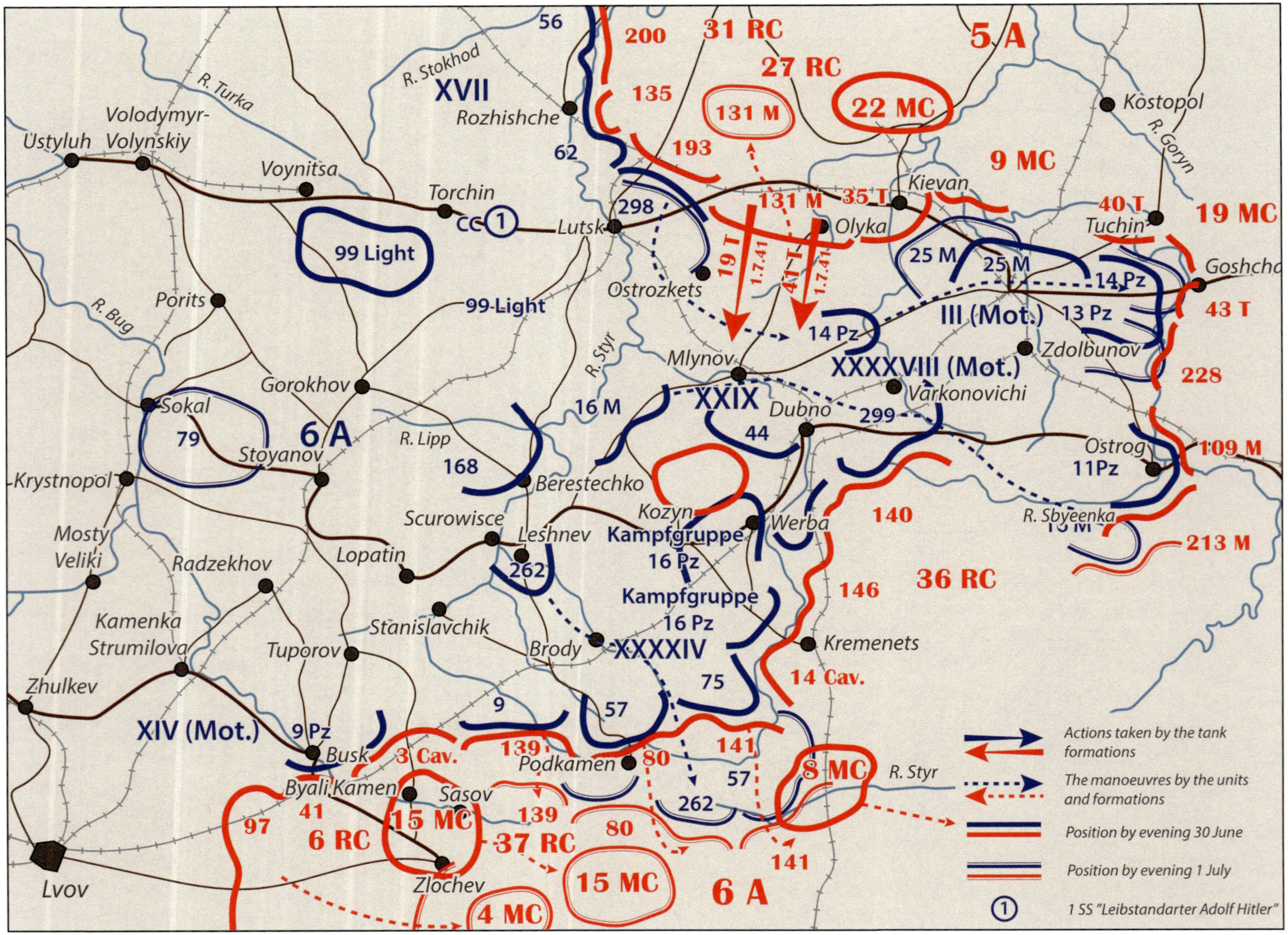

Map 8 Combat activity on 30 June-1 July 1941.

No confirmation is evident either of the suggestion that the enemies just did not see each other and acted independently. Tsibin, in his report, identifies the settlement of Krylov as one of the starting points for his attack, which was located just a few kilometres from to the north of Varkovichi. The Germans noticed the advance of Soviet forces and the following was recorded in the combat journal of the *XXXXVIII Corps*: "Our pilots report that enemy tanks have been advancing slowly towards Mlodava from Khruzvitsa from 1300 hrs. Our tanks have been engaged in combat with the enemy in the area around Varkovichi since 1400 hrs." Thus it simply would not have been possible for Tsibin to pass the tank group in Crüwell's division by owing to the lack of a consolidated front line. There is no denial of a tank battle in his report.

Put simply, it has to be acknowledged that in the case of Tsibin's report we are dealing with a dubious account. If the many other reports more or less coincide with the enemy's information then there would be no confirmation of the breakthrough made by the 43rd Division towards Dubno. This episode stands out starkly from the overall series of battles and appears somewhat strange. After having only just beaten back an attack by T-34s outside Radzekhov the units of the *11th Panzer Division* would have passed in front of a crowd of T-26s supported by two KVs and two T-34s. The chances are that the formations of the 43rd Tank Division were engaged in combat near Varkovichi, almost without advancing forward. The most that the Germans could have blown up was the river crossing over the Stulba at Krylov, to the north of the '*Panzerstrasse*.' Correspondingly the next step taken by the 43rd Tank Division was an attempt to break through to the rear of the enemy bridgehead over the railway bridge to the south of Varkovichi. The marshy nature of the banks of the Stulba was also prevalent and was illustrated on maps of that day. Put simply a report by the 43rd Tank Division becomes a great deal more plausible if 'Dubno' is replaced with 'Varkovichi.'

If we are to consider that at least the overall idea of the battle on 26 June was described accurately by Tsibin, then his division spent a number of hours attempting to prevent a breakthrough by the enemy from the bridgehead at Varkovichi using their own river crossing with an exit to the rear of the bridgehead. There is nothing shameful in this tactic: The *panzer kampfgruppe* in the *11th Panzer Division* remained in place over the entire course of the day on 26 June. Of itself the constraint of what was a powerful *kampfgruppe* in terms of their armoured vehicles, over the course of an entire day, was not a bad achievement for a formation that was equipped predominantly with T-26 tanks. That is to say the Germans would have been able to breakdown the shield and surge forward but this would automatically mean that after their departure to the east the river crossing at Varkovichi would have been lost, and the '*Panzerstrasse*' would be recaptured. Correspondingly they would have to forget about the supply columns. This forced them to hold on to the river crossing, remaining in position and engaging the enemy in a shootout. Furthermore the 43rd Tank Division's results for the day were not all that great: the two KV tanks were lost (they both caught fire), as well as 15 T-26 tanks (of these four were flame-throwing tanks) and 128 men had either been killed or injured.

It has to be said that the assessment by the enemy of the clash with the 43rd Tank Division was far from rousing. In the history of the *11th Panzer Division* this episode is described as follows:

> The Russians attempted to break through everywhere, and at times they created some really critical situations. Within a short space of time following the attack on the flank the Russians succeeded in obstructing the path to an offensive towards Ostrog. Despite this Soviet command did not understand that in order to achieve great success they could make use of the confusion that was present on the German side.[4]

4 Schrodek, p.131.

That is to say, from a German perspective, the Soviet counterattack did not enable the *panzer kampfgruppe* in Crüwell's division to follow the motorised infantry in the direction of Ostrov.

Changes in this environment occurred on the night of 26–27 June. With the onset of darkness the 43rd Tank Division was outflanked on both sides. In view of the withdrawal of the neighbouring 40th Tank Division a threat arose of an attack against the flank and the rear from the German *13th Panzer Division* that was advancing towards Rovno. After encountering fierce resistance at Lutsk, Mackensen sent the *13th Panzer Division* to go around the town to the south. This is how it ended up on the flank of the 19th Mechanised Corps. Simultaneously in their strivings to breakthrough from the bridgehead at Varkovichi the German *panzers* began to bypass the left flank of Tsibin's division. In view of the obvious threat of encirclement the commander of the 19th Mechanised Corps gave the 43rd Tank Division an order to depart in the direction of Rivne at 0300 hrs in the morning.

Incidentally another of the discrepancies in Tsibin's report is linked to this withdrawal: He writes: "According to the order given by the commander of the 19th Mechanised Corps at 0300 hrs on 27 June 1941 the 43rd Tank Division had been led away from the vicinity of Dubno and by 0600 hrs had been concentrated on the western edge of Rivne." That is to say the withdrawal from Dubno to Rivne (a distance of around 30km) was undertaken in the space of just three hours. The division was to return much more slowly. A withdrawal from Varkovichi in this timescale seems more convincing. Subsequently the 19th Mechanised Corps would depart from the *XXXXVIII Motorised Corps*' area of responsibility and, in doing so, depart from the scene of the battle along the central '*Panzerstrasse*'.

Combat operations to the east of Dubno did not cease with the withdrawal of the 19th Mechanised Corps towards Rivne. The last act in the drama of the routing by the tanks of the 228th Rifle Division followed. The hurried withdrawal of Feklenko's corps left the division under Colonel Ilina face to face with enemy tanks and with the flanks unprotected. The depleted rifle regiments were truly a small island in the path of the violent stream of German *panzers* advancing towards Rivne and Ostrog. The position that the 228th Rifle Division occupied by the middle of the day on 27 June was not an enviable one. To the right the *13th Panzer Division* was attacking via Mlynuv, cutting off a withdrawal towards Rivne. On the left the *panzer kampfgruppe* of the *11th Panzer Division* had commenced their withdrawal. The 795th Rifle Regiment was deployed in a counterattack against this division, however on encountering powerful artillery, mortar and machine gun fire, as well as fire from tanks, they departed back to their starting position.

Under the threat of total destruction the remnants of the 228th Rifle Division began to withdraw towards Zdoblunov (to the south of Rivne). The assessment by command of the condition of the formation after three days of fierce fighting needs no further comment: "The division has lost its entire howitzer artillery; their squadron of light artillery; all its mortars; and up to 50 percent of its me[medium] machine guns; and the 799th Rifle Regiment has lost 75 percent of its personnel, either killed, wounded or missing."[5] Apart from that the division had lost all its communications equipment, as well as its regimental and battalion artillery.

The withdrawal of the 228th Rifle Division to the north-east opened the way for the Germans to Ostrog. The threat of an interruption in supply had been liquidated. The following entry appears in the combat journal of the *XXXXVIII Corps*: "The Tank Corps [the *11th Panzer Division*] repelled the enemy to the west of Mizoch, capturing a multitude of heavy armament, and is moving towards Ostrog." The 'multitude of heavy armament' belonged to the 205th, and 458th Corps Artillery Regiments in the 36th Rifle Corps. Having fired all their shells, and without fuel, the regiments were literally smashed to pieces by the attacking *panzers*. The 205th Regiment

5 The Central Archive of the Ministry of Defence, fund 229, inventory 161, file 89, p. 31.

suffered even more; losing 33 items of weaponry (twenty-two 122mm A-19s and eleven 152mm ML-20s); their tractor fleet and their communications equipment. The regiment only managed to retain three items of weaponry. The 458th Artillery Regiment lost 15 items of weaponry in this battle. Thus the idea of forming a shield along the Ikva from Mlynuv to Dubno finally crumbled. A rifle division, which was relying on a river with marshy banks and which was supported by corps artillery, could create serious problems for the Germans. However owing to their arrival being a few hours late, the elements of the 228th Rifle Division that were present were smashed, and the two corps artillery regiments were routed by tanks.

The 8th Mechanised Corps

Despite the dramatic development of the counterattack by the 19th Mechanised Corps, command had placed a great deal of faith in the mechanised corps from the Lvov salient with their large numbers of new tanks. By the morning of 26 June the command of the South-Western Front had nevertheless succeeded in withdrawing one of their most powerful mobile formations to their starting position for the counterattack—the 8th Mechanised Corps. Combat order No. 0015 that ordered the attack to commence at 0700 on 25 June was only received by corps command at 0920 hrs on 25 June, and at that time they were located in the area around Busk. Up until that moment the units in the corps had still been marching. Therefore going on the offensive on 25 June was out of the question. As a result of this a new combat order No. 0016 was issued, which stated:

> The principle attack on the enemy's mechanised alignment is to be carried out by the 8th and 15th Mechanised Corps, and the last attack is to be conducted using the 8th Tank Division in accordance with the objectives that had been set by these formations under order No. 0015 dated 25 June 1941. The starting positions for the attack were to be taken by 0430 hrs on 26 June 1941. The beginning of the attack was set for 0900 hrs on 26 June 1941.[6]

By evening on 25 June the main forces of the 8th Mechanised Corps had withdrawn to the area around Brody. Before them lay an entire night of preparations for the counterattack. Nevertheless the corps still did not manage to concentrate their forces in accordance with the deadline set, that is to say by the morning of 26 June. The 7th Motorised Division had not withdrawn to their starting point by the appointed time, and was moving through the forests to the north-west of Brody in difficult terrain. If a map from that time were to be consulted then it would show that the terrain in these locations was certainly bereft of roads and was poorly suited to a large number of vehicles in a motorised division being able to move quickly. Of itself one division being delayed, while the other forces allocated to the counterattack went into battle piecemeal was not without precedent in the history of the war. Putting formations into battle as they arrived was widespread both in the Red Army and in the *Wehrmacht*. The delay of the motorised division however, significantly reduced the weight of the infantry component in the alignment that had concentrated around the town of Brody.

The long march, which was conducted at an accelerated rate, led to a significant reduction in the strike capabilities of the 8th Mechanised Corps. The Commander of the 8th Corps, D.I. Ryabishev, and his chief of staff, A.V. Tsinchenko, in their reports on the results of the corps' combat activity assessed the number of combat vehicles that had withdrawn to the area around Brody as between 40–50 percent of their number on the first day of the war. These assessments however were done 'by sight'. Thus the 12th Tank Division had withdrawn to their starting

6 *Collection of Combat Documents from the Great Patriotic War* Issue No. 36, p. 29.

positions for the attack on 26 June formed of two of its tank regiments, just 75 tanks, compared to the approximately 300 that the division had on 22 June.[7] According to an assessment made by divisional headquarters they had covered on average of 415km and had amassed between 30–35 engine hours. Moreover inspection and servicing was not being carried out owing to the fact that the vehicles were constantly on the move. Even if the repair brigade did arrive on time they would never be able to reach the machines that had broken down in their own units. All this meant that only a pale shadow of the division led by T.A. Mishanin remained.

Things were only slightly better in the 34th Tank Division, and D.I. Ryabishev added just 10 T-35s and 15 T-26s, which were 18 wheeled machines, in total to the tanks of the 34th Tank Division that were still on the march towards the forests to the south of Yavorov. The division's howitzer regiment had fallen far behind, as had a separate anti-aircraft battalion and one battalion of the motorised rifle regiment. As strange as it may seem the KVs in the 34th Tank Division were still holding the formation. From the point of view of the potential to fulfil the tasks set for the 34th Tank Division the most painful loss was in terms of artillery. The STZ-5 tractors in the howitzer artillery regiment in the division would simply break down in the middle of a march and the formation would be left bereft of artillery support at the most inopportune moment. The availability of tractors in the division was not great: of the 39 standard STZ-5s there were only 14 in the regiment. Of these four remained in Grudek-Yagelonskiy on 24 June as a result of breakdowns. A further five tractors remained in Lvov. As a result there were only enough tractors for three howitzers. There could be no question of any effective suppression of anti-tank artillery or of a duel with enemy artillery.

It cannot be said that the situation in the 8th Mechanised Corps was a typical one. The march this corps undertook was unprecedentedly long by the standards of any battle. However D.I. Ryabishev's corps as the only mechanised corps on the South-Western Front to have withdrawn to their initial positions for the counterattack on the flank of *Panzergruppe 1*, suffered the most from the lack of materiel. The 'teething troubles' of the new materiel and the wear and tear in the old machines would have the most dramatic effect on its counterattack. It would be no exaggeration to add 'for the entire Border battle.'

The next operational factor to have had an effect on the development of the 8th Mechanised Corps' counterattack was the terrain. In the path of the offensive by two divisions of D.I. Ryabishev's corps were two rivers that flowed from east to west – the Slonuvka and the Plyashevka – which had marshy banks. A report written by the 12th Tank Division later recorded that even the 75 tanks that remained in service "could not be utilised fully as a result of the marshy terrain." Naturally the rivers in themselves did not represent an insurmountable barrier for mechanised formations even if they did have marshy banks. Their presence however increased the requirement for the number of infantry, since the tactic of 'infantry first' had to be employed and the tanks could only be used efficiently after a bridgehead had been secured and a river crossing had been put in place.

To some degree the enemy's mood favoured the counterattack that had been prepared. Firstly the area around Leshnev, which stood in the path of D.I. Ryabishev's corps, had only been occupied by sub-divisions from the *57th Infantry Division* at 1500 hrs on 25 June. Secondly the division did not need to construct a solid defence in this direction. Thirdly units of the *16th Panzer Division* that were moving along the central '*Panzerstrasse*' had not taken up defensive positions. Early in the morning of 26 June the formations that were active in this direction were orientated around the actions of the Red Army Air Force's mechanised formations as follows: "On the basis of the order broadcast over the radio from the headquarters of the *Panzergruppe 1*, the *57th Infantry Division* and the *16th Panzer Division* are again reminded not to ignore the threat of an

7 The Central Archive of the Ministry of Defence, fund 229, inventory 157, file 7, volume 1, p.168.

enemy tank offensive from the area around Toporuv to the north."[8] That is to say the German command had anticipated a repeat of the offensive undertaken by the 15th Mechanised Corps and the concentration of the 8th Mechanised Corps in the area around Brody was not discovered in time and correctly interpreted. Apart from that *Panzerjäger-Abteilung 670* nevertheless became involved in the battle with the 'wandering pocket' of the 124th Rifle Division and they did not participate in the battles outside Leshnev on 26 June. Put simply a hastily mounted defence stood in the path of the KVs, T-34s, BTs, T-26s and T-35s of Ryabishev's corps. A sufficiently powerful blow could lead to Soviet tanks coming into contact with the *panzer* divisions in *Panzergruppe 1* that were advancing to the east.

Finally on the morning of 26 June, following several days of tiresome marching, the tanks of the 8th Mechanised Corps went on the offensive. The hardest mission of all was that of the 12th Tank Division. At the same time, by all accounts, great hopes were placed on this division. At least the commander of the corps, Raybishev, and the commissar, Popel, followed the course of the counterattack from the location that this same division occupied. The division was the best equipped of all of them, had been formed before any of the others and had a relatively high number of the new types of tanks. The forward detachment had not been successful in securing a bridgehead before them and now a marshy river had to be crossed under enemy fire. In fact it was only possible to advance along a single road. The bridge on this road over the river Slonuvka had been blown up by the Germans and the combat vehicles in the division huddled before it. As was subsequently recorded in the divisional report: "The tanks were standing so close together that the tracks became stuck." The motorised infantry needed to push forward to secure a bridgehead. With artillery support, as well as tank fire at very close range, the motorised rifles crossed the river, set up a bridgehead and provided the sappers with an opportunity to rebuild a bridge and lay a path of logs across the marshy floodplain. By around 1100 hrs in the morning the bridge had been rebuilt and the offensive continued.

At around midday on 26 June the command of the *XXXXVIII Corps* were, it appears, forced to act to counter the Soviet offensive by units of the 16th Tank Division. The *kampfgruppe* in the division led by Hans-Valentin Hube, which had been formed around a *Schützen-Brigade,* was at that moment on a march in the area around Leshnev, and Berestechko. This *kampfgruppe* was named the '*Wanger kampfgruppe*' in honour of the commander of the motorised brigade in the formation. After having broken away from the bridgehead close to Leshnev, the units of the 12th Tank Division encountered the counterattack by German *panzers.* Popel wrote: "We were already able to distinguish the black and white crosses and the fleeting treads of their moving tracks."

Unfortunately in the Soviet memoirs German tanks are encountered on a very regular basis, and furthermore in places where they could not possibly have been. However in this case the information that is available concerning the disposition of German forces does not contradict the possibility of a clash between the formations of the 12th Tank Division and the German *16th Panzer Division* at all. The tanks in the *Wanger Kampfgruppe* were available and were drafted in to counter the Soviet offensive. Also in the history of the *16th Panzer Division* there is a mention of a clash with Soviet tanks on 26 June. It was true that this is linked to the action outside Kremenets, but there was just a single KV tank from the Kremenets group of the 37th Tank Division in that location (there were no T-34s there at all). It is doubtful that this tank could have left such an impression. Therefore any clash of tank crews in Hube's division with KVs and T-34s took place most likely outside Leshnev. The formation's historiographer wrote:

8 NARA T314 R1138 f499.

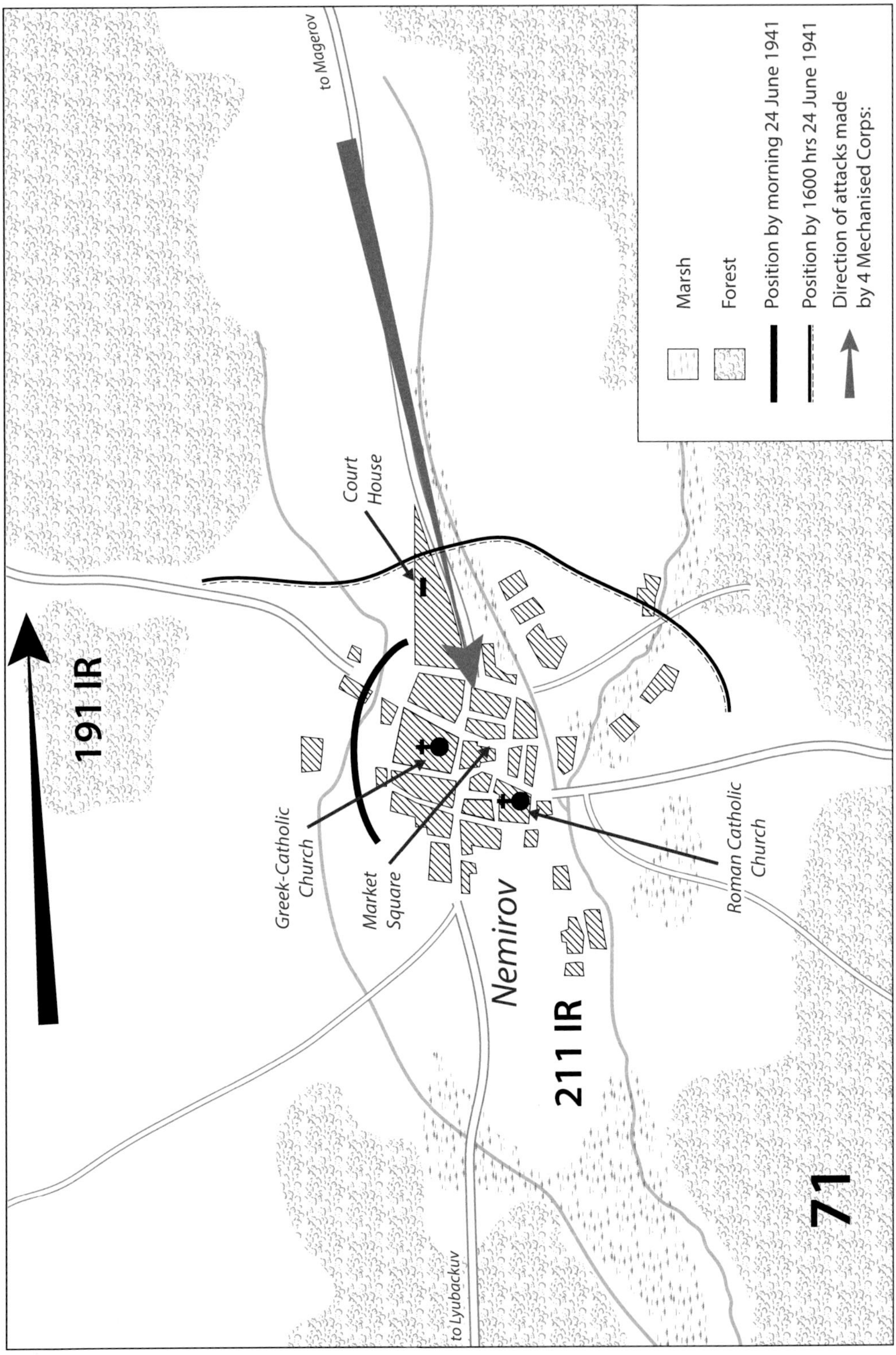

Map 6 The battle for Nemirov 24 June 1941.

> The soldiers were given their first taste of the tenacity with which the Russians defended their positions, their motherland. They 'encountered' the Soviet T-34 tanks, which were technically superior to our combat vehicles. The giant KV-1s and KV-2s with their 76.2mm long-barrelled guns would hardly be an even match for the German *Panzer III* with its short 5cm gun. In order to suppress enemy tanks it was necessary to draft in anti-aircraft and field artillery.[9]

Somehow or other the counterattack by German tanks on the bridgehead that had been captured was not successful. The Soviet claims of the number of enemy tanks that had been disabled was, it has to be said, relatively modest. The 12th Tank Division recorded just four enemy tanks on their tally. By 1400 hrs the tanks in Mishanin's division had broken through to Height 241.0 that dominated the landscape from which it was possible, most likely, to see Berestechko.

The entries in the combat journals of the *XXXXVIII Motorised Corps* demonstrate that the counterattack by two divisions under D.I. Ryabishev led to the onset of a crisis situation:

> The situation near Leshnev was becoming critical by midday. Despite the courageous resistance of the augmented battalion of the *179th Regiment*, which incurred heavy losses, the Russians managed, with powerful artillery support, to cross the rivers and bypass the settlement with a considerable tank force. The bridge to the south of Leshnev could not be destroyed the evening before due to heavy enemy fire. Separate enemy tank detachments advanced up to Mytnik and to Styr to the west of Berestechko. In places the infantry and artillery locked in combat to the north of Leshnev were forced back under intense pressure from the enemy.[10]

The eyes are immediately drawn to a contradiction: the Germans affirm that they were not able to destroy the bridge to the south of Leshnev. At the same time the Soviet side affirm that they were able to cross the river even though the bridge had been destroyed. These two affirmations can be solved by a single glance at a map: on the road from Brody to Pleshnev there are two bridges over the Slonuvka. The river channels split into two and two crossings need to be made.

The attacks by Soviet tanks posed a threat not only to the German artillery positions, but even to Werner Kempf's command post in Berestechko: "Since the Russian tanks had come within 6km of the corps command post, and the fact that this coupled with constant air raids made it impossible to operate the command post, it was moved to a farm 2km to the north of Berestechko."[11] The command post had to be moved by evening to avoid an interruption in the management of forces.

However the forces of the 8th Mechanised Corps were not able to keep up the pace. Further on in the combat journal of the *XXXXVIII Corps* the following entry can be found:

> The haphazard nature of the subsequent Russian attacks and the personal confusion of the Commander of the *57th* prevented this from becoming a success. On the order of the corps the units in the reinforced *199th Infantry Regiment*, who were on the march in the direction of Sitno to provide cover for the flank, have been deployed to the south with the aim of driving back the enemy that had broken through.[12]

Sitno lay to the east of Berestechko and Leshnev, that is to say the units in the *57th Infantry Division* were turned back to meet the Soviet counterattack.

9 Werthen, *Geschichte der 16.Panzer-Division 1939-1945* (Bad Nauheim: Verlag Hans-Henning Podzun, 1958), p.45.

10 NARA T314 R1138 f499.

11 NARA T314 R1138 f501.

12 NARA T314 R1138 f499.

Aside from a controversial and poorly formulated factor, such as the personal confusion of Lieutenant-General Oskar Blumm, who commanded the *57th Infantry Division*, circumstances that were evidently much more calculable worked against the Germans. The forward subdivisions of the *16th Panzer Division* departed for the approaches to Kremenets but the core of Hube's division was still on the march along the central '*Panzerstrasse*' on 26 June. They participated in countering the offensive by the 8th Mechanised Corps along with the *57th Infantry Division*. It was mentioned above that the *panzers* in the formation took part in the battles outside Leshnev. Aside from the *panzers* however, the *kampfgruppe* threw both their infantry weapons and the 50mm PAK-38 anti-tank guns into the balance of the battle. The history of the *16th Panzer Division* recounts this event as follows:

> The units in the infantry regiments had already come under attack from Russian tanks close to the settlements of Scurowisce and Storovitse on the River Styr. The *16th Panzerjäger Battalion* engaged them in combat. The field guns opened fire from a distance of up to 100m on the steel giants...21...23...a direct hit! The Russian tank moved backwards slowly. Only the turret rotating mechanism was damaged. The soldiers wanted to cry with resentment! It turned out that neither the 3.7cm, nor the 5cm field guns with their short muzzles were able to do anything to Russian tanks at a distance of more than 500m. Other tanks rained down fire on the field gun positions. Only the light tanks in the anti-tank gun groups were able to achieve any success. Just one, the 3rd Company, *16th Panzerjäger Battalion* destroyed 18 enemy tanks that day on 26 June 1941.[13]

On the one hand these words are very similar to a traditional German complaint about the 'door knocker' PAK-35/36 guns. However if we were to become absorbed in this pen-picture we would discover that the tank crews 'cried with resentment' at not being able to hit the Soviet tanks at a distance of more than 500m, or if it were written out in full; five hundred metres. Strictly speaking the Soviet 1937 standard 45mm guns did not penetrate German tanks either, which were protected with 50mm of armour, at a distance of 500m. Correspondingly at distances of less than 500m Soviet tanks could still be hit, at least from a PAK-38, but if it were to hit a heavy KV, as the description suggests it would just lock up the turret.

If the 12th Tank Division had succeeded in engaging only half of its armoured vehicles in combat then the 8th Mechanised Corps would have had every chance of achieving a decisive result in the counterattack of 26 June. The units of the *16th Panzer* and *57th Infantry Divisions* were able to counter an offensive using 75 tanks (that is to say an augmented tank brigade if the standards for 1942–1945 are applied).

According to a report that was compiled on the results of the battles, the losses in terms of combat vehicles for the 12th Tank Division on 26 June were as follows:

> Five KVs
> Eighteen T-34s
> Ten BT-7s.[14]

The formation lost 33 tanks; almost half of the 75 machines from two tank regiments that participated in the counterattack. According to a report by the commander of the corps at least two tanks from the 12th Tank Division became stuck in the mire. Incidentally Ryabishev and

13 Werthen, p.45.

14 The Central Archive of the Ministry of Defence, fund 229, inventory 157, file 7, volume. 1, p. 169.

Tsinchenko, in their report, assessed the losses for the formation under T.A. Mishanin as just eight combat vehicles, as 18 T-34s alone suffered a failure. If the figures from the headquarters of the 12th Tank Division are taken as a basis then it is possible to draw a conclusion that the anti-tank crews of the *16th Panzer Division* underestimated somewhat their successes. They counted the newest 'thirty-fours' as being among the Soviet light tanks that had been destroyed.

The delay in crossing the marshy rivers afforded the Germans a chance to recover from the initial shock and to call in air strikes. The *V Fliegerkorps*, which had previously concentrated on bombing the airfields of the Air Forces of the South-Western Front, had transferred to bombing the mechanised corps. The 12th Tank Division was the hardest hit. At least the impact of enemy aviation on 26 June is not mentioned at all in the reports written by the 34th Tank Division. The chief of staff of the 8th Mechanised Corps, Tsinchenko, writes very pointedly about these air strikes. "First and foremost they were on the 12th Tank Division." It is possible that the *Luftwaffe* were aiming at the division that was advancing specifically towards Berestechko. It is also possible that the fact of the terrain around Leshnev being more open played its role, as it was more conducive to using aviation. It would have been complicated to pound the 34th Tank Division in the surrounding woods. Somehow or other at 1400 hrs the skies above the heads of the soldiers and the commanders of the 12th Tank Division opened at 1400 hrs. Up until 2000 hrs some 20 air raids bore down on the units in the division led by T.A. Mishanin. The enemy bombers literally passed over their heads. Naturally Soviet tanks of all kinds were a difficult target for the twin-engine *Heinkel He-111* and *Ju-88* twin-engine bombers. However the logistics and artillery divisions were subjected to a decisive routing. The majority of the vehicles with ammunition, fuel and other equipment on board were set on fire. The memoirs of the commissar of the corps, N.K. Popel, contain a multitude of mistakes and inconsistencies but they describe the picture of the burning forest that was left in the wake of the air raids so vividly, it was as though Nikolai Kirillovich had really seen it with his own eyes: "The upturned shells of radio-vehicles burnt themselves out over a distance of 15m. The forest was also burning. Flames were running up the bronze coloured bark of the pine trees. Up and down, along the branches and on to neighbouring trunks. The burning trees fell, setting the lorries, tents and motorcycles on fire."

All the tractors in the artillery regiment of the 12th Tank Division were also destroyed in the air raids and the majority of the artillery crews were killed. T.A. Mishanin's formation was left bereft of artillery. This was the same artillery, the impact of which had been assessed so highly by *XXXXVIII Corps* command in all the documents that have been cited above. The success in terms of the routing of the logistics and the artillery in the Soviet divisions cost *Kampfgeschwader 55* one *He-111*, which was shot down by ground fire in the area around Brody. *Kampfgeschwader 51 Edelweiss* lost two *Ju-88*s in the area to the south of Leshnev, as well as one in the area around Brody. In all three cases the reason for the loss of the aircraft was ground fire.

On the whole one cannot fail to agree with the headquarters staff officers of *Army Group South* who, in the combat journal, wrote: "The attacks by tanks on the areas around Radzekhov, and Leshnev were stopped as a result of stubborn defensive battles and effective support from the *V Fliegerkorps*." This was probably one of the first instances in which an advance by a Soviet mechanised formation has been stopped by air strikes. The 6th Mechanised Corps, having been subject to a powerful enemy air attack outside Grodno carries the garland of the first unit to achieve this. Subsequently the *Luftwaffe* was to prove a formidable opponent. Aviation was a more manoeuvrable weapon in the hands of its commanders. It was easier to redirect aviation than it was to send tanks and artillery on the march along front line roads. The strength of German aviation lay in its ability to operate with a high degree of intensity, that is to say to complete a large number of combat sorties in a comparatively short space of time. Air strikes became a serious obstacle in the path of the advancing Soviet tank corps both in the summer of 1941 and the summer of 1942 and even in the summer of 1943 (during Operation 'Kutuzov'). It had become difficult for the

Germans to beat back tanks even in 1943, but artillery, logistics and motorised rifles were much more vulnerable on the battlefield. The effect on morale of constant air attacks also had a huge impact.

In the meantime, having lost less time crossing the marshy river and having only engaged the infantry, the 34th Tank Division passed through the wooded area and tore out of it like a jack in the box. The division led by Colonel Vasilyev reached the area around Khotyn and Redkuv rapidly and from there it was less than 10km to Berestechko. The Germans wrote specifically of the actions of this division: "Separate Russian tank divisions reached Mytinik." Mytinik is the last town on the road to Berestechko from Redkuv. The Germans, having turned the *16th Panzer Division* around, and after calling in air strikes, managed to fend off the attack by the 12th Tank Division, 8th Mechanised Corps. However the 34th Division, in this same corps, was able to create another crisis in the afternoon of that day. Again we turn to the combat journal of the corps led by Kempf:

> Up until the evening the position to the south of Berestechko remained critical. The enemy was attacking with their tanks to the north-east from Leshnev via Redkuv out to Ostrov, as a result of which the enemy managed to traverse the highway close to Ostrov. In the wake of this situation the corps was forced to issue an order at 1800 hrs to prepare the bridges over the Styr for destruction.[15]

In order to counter the Soviet offensive all remaining anti-tank weapons in Berestechko that had been united under the control of the commander of the *'Herman Goering' Luftwaffe Regiment* were mobilised. However the penetrating force of the 34th Tank Division was much lower than that of its neighbour. The majority of the tanks that took part in the attack were T-26s of various modifications. According to the memoirs of Ryabishev, by the time his corps went into battle "All the T-35 tanks had been stopped en route." This is indirectly confirmed by the fact that not one of the five-turret giants was lost in the area around Khotyn and Redkuv. Whether six KVs from Vasilyev's division participated in the attack is not known. In the end the 34th Tank Division was brought to a halt in the area around Mytnik by heavy artillery fire and lost around 30 tanks that either caught fire, or were destroyed, and the division did not enjoy any further success in this offensive. Having stretched out along the highway in the direction of Berestechko parts of the division came under fire from both sides and from the front line, from Teslugov, Ostrov and Mytitsa (Mytnik). Furthermore there was another marshy river—the Plyashevka—that was getting in the way of dealing with the enemy that lay in wait in Teslugov. A further offensive towards Berestechko was possible should the neighbouring 12th Tank Division be successful in liquidating even just one of the threats from the flanks. On the contrary, by the end of the day concerns over the threat from the flanks had only grown. Reconnaissance had noted movement from Teslugov to Kozin of up to 100 tanks as well as concentrations of up to 100 tanks in the forests close to Antonushka (to the south of Berestechko). These most likely, were units of the *16th Panzer Division* that were attempting to reach the forward detachment near Kremenets. At the same time however this route left the rear and the flank open to the 8th Mechanised Corps. The corps did not have any neighbouring forces on the right flank, and it was not possible to close the flanks using the detachments that had been active close to Kremenets either. I.V. Vasilyev, who was concerned about being outmanoeuvred and outflanked from the right, called his forward units back and concentrated his divisions in the forests to the south of Khotyn. The total losses for the 34th Tank Division for 26 June were 31 T-26s, five BTs and three armoured cars.

15 NARA T314 R1138 f499.

Theoretically Ryabishev could have turned the situation round to his advantage by introducing the third division in his corps into the battle. In the second half of the day the 7th Motorised Division finally occupied its starting position for the attack. At 1300 hrs the division under A.V.Gerasimov went on the offensive in the marshy areas of Bordulyaki Stanislavchik and Manastyrek but did not enjoy any specific success in this battle and remained on the line it had secured up until the onset of darkness. The character of the terrain in the area around the offensive was little different to the area the formation had been marching through, which has already been described above. Namely forests, which were interspersed by one or two marshy streams; the mediocre result of the counterattack by the motorised division in Ryabishev's Corps came as no surprise. In this forested area movement was only possible along the small number of roads and clearings, which could easily be covered by the enemy.

The War in the Air

The debut of the German bombers near Leshnev as a weapon of war on the battlefield was without a doubt, frightening. However the contribution of von Greim's corps was not just limited to air strikes on the advancing Soviet forces. The fighters of the *V Fliegerkorps* began to actively cover the advancing formations in *Panzergruppe 1.* It can be said that German aviation on 26 June turned to face the requirements of their ground forces. To some degree this supported a change in the airfields on which the '*Messerschmitts*' were based. On the morning of 26 June two groups from the three squadrons in *JG3* fighter squadron were moved to an airfield very close to the area where the tank battle was unfolding. *Group III/JG3* was now based outside Lutsk on a Soviet airfield that had only just been captured by German *panzer* crews.

In contrast no changes in strategy were forthcoming in Soviet aviation. The commanders of the South-Western Front set their aviation formations a mission in a single order along with the mechanised corps. This was the first order No. 0016 dated 25 June, which stated: "The air forces of the front line are to begin bombing concentrations of tanks with the aim of effecting maximum suppression by the start of the attack. The attack is to be preceded and supported by large-scale air attacks."[16]

As they were finally coming to after the shock of the first few days the Air Forces of the South-Western Front began to operate with an increasing intensiveness. Thus the 17th Aviation Division increased its activity level sharply on 26 June in comparison with the previous few days. The pilots in this division flew 235 combat sorties, dropping 280 FAB-100, 424 FAB-50 and 30 AO-25 bombs. The main targets were the enemy columns as well as the concentrations of materiel in the area around Berestechko, Ostrov and Radzekhov. The 225th High-Speed Bomber Aviation Regiment carried out three sorties with the entire regiment, the 224th and 48th High-Speed Bomber Aviation Regiments flew two sorties each with their entire regiments. The formation's losses, despite the high level of intensity, were not great: one aircraft failed to return from its sortie and two SBs were shot down in the area around the target. The 48th Bomber Aviation Regiment in this division (which consisted of 17 Pe-2s), and which were covered by the 20th Fighter Aviation Regiment (consisting of 28 Yak-1s), did not incur any combat losses at all. Only one of the '*Peshkas*' was forced to make an emergency landing. In turn the '*Yakovlevs*' in the 20th Fighter Aviation Regiment lost just one single aircraft in all, after flying 64 combat sorties (which amounted to between two to three sorties per aircraft) and covering not only the '*Peshkas*' but also the DB-3s of a neighbouring aviation division.

16 *Collection of Combat Documents from the Great Patriotic War* Issue No. 36, p. 28.

The reconnaissance aircraft of the 316th Reconnaissance Aviation Regiment also operated without incurring losses. Normally the Yak-2 and Yak-4 aircraft were assessed with some scepticism but they nevertheless proved the speed characteristics that were laid down by A.S. Yakovlev. Thus an operational intelligence report compiled by the regiment on 26 June states: "During the course of reconnaissance flights the Yak-2 and Yak-4 aircraft encountered enemy fighter aircraft on five occasions [...] in each case these aircraft were not able to attack our aircraft, since the reconnaissance machines had the edge in terms of speed and managed to evade the fighters without incurring damage."[17] As far as the tasks they were able to perform were concerned they were set to some depth: on 26 June the Soviet 'mosquitoes' flew to the area around Lutsk, Berestechko and Sokal on reconnaissance missions.

Not everyone was that lucky however. The re-basing of the *II* and *III Groups* of *JG3* immediately began to have an effect on the environment in the air; the 19th Aviation Division immediately lost 11 SB aircraft. With a reduced operational intensiveness (107 sorties), the SBs did not return from their sorties and a further Yak-2 was shot down over the target by enemy fighters. In one case an entire flight of SBs from the 138th Regiment failed to return from their sortie. The pilots of another bomber aviation regiment then reported that they had witnessed a battle between the SBs and *Me-109* fighters, and that one of the SBs caught fire in front of their eyes. The targets for the 19th Aviation Division were Sokal, Krystynopol and Radzekhov. Despite the enemy resistance the regiments in the division were still able to drop 385 FAB-100 bombs and 68 FAB-50s.

Even MiG-3s from the 15th Aviation Division were drafted in for air attacks on the columns on the central '*Panzerstrasse*'. Betweeen 0615–0925 hrs on 26 June some 28 FAB-100 and six FAB-50 bombs were dropped by 17 MiG-3s on the columns of enemy tanks and motorised formations. Uncharacteristically for fighters the '*sotki*' were suspended under the wings of the 'MiGs'. In the opinion of the command of the 15th Mixed Aviation Division the increase in the take-off weight of 200 kg did not fatally affect the handling. The MiGs of the 15th Aviation Division escorted the SB bombers to the target, losing four aircraft in the aerial combat. The aviation divisions were almost exclusively concentrated on Zubov airfield.

In the 16th Aviation Division the 'MiGs' covered four aircraft of the 86th Bomber Aviation Regiment but lost sight of them in air combat. The results of this interruption in the bomber escort immediately began to tell on the outcome of their sortie. One Pe-2 (the lead aircraft of Lieutenant-Colonel Sorokin's group) and three SBs failed to return from their sortie and one 'MiG' was also shot down. A flight of SBs of this same regiment that took off on a sortie, escorted by I-16s from the neighbouring aviation division, also disappeared without trace and not one aircraft from this flight returned to its airfield. According to the tally for the day in the 86th Bomber Aviation Regiment only three serviceable SBs and one Pe-2 remained in this regiment. On top of that the regiment was subject to a powerful attack on 22 June and by 26 June the regiment had almost lost its combat capability completely. An operations report written by the 16th Aviation Division notes the following on the tally for the day: "In the course of 26 June 1941 fierce resistance was observed from enemy fighters, which had been escorting the tank columns [and] patrolling in large groups of between nine to 12 aircraft, activity by all anti-aircraft weapons was also observed in the direction in which the tank columns were moving."[18]

The day of 26 June was just as unsuccessful for the 18th Aviation Division. Its DB-3 bombers flew 61 combat sorties (almost double the number they had flown on the previous day) and dropped 347 FAB-100 bombs on the area around Sokal, Radzekhov and Berestechko. Furthermore the 93rd Regiment lost seven bombers that failed to return from their sorties. The regiment also

17 The Central Archive of the Ministry of Defence, fund 229, inventory 181, file 19, p.311.
18 The Central Archive of the Ministry of Defence, fund 229, inventory 181, file 14, p.72.

survived an attack on their airfield on that same day, but the bombs landed on the edge of the airfield without doing any damage.

The 62nd Aviation Division incurred the highest losses on 26 June, this regiment conducted 73 combat sorties in total and furthermore 14 SBs and one Pe-2 were immediately lost. Following the diversion in the direction of Kovel on 25 June the division 'worked' these same targets on 26 June as well as the other aviation formations of the South-Western Front—namely Radzekhov, Berestechko and Stoyanuv. Some 152 FAB-100s and 350 FAB-50s were dropped. In total, according to German data, on 26 June some 68 Soviet aircraft were shot down in aerial combat and a further five were downed by anti-aircraft artillery. Losses of DB-3 aircraft were the most commonly reported and the Germans considered they had shot down 26 examples of this aircraft. This is quite strange since the most common type to be shot down were the SBs, which were in German terminology known as 'Martin-bombers.' The pilots of *I/JG3* achieved the greatest success claiming 31 aircraft shot down. The area the group operated in was relatively broad: Berestechko, Brody and Dubno, the 26 Squadron's own losses on 26 June amounted to 10 aircraft. Overall the 26 June 1941 could to some degree be called a 'black day' for the Air Forces of the South-Western Front. Heavy losses were inflicted and furthermore, in contrast to the attacks on the airfields that predominantly destroyed the materiel, losses in aerial combat more often than not meant the loss of the crews. There was no agreement strictly speaking on how the mechanised corps were to work together. Specifically Leshnev did not figure in the targets for the bombers, neither were the enemy defences ahead of the front line of the advance by the 8th Mechanised Corps. Also absent was any air cover for Ryabishev's corps. Fighters from the front line aviation divisions almost exclusively escorted their own bombers.

The reason for the absence of Soviet fighters over the 12th Tank Division deployments was far from the air raids on the airfields of 22 June. Quite a few combat aircraft still remained in service, including those that belonged to the newest types. On 27 June some 37 MiG-3 fighters remained in the 15th Aviation Division. Given the above system of communications and cooperation the 'MiGs' were capable of, if not driving away the German bombers, at least of seriously inhibiting their work.

It has to be said that Soviet aviation was active in more or less the self-same area, without shifting its targets, as the German *panzer* spearhead moved eastwards. This afforded the *11th Panzer Division* a short respite. Schrodek wrote with some satisfaction: "The deployment of our aviation will lead today to the weakening of Soviet aviation activity, which in general is pleasing to see." It was possible that the German tank crewman was witness to the battle with 18 I-153s from the 92nd Fighter Aviation Regiment against an *Me-109* above Dubno in the middle of the day, in which two I-153s were lost. However the *11th Panzer Division* was still some distance from the fiery corridor near Berestechko and Radzekhov. Let us remind ourselves that Kempf was forced to transfer his headquarters from Berestechko under the impact of air attacks from 'Stalin's falcons.'

The results of the counterattacks of 26 June

Summing up the combat activity of 26 June it has to be said that the Germans succeeded in containing the first attack by the 8th Mechanised Corps and in preparing for the next attacks.

If the Soviet tank crews decided to continue the offensive the following day in the previous directions they would have encountered a much more powerful defence. Ryabishev set off towards the 34th Tank Division at the close of the day. In his memoirs he explains that this was due to the absence of reports from this division, however this reason was clearly one made on reflection: in order to clarify the environment and to receive a daily report all that was necessary was to send a signals delegate. The corps commander evidently did communicate his hopes for the development of the counterattack conducted by the corps to the 34th Tank Division. This division was not on the receiving end of a crushing air attack and was in the most advantageous position. However on the night of 26–27 June events occurred, which changed the course of the counterattack drastically and which led to unexpected circumstances.

In the evening of 26 June the commander of the 12th Tank Division, T.A. Mishanin, took what was, to be honest, a controversial decision to withdraw his forces from the battle. Unfortunately the General, who was subsequently killed, did not explain the reasons for his order to anyone. From the data now available on the environment at the time it is possible to propose that he was trying to take the division (or to be more accurate what he had left) under the protection of the forested area and to move up the rest of the materiel. The forest provided cover from being observed by aerial reconnaissance and in doing so reduced the effectiveness of air attacks. Apart from that, after the day battle, Mishanin only had 40 tanks left at his disposal and his artillery was almost completely destroyed. In that environment an enemy counterattack could lead to the encirclement and to the routing of the formation. It should be noted that his neighbouring commander on the right flank, I.V. Vasilyev, made a similar decision in drawing his division back slightly into the forest on the northern bank of the Slonuvka. It cannot be ruled out also that Mishanin had agreed his withdrawal with Ryabishev and that his goal was to reshuffle the 12th Tank Division towards the 34th Tank Division's zone. These manoeuvres were quite often employed by Soviet troops between 1944–1945: during offensives along parallel routes the corps that was advancing more slowly would form up in line with the more successful corps and contribute to its success.

Somehow or other by midnight Mishanin's order had been fulfilled, the 12th Tank Division had withdrawn from the battle. This step, in terms of retaining the orders for a counterattack in the direction of Berestechko, could have cost the general dear. However new orders from front line headquarters unexpectedly coincided with his decision to withdraw the 12th Tank Division from the battle. At 0230 hrs on 27 June 1941 Major-General Panyukhov arrived at the headquarters of the 8th Mechanised Corps and relayed to D.I. Ryabishev a verbal order from the commander of the South-Western Front, which stated: "The 37th Rifle Corps is mounting a defence on the front line between Pochayuv Novy, Podkamen and Zolochiv. The 8th Mechanised Corps is to withdraw behind the lines of the 37th Rifle Corps infantry and is to augment its deployment using its own fire-power. This withdrawal is to commence immediately"

Thus, worn out by German aviation, the 12th Tank Division had already been taken out of the battle by 2400 hrs on 26 June. The decision by T.A. Mishanin just went unnoticed and as it turned out he had just predated the next order form front line headquarters. Otherwise he risked being put on trial, just like commander of the 14th Mechanised Corps Oborin, who was shot.

After receiving the next order Ryabishev wasted no time in passing this order on to the formations subordinate to him:

> The 34th Tank Division is to withdraw from the battle and moving along the route from Chernoarmeysk, to the monastery at Pochayuv Novy, is to concentrate in an area south-east of Pochayuv Novy.
>
> The 12th Tank Division and the 7th Motorised Rifle Division are to move along a route between Brody and Pidkamin, concentrating to the south, and south-east of Pidkamin.

We note that these words concerning a withdrawal from the battle only relate to the 34th Tank Division. The only indications for the other two divisions are the routes along which they were to move. Subsequently in his memoirs Ryabishev corrected the course and the chronology of the events slightly in order to fence off the withdrawal of Mishanin's division. To do this he had to shift Panyukhov's arrival to 0400 hrs, one and a half hours different to the actual time he provided in a report in July 1941. The corps commander later wrote in his memoirs:

> Now one question worried me. Whether we would have time to get this order out to the troops before they went on the offensive. If they were to start the battle then fulfilling the commander's order in daylight would have been very difficult. We had to hurry. Everything that corps headquarters were able to do had been done. The 7th Motorised and 12th Tank Divisions managed to receive the order before the offensive had commenced. The 34th Tank Division on the other hand had already attacked the enemy to the north of Berestechko and their withdrawal from the battle was delayed by two and a half hours.[19]

There could be no question of going on the offensive in the middle of the night. Apart from that counterattacks more often than not began at 0900 hrs. Therefore there was more than enough time to inform the troops. The only difference being that the 12th Tank Division had already fallen in with the marching columns. Signals delegates were sent to the other two divisions following Panyukhov's arrival. Interestingly in the reports written by the 34th Tank Division no mention is made of any orders for their withdrawal from the battle in the hours of darkness of 27 June. If the delegates did get to Vasilyev's headquarters then the withdrawal would not have taken place until the next order. On the contrary, the marching columns that had already been formed in the 12th Tank Division set off immediately to the area around the settlement of Pidkamin, to the south of Brody.

While the 12th Tank Division were withdrawing from the battlefield we will try and sort out how such a drastic change of strategy from front line command came about. Naturally it cannot be said that the 8th Mechanised Corps succeeded in achieving any outstanding results. The corps was not able to break through to Berestechko. In addition, as is evident from the documents cited above, Ryabishev's divisions managed to create a local crisis. In an operations report however, written by the headquarters of the South-Western Front, from 2000 hrs onwards on 26 June the outcome of the battle is described in a very disparaging way: "At 0900 hrs on 26 June 1941 the 8th Mechanised Corps attacked the enemy mechanised corps from the area around Brody in the direction of Berestechko, half-heartedly and without sufficient support either from the air or from its neighbouring 15th Mechanised Corps, which were being held by the enemy in what were their initial attack positions."

Karpezo's corps also found its way into the operations report: "The 15th Mechanised Corps, also operating with the same half-heartedness, failed to fulfil the order to attack. By 0900 hrs on 26 June 1941 (the beginning of the attack for the mechanised corps) they had still not concentrated at their attack positions." These words are justified, but only partially.

What then happened? In the memoirs of I.Kh. Bagramyan (or to be more precise in the memoirs of Ivan Khristoforovich, which were subject to a shameless 'literary adaptation' with dialogues added in that nobody was able to recall several years later) this is explained as a rejection of the counterattack strategy in support of building up a 'stubborn defence' based on the rifle corps.

The reason behind the withdrawal of Ryabishev and Karpezo's corps from the battle was completely different. The main mistake that front line command made was probably in their assessment of the direction that the development of the German offensive would take. In a reconnaissance report from the front line from 2200 hrs on 26 June we read: "The Radzekhov–Brody direction. The enemy, with the main force of the motorised and mechanised alignment that had broken through still intact in the area around Berestechko, and the forward units towards Dubno, Werba and Razdvilluv, attempted to expand this breakthrough in the direction of Brody and Ternopil. However on encountering resistance from our forces was unsuccessful." In the meantime *Panzergruppe 1* was striving to develop the advance not in a south-easterly direction towards Ternopil, as South-Western Front headquarters had proposed, but further east in the direction of

19 Riabyshev, 'The first year of the war' (Moscow: Voenizdat, 1990), p.31.

Ostrog and Shepetovka. M.A. Purkayev and M.P. Kirponos incorrectly assessed the movement of the 'pincers' in the Germans' planned encirclement of the front line troops. It is possible that the attack in the direction of Kremenets was incorrectly interpreted. As we now know it was dictated simply by a striving to use the *11th* and *16th Panzer Divisions*, not in line with one another, but along different routes. *Army Group South* command actually planned to perform an encirclement of the Soviet forces located opposite one another. The plan however was much more ambitious. The Germans were planning, in conjunction with the *11.Armee*, under Eugen Ritter von Schobert, that had been concentrated in Romania, to encircle the 6th, 26th, and 12th Armies. This is just how the entry for 26 June in the combat journal of *Army Group South* looks:

"Considering the course of the operation up until this point the issue of the expediency of a transfer from a deep strategic breakthrough in the direction of Kiev to a narrow, strategic encirclement of Soviet forces actively engaged in combat in the area around Ternopil–Lemberg (Lvov) is proposed for your detailed examination."

Furthermore the beginning of the encirclement operation was delayed to allow enough time to bring the *11.Armee* up to full readiness for the offensive (which was on 2 July). Correspondingly the mission of the *11th Panzer Division* remained a breakthrough "With three leading columns in the direction of Berdichev–Zhitomir in spite of the presence of flanks to some depth, and using any of the available roads." In order to contain the enemy breakthrough in the direction of Berdichev and Zhitomir the mechanised corps would need to maintain the counterattacks. Driving them backwards would actually take them out of the battle. If the South-Western Front command had assessed the enemy's intentions correctly no withdrawal would have taken place.

Thus the mechanised corps of the South-Western Front withdrew behind the line of the 37th Rifle Corps since it was proposed that they be used in a counterattack on the flanks, against a turn that it was anticipated *Panzergruppe 1* would make to the south. At the same time front line command decided to commence the withdrawal of forces to the east away from the proposed 'pocket'. In a private combat order, No. 0016, the 6th Army was withdrawn to a boundary formed by Pochayuv Novy, Ponikva, Ushnya, Zolochiv, Gologury and Ganachuv. The 37th Rifle Corps came under the 6th Army along with the 141st and 139th Rifle Divisions. In accordance with this same order the 12th Army withdrew to a front line formed of Styr, Dolina and Vyshkuv. In doing so the convex front line, which encroached on enemy territory in the Lvov salient was contracted and the Army was deployed to a line that faced north-west. A chasm was also eradicated between the covering army formations and the 'remote' rifle corps. The 37th Rifle Corps now came under the 6th Army.

Moscow however did not support the decision that front line command had made. I.Kh. Bagramyan recalls:

> ...Comrade Colonel! Comrade Colonel! I am listening to the voice of the Duty Officer—Moscow is on the line!
>
> I ran to the conference room. To my surprise the radio-operator had got through to Moscow. "Colonel Bagramyan speaking." I grabbed the report, and started reading: 'It is General Malandin speaking. Hello. Please tell your leadership immediately that General Headquarters have banned the withdrawal and demand you continue the counterattack. Do not give the aggressor one day of peace. That's all."[20]

M.P. Kirponos attempted to explain his decisions but was not able to defend them. The subsequent turn of events were to prove that General Headquarters had been correct in their

20 Bagramyan, p.141.

assessment—the tip of the German *panzer* spearhead had turned south much later, only after they had crossed the 'Stalin Line'. Since the missions for the mechanised corps had already been set on the basis of the environment as it had been between 24–25 June it would have been inexpedient to send them back into battle in the previous directions. The direction of the attacks was therefore changed: Bagramyan wrote:

> Kirponos leaned over the map once more.
>
> Give our mechanised corps new orders—he turned to Purkayev—we are going to turn the Eighth to the north-east so that they can advance straight towards Dubno, and the Fifteenth will launch an all-out attack on Berestechko. If Ryabishev is going to join Rokossovskiy and Feklenko's corps in the area around Dubno then the enemy units that have broken through will end up with their back against the wall.[21]

On the one hand a change in direction of the attacks would have allowed the combat activities of Ryabishev and Kirponos' corps to be coordinated to some extent with those of Feklenko and Rokossovskiy. On the other hand turning the 8th Mechanised Corps would make it possible to strike a blow on the flank of the German alignment that had pushed towards Kremenets and in doing so eradicate the threat to Ternopil. The instructions were conveyed to the 8th and 15th Mechanised Corps by brigade commissar A.I. Mikhaylov and brigade commander N.S. Petukhov. N.N. Vashugin, a member of the Military Council, visited this mechanised corps a short time later.

The delegates reached the location of the 8th Mechanised Corps early in the morning. At 0600 hrs on 27 June 1941, in an area 2km south of Brody, the brigade commissar A.I. Mikhaylov handed D.I. Ryabishev a second order form the commander of the South-Western Front, No. 2121, dated 27 June 1941. In accordance with this order from the commander the 8th Mechanised Corps was to commence an offensive towards Brody, Werba and Dubno at 0900 hrs on 27 June 1941 and by the end of the day was to concentrate in the area around Dubno, Volkoviye and Werba.

If the 12th Tank Division had not been withdrawn from the battle back in the evening of 26 June the night time ambivalence that the command showed towards the corps' objectives could have passed completely unnoticed by division. The withdrawal however of Mishanin's division was in full swing. At the time order No. 2121 was received from the South-Western Front the 12th Tank Division was already on the move from Brody to Podkamen and its column was spread out over 20–25km. Reluctantly Ryabishev gave the order at 0700 hrs:

> The 34th Tank Division is to attack in the direction of Kozin, Werba and Dubno, and by the end of the day is to advance towards the area around Dubno, Zagortse Male and Semyduby.
>
> The 12th Tank Division is to attack in the direction of Sitno, Kozin Werba, and by the end of the day on 27 June 1941 is to advance towards the area around Podluzhe, Werba and Sudobiche.
>
> The 7th Motorised Rifle Division is to advance towards the area around Brody, Chernoarmeysk and Werba and by the end of the day on 27 June 1941 is to concentrate in the area around Werba, Rudnya and Bereg exclusively, supporting the corps' action to the north-west, and south-west.
>
> The offensive is to commence at 0900 hrs on 27 June 1941.

It is worth paying attention to the final phrase: the corps commander set the time of 0700 hrs to go onto the offensive. Later, in his memoirs, Ryabishev gave a very different time: "The starting point

21 Bagramyan, p.142.

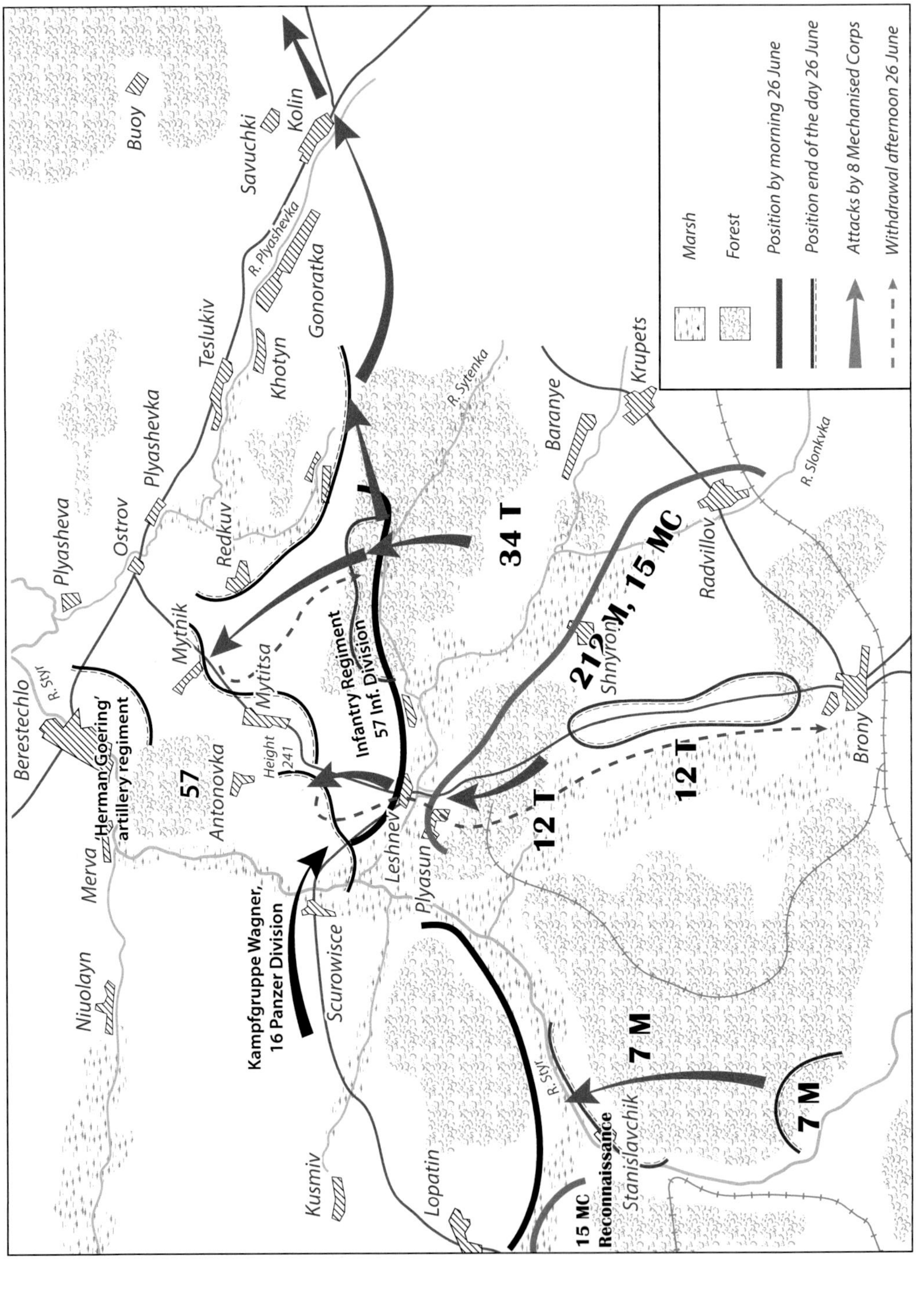

Map 7 The counterattack by the 8th Mechanised Corps 26 June 1941.

for the offensive was the Rudnya-Setsratin station. The division was to concentrate in this area by 0200 hrs on 28 June and the offensive was to commence two hours later."

After 0900 hrs in the morning N.N. Vashugin arrived at the location of corps headquarters and according to N.K. Popel's verbal testimony (which was later confirmed by D.I. Ryabishev) he demanded that the division go on the offensive immediately by way of an ultimatum. This version does not correspond to the documents at all. The objective of this version was to prove that the mechanised corps had entered combat in a slapdash and piecemeal fashion. In his memoirs Ryabishev attempted to portray himself as a judicious person not given to cramming.

> I had despatched reconnaissance with the aim of establishing the location, forces and alignment of the enemy. This objective is being carried out by the corps' motorcycle regiment. The corps' forces will be able to concentrate at their starting point by the end of the day and will only be able to commence the offensive from the morning of 28 June—this was how I ended my report.
>
> What!? Exclaimed the Member of the Military Council—an immediate decision—and then you move forward![22]

Correspondingly in the eyes of the corps commander there was no need for a new order in this melee. It had been prepared two hours before his visit. The signing by Vashugin of an order that had already been signed by the corps commander seems to be an even bigger idiocy. Popel describes this process with no expense spared: "The corps commissar grabbed the fountain pen and signed so quickly that splashes of ink were flying up." There was nowhere for the aforementioned command to sign the order and there would not be, since it is signed by the commander, the commissar and the chief of staff of the formation. Vashunin's signature was on the front line order anyway. Put simply this entire episode is poorly concealed in the memoirs. Subsequently these heart-rending stories were used to make N.N. Vashugin the fall guy and the person who was responsible for this entire failure. Subsequently this naturally developed into the 'role of the party' as the whole thing took a new twist. That is to say as a way of blaming the political system of the USSR for military failures.

In reality corps command went out of their way to fulfil this new order within the timescales set. Between 0730–0830 hrs on 27 June Ryabishev personally visited the 34th Tank Division and gave the order for the offensive towards Dubno. The corps commander had realistically assessed the environment and understood that the 12th Tank Division, which had been withdrawn back behind the lines, and the 7th Motorised Division that had become trapped in the forests, would be unlikely to be able to realise a plan that front line headquarters had developed. Therefore Ryabishev left for the formation at a point when the achievement of the objective that had been set was as close as it could have been. However it is possible an incident of some kind involving N.N. Vashugin nevertheless took place. This naturally enough was not over the planning of the counterattack, since as we have seen all the necessary decisions had been taken, and the orders were already signed. The corps commander's concerns could have been about the pace with which the division was to go into battle. Despite the fact that that Ryabishev personally took it upon himself to deploy the 34th Tank Division, at 0900 hrs it had still not gone on the offensive in this new direction. The documents that have survived indicate a time between 1400 hrs and 1430 hrs on 27 June. As subsequent events were to illustrate this delay in the advance was to play a fateful role.

A chronology of this gathering of forces and their advancement in the given direction illustrates the following: At 1000 hrs on 27 June a front line headquarters delegate deployed a column in

22 Riabyshev, pp.34–35.

this new direction consisting of the 12th Tank Division with 25 heavy and medium machines. Between 1400 hrs and 1430 hrs on 27 June 1941 the 34th Tank Division went after them (between 150–160 tanks, as well as motorised rifle and artillery regiments). At 1700 hrs, from the area around Chernoarmeysk, the remaining units from the 23rd and 24th Tank Regiments (up to 30 tanks) set off for the area around Werba for their joint combat operations with the 34th Tank Division. N.K. Popel was made commander of this composite group. Correspondingly the 7th Motorised Division was on the march on 27 June and the rest of the units in the 12th Tank Division were withdrawn to the area around Podkamen, where they were able to regroup, draw up the rest of the tanks and refuel.

However despite all the inconsistencies and difficulties the deployment of units from the forces of the 8th Mechanised Corps towards Dubno did bring unexpected success. At that time there was no consolidated front line and Popel's group struck an area where the forward units of the *16th Panzer Division*, outside Kremenets, and the *57th Infantry Division* joined. Furthermore Popel's group had to drive a wedge in between the *kampfgruppen* of the *16th Panzer Division*. There was a gap in the alignment of German forces that was more or less unoccupied, which enabled more than 200 tanks to be deployed towards Dubno unopposed.

The factor of the enemy's plans being unpredictable did have an effect on both sides, but in different ways. The Germans were overly concerned with building their defence on the approaches to Berestechko, thinking that the counterattack would be launched at this location once again. In accordance with an order issued by *Panzergruppe 1* command a special mobile detachment from *Panzerjäger-Abteilung 670* was formed as well as a motorcycle battalion. However the direction of the attack shifted suddenly and the Germans did not have anything with which to counteract it.

The environment that had developed by the evening of 27 June is described in the combat journal of the *XXXXVIII Corps*:

> At 1900 hrs the situation in the area around Berestechko grew more serious. A strong enemy tank unit was trying to break through towards Dubno from Brody. For the third time in the last few days the corps' highway was cut off and an extraordinarily difficult situation arose. The rifle brigade did not manage to join up with the forward units of the *16th Panzer Division*. It was engaged in combat with a powerful enemy near Honoratka and destroyed a large number of enemy tanks. An advanced guard of enemy tank units preliminarily reached Dubno and in the area around Tarakanova attacked the corps' signals and transport battalion. The principle section of the enemy group is located to the south of the highway and only around 50 super-heavy tanks were noted at Tarnawka. It is still not possible to draw a clear picture of the forward units near Kremenets. General Hube is probably surrounded at Kam'yana Werba along with part of his headquarters.[23]

Curiously rumours concerning certain problems with divisional headquarters had reached Popel's group as they went on the attack. In his memoirs he wrote: "And then a small German aircraft, a 'storch', which had been hidden up until that moment by the tall rye grass, took off. This, we learned that night from prisoners of war, was General Milche, the commander of the *11th Panzer Division*, abandoning his troops." The commander of the *11th Panzer Division*, Ludwig Crüwell, at that time was way out in front at Ostrog, and Hube was named as the commander of the *16th Panzer Division* and he did not fly off in any 'Storch.' Subsequently Popel's stories about the 'Infantry combing the field, getting hold of the chief of staff of the *11th Panzer Division*, and then the head of reconnaissance, and then someone else and getting rid of them is a complete

23 NARA T314 R1138 f507.

fabrication. Popel hastened events slightly. Hans-Valentin Hube escaped the Stalingrad '*kessel*' in an aircraft, he was already the commander of the *XIV Motorised Corps*. In general the encirclement in the first few days of the war did make an impression, as it were, on Hube's subsequent career. He ended up in the encirclement in Stalingrad but his final battle on the Eastern Front (and by then he was a commander) was the encirclement of the *1. Panzerarmee* in Ukraine in spring of 1944.

Specifically Popel's group had only reached Dubno by the evening of 27 June. In his report Popel wrote tactfully: "By 2300 hrs the southern edge of Dubno had been captured."[24] Later he wrote in his memoirs: "As we entered Dubno it was completely dark. Clouds obscured a young moon. There were no stars in the sky, no lights in the windows, nor any living soul on the streets. Shells and mortars pounded the darkened streets and empty houses."[25]

Table 5.1 Losses in the Air Forces of the South-Western Front in the period from 25–27 June 1941[26]

	SB	Pe-2	MiG-3	I-16	I-153 (I-15)	Yak-2	DB-3	Ar-2
Shot down in combat	20	1	3	8	5	3	4	5
Shot down by anti-aircraft artillery	2	1	1	3	–	–	1	1
Destroyed on the airfields	–	–	–	11	22(1)	–	–	–
Failed to return from its sortie	8	1	9	2	8(5)	3	3	1
Destroyed during withdrawal	5	–	–	–	5(4)	1	–	–
Abandoned on enemy territory	8	–	–	–	–	–	1	–
Catastrophes and accidents	1	–	2	8	3(1)	1	–	–

However, according to a report written by the 34th Tank Division, as well as their combat journal, the 67th Tank Regiment that had reached the town: "Came under heavy fire from anti-tank guns and artillery from the southern edge of Dubno and Zabrame."[27] Zabrame is a western suburb of Dubno. Correspondingly that night the 34th Tank Division was planning to head for Podluzhye, a village to the south-west of the town. They did not take the risk and attack Dubno by night to come out onto the 'darkened streets.' This decision was to have fateful consequences.

The War in the Air

German aviation, which had hardly played a decisive role in repelling the counterattack on 26 June turned out to be all but useless: "The air raids that the division [the *16th Panzer Division* – author] needed to be made against enemy tanks met with difficulties, in as much as it was impossible to draw a precise boundary between the warring sides owing to the ambiguity of their position."[28]

Soviet aviation had also reduced its activity somewhat. The 17th Aviation Division had not been given any orders since the morning of that day.

The 14th Aviation Division covered the forces in their movement along the roads in groups of between seven to ten aircraft, flying 56 combat sorties, including 19 made in I-16s, and 37 in I-153s. Considering they had 37 serviceable aircraft this was a small number of sorties, one and a half sorties per aircraft. The 15th Aviation Division took off to cover the 15th Mechanised Corps (over the course of 50 combat sorties) and to attack an enemy column in the area around

24 The Central Archive of the Ministry of Defence, fund 229, inventory 161, file 89, p. 67.
25 Popel, 'In a difficult time' (St. Petersburg: Terra Fantastica, 2001), p.145.
26 The Central Archive of the Ministry of Defence, fund 229, inventory 181, file 47, volume 76, p.77
27 The Central Archive of the Ministry of Defence, fund 229, inventory 157, file 7, volume 1, p. 65.
28 NARA T314 R1138 f506.

Scurowisce, Berestechko and Werba (over the course of 30 combat sorties), as well as covering the airfields and performing reconnaissance. In total some 126 combat sorties were flown and 5,600 kg of bombs were dropped. Losses were also modest; a single I-153. The 16th Aviation Division also provided cover for the 15th Mechanised Corps (over the course of 40 combat sorties). This cover was provided by a relatively large force—groups of nine aircraft. In the course of a patrol the pilots of the 87th Fighter Aviation Regiment repelled a raid by *Ju-88*s, shooting down one of them. Apart from that the division attacked enemy tanks around Scurowisce, Berestechko and Werba using fighters fitted with bombs (in the course of 70 combat sorties). In total the pilots of the 16th Division flew 156 combat sorties, dropping six tonnes of bombs. The 86th Bomber Aviation Regiment saw no action at all on 27 June. In accordance with this drop in Soviet aviation activity the number of claims for aircraft shot down by German aces also fell. On 27 June the fighter pilots of *JG3* fighter squadron only claimed 14 red star aircraft shot down.

In total therefore only 173 aircraft were lost between 25–27 June.

Ostrog

These scenarios for the course of events outside Dubno were in many ways reminiscent of the second day of the war. While the *'panzer' kampfgruppe* on 26 June were engaged in combat with the advancing Soviet tanks, the other units in Crüwell's division were heading east. In fact they were put into action in the gap in the front line formed by the 228th Rifle Division being pushed back to Dubno. The *Angern 'infantry' kampfgruppe* advanced forward, covering 35km in a day. The motorcycle battalion moved with even more haste and had by the evening of 26 June reached Ostrog after advancing more than 50km from Dubno. Here the battalion encountered the spectre of the Red Army's Second Strategic Echelon in the shape of the 109th Motorised Division from the Far East.

At the end of May 1941 the 109th Motorised Division, which was stationed at Haranor, had departed westward under strict secrecy. The first echelons, along with the divisional headquarters, the formations of the 381st Motorised Rifle Regiment, part of the sub-divisions of the 602nd Motorised Rifle Regiment and some other units from this division disembarked at Berdichev station on 18 June 1941. The arriving division was billeted 10km from the station, in the Skrulev camps. In connection with the crisis situation that had unfolded on the western front on 26 June 1941 an order arrived for the redeployment of the 16th Army in the area around Orsha–Smolensk. The division began a 120km march to the Shepetovka station in accordance with an order issued by the Chief of Staff of the Army Lieutenant-General M.F. Lukin. It was in this location that the equipment was to be loaded onto railway trains and depart for Belarus. The breakthrough by the *11th Panzer Division* in the direction of Ostrog in the second half of the day of 26 June required extraordinary countermeasures. M.F. Lukin, at his personal risk, took part of the 109th Motorised Division away from the loading and sent them to meet the Germans. This required a certain decisiveness and, in fact, the initial arrival of the Germans in the area of Ostrog was assessed as an airborne drop. The first to reach Ostrog and engage the Germans in combat was the 173rd Reconnaissance Battalion under Major Yulborisov. This reconnaissance battalion was the first to enter Ostrog and mount a defence there. The motorcycle units that were approaching on the evening of 26 June became dragged into the battle for the town and the subdivision under Major Yulborisov ended up being blocked. This is a sufficiently typical example of the Soviets using motorcycle units. As mentioned above the practice of using motorcycle units raised questions among Red Army tank commanders. They were in reality barely suitable in terms of using tank formations to make a breakthrough. In a mobile warfare however, without a consolidated front line, these sub-divisions found their niche. A situation would often arise for a tank division when there would be an interval that would be empty and which would be filled by the most mobile formation. The motorcycle crews were naturally not able to counter an organised defence in a slapdash fashion, but they were very capable of engaging medium size detachments and logistics units in combat. Capturing a position in the path of the division afforded an opportunity to take the next step in more favourable conditions. Thus, the reconnaissance under Yulborisov were able to entrench themselves in Ostrog and await the formations in the morning and the day would then begin with them storming the *'Angern kampfgruppe'* in Ostrog. In reality the exact opposite happened—it was the motorcycle crews that entrenched themselves in Ostrog and the 109th Motorised Division that had to drive the enemy out of the town.

The balance of forces, by the morning of 27 June, began to change in favour of the Germans. The *Angern 'Infantry' kampfgruppe* from the *11th Panzer Division* reached Ostrog, after a night time march, at 0500 hrs. The battle for the town took place in the daytime on 27 June. In the morning of the 27 June the 381st and 602nd Motorised Rifle Regiments, 109th Motorised Division ordered an offensive towards Ostrog from the settlement of Vilbovnoe, which was situated to the north-west of the town. There was almost no artillery support for the attack, in as much as the 404th Artillery Regiment had not managed to reach their starting point. The regiments attacked solely with the support of the 76mm regimental artillery and the fire from 45mm guns mounted on T-26 tanks, as well as BTs from detachments from the 57th, and 13th Tank Divisions. The majority of the latter had already been loaded onto trains and were on the way to Orsha. Having crossed the Viliya River on the only bridge, and by swimming across, the units of the 109th Division began to fight for the town. In the first few hours of combat the division lost its commander. At 1000 hrs in the morning the formation's command post came under artillery fire from the Germans that were housed in the bell tower. The commander of the 109th Motorised Division, Colonel N.P. Krasnoretskiy, was seriously injured by a piece of shrapnel from one of the shells. He was replaced as commander by his deputy N.I. Sidorenko.

In the second half of the day the *'panzer' kampfgruppe* of the *11th Panzer Division* drew up to Ostrog and the balance of forces shifted immediately in favour of the enemy. Colonel Sidorenko brought part of the reconnaissance battalion of the 13th Tank Division comprising of a tank company made up of 17 BT tanks, a company of armoured cars (consisting of 15 armoured cars), transport companies and a motorcycle platoon under his authority and sent them to assist the 318th Motorised Rifle Regiment. He was however not able to influence the outcome of the battle. The Germans drove out the Soviet forces that had been in the town itself, forcing them to retreat beyond the River Viliya under artillery and machine gun fire. By nightfall everything that had managed to cross the Viliya had been concentrated in the forest to the east of Vilbovnoe. By evening the 404th Artillery Regiment, 109th Motorised Division, approached Ostrog but there was insufficient support for them in the daytime battle. The offensive of Lukin's group, though it did not lead to the liberation of Ostrog from the enemy, did obstruct any further advance by the enemy. For the first time since the beginning of the campaign the *11th Panzer Division* was concentrated in one place and any advance forward was stopped. At that moment there were no obstructions to the development of the offensive. The threat to the flank of the *11th Panzer Division* had been liquidated. The offensive by the *III Motorised Corps* had completely contained the actions of the 40th and 43rd Tank Divisions. In the second half of the day on 27 June even the 228th Rifle Division and both tank divisions of the 19th Mechanised Corps withdrew from Dubno to the edges of Rivne. Only Lukin's group stood between Crüwell's division and Shepetovka.

28 June. A retaliatory strike

Having been deployed towards Dubno by order of front line command the 8th Mechanised Corps had dangerously overstretched their flank. In fact between the right flank of the 212th Motorised Division, 15th Mechanised Corps and the left flank of the 7th Motorised Division, 8th Mechanised Corps a 30km gap had opened up, which partially cut through the forested areas.

At 2045 hrs on 27 June an order, No. 6, was issued by the *6. Armee* in which Reichenau ordered an attack on Soviet forces in the area around Brody:

> The *XXXXVIII Artillery Corps* is to concentrate as many forces as possible in the area around Lopatina and Leshnev in order to enable an attack on Brody on 29 June. The focus for the artillery is to be the eastern flank. South of Radzekhov a sector needs to be captured north of Toropov. Any patch of land abandoned by the enemy needs to be captured immediately. Up until the beginning of the offensive the heights to the north of Leshnev need to be held in the event of any possible enemy tank attacks. The mission for the corps is to further support the flanks from Holoyuv to Brody from the enemy's motorised, and tank forces, which could still be expected from the direction of Lvov and Zlochev.[29]

We note that German command did not have a clear picture of the environment that had developed and in no way was a repeat of the counterattack in the direction of Leshnev ruled out. There was however nobody left to make this happen. It was more than likely that the Germans did not suspect that the gap between the 15th Mechanised Corps and the principal forces of the 8th Mechanised Corps existed. At least this cannot be gleaned from the order that was given. However in solving the task of providing active support for the flank of the *Panzergruppe 1* the German divisions made a move, which was symmetrical to the deployment of Popel's group, in the direction of Dubno and ended up in a vulnerable position in the Soviet troop alignment. .

Both sides went on the offensive at almost the same time but in different sectors and in different directions. The rest of the formations in the 8th Mechanised Corps gradually drew up towards N.K. Popel's. By 1100 hrs on 28 June an advanced guard from the 7th Motorised Rifle Division (one battalion of the 300th Motorised Rifle Regiment with an artillery battery) headed the approach to Werba, where they engaged the enemy's motorised infantry and tanks in combat. The principal forces of the 7th Motorised Division, and the remainder of the 12th Tank Division, by that time had lagged behind the forward detachment by 20km. Units from the *75th Infantry Division* and the infantry brigades from the *16th Panzer Division* immediately wedged themselves into this gap.

When by 1300 hrs the units that remained under the command of D.I. Ryabishev had approached the boundary formed by the River Plyashevka a nasty surprise awaited them. The gap between the corps' main forces had reduced by up to 10km, however overcoming the other 10km proved to be no easy task. Ryabishev's group encountered fierce German anti-tank resistance.

At that moment the 12th Tank Division, which had been pulled back on 27 June arrived on the battlefield. Over the course of the day on 27 June the units in T.A. Mishanin's division, which had pulled back to Podkamen, had still not sorted themselves out and pulled the remainder of their materiel back. At 1500 hrs the 12th Tank Division joined the battle with their renewed forces. All attempts however to break through the enemy's defences, which continued up until 1900 hrs, proved unsuccessful. The German side described the attempts by Ryabishev's group to advance towards Dubno thus:

> The regiment's principal forces continued to move in the direction of Kozin, and then turned east. Only the 11th Battalion of *Infanterie-Regiment 64*, which had been augmented by the 11th Company, *16th Panzerjäger Battalion,* and a battery of 88mm guns destroyed the enemy in the forests to the north and south of Tarnovka. Infantry companies occupied starting positions on the edge of Tarnovka. The 8th Company, *Infanterie-Regiment 64* under the command of Senior Lieutenant Muusa set about attacking Ivani-Pusto with the aim of 'trapping the

29 NARA T313 R4 f1100.

> enemy in a vice' from the east. The soldiers of the 8th Company, *Infanterie-Regiment 64* found fighting a heavy Russian tank hard going. It would hold down the infantry by keeping them under fire, and slow the capture of the villages down, from constantly changing firing positions. The Russian troops up to battalion level were nevertheless captured in a pincer movement and were pushed back. From their perspective however the tank based counterattack would follow shortly, and the *Infanterie-Regiment 64* was forced to return to its starting position. Tarnovka itself shook from the exploding anti-tank grenades, houses caught fire, and all the available weaponry was sent to destroy tanks. The wind scattered the dust and powder everywhere. One of the heavy infantry guns [this refers to a 150mm *sIG 33* gun—author] succeeded in taking out two medium tanks. The 5cm anti-tank guns were no use at a range of over 400m. All the new steel giants entered Tarnovka but the soldiers of the *16th Panzer Division* held fast. One of the 8.8cm anti-aircraft guns destroyed four tanks in the space of half an hour. When the attack had been repelled, the dead and injured had been gathered, and the dust had settled, the wrecks of 22 tanks could be counted on the battlefield. In the village of Ivanits-Ivnitskiy the fighting continued.[30]

While Ryabishev was trying to break through to join up with Popel's group, an enormous threat was building in respect of his logistics forces. At 0900 hrs on 28 June the *57th* and *75th Infantry Divisions* commenced an offensive to the south. After having overwhelmed the 212th Motorised Division that was stretched out on a broad front line, the Germans were already in Brody by 1530 hrs. By 1900 hrs the 7th Motorised and 12th Tank Divisions of the 8th Mechanised Corps were overcome on three sides and were practically surrounded. Their order of battle was utterly exposed to artillery fire and subject to intensive air attacks. This forced D.I. Ryabishev to issue an order to withdraw from the encirclement to the south-east. During the course of the exit from the encirclement the commander of the 12th Tank Division's own tank was hit and caught fire, T.A. Mishanin was killed. By 2400 hrs units of the 7th Motorised and 12th Tank Divisions, 8th Mechanised Corps had escaped the encirclement and had concentrated in the area to the south-east of Brody. The 12th Tank Division's losses in the battle outside Sidno were six KVs, 15 T-34s, seven BT-7s, 11 T-26s, 15 BA-10s, three BA-20s, 14 guns and more than 190 vehicles. The two battered divisions that remained from the 8th Mechanised Corps were withdrawn from the battle. Their participation in the Border battle ceased at that point.

On the periphery of the battle the Germans successfully repelled attacks by the 15th Mechanised Corps from the direction of Toporuv that they had anticipated. The counterattack that was conducted by units of the 10th Tank Division ran into a strong anti-tank defence and led to the loss of four KV tanks and seven BT-7 tanks. Only a small part of the 10th Tank Division was not involved in the immobilising clashes with German units that continued to arrive. After rushing around fruitlessly along the roads to Brody and back the 19th Tank Regiment, 10th Tank Division leapt into action. At 1000 hrs in the morning, in accordance with a private initiative on the part of the commander of the regiment Lieutenant-Colonel Proleyev, an attack was organised from the area around the heights to the south-east of Radzekhov. However, by that time Radzekhov represented a fortress, which was defended by the *297th Infantry Division* with the support of the 88mm anti-aircraft guns of the *'Hermann Goering' Regiment* that had been there since 23 June. Proleyev's regiment was met with organised fire from guns of different calibres, including heavy howitzers that were set at close range. In this attack the regiment lost nine KV tanks and five BT-7 tanks. One of the participants in this battle, the commander of the 1st Battalion, Captain Z.K. Slyusarenko described the battle as follows:

30 Werthen, p.45.

> Enemy shells could not penetrate our armour, but they could break the tracks, and destroy the turrets. The KV to the left of me is bursting into flames. A plume of smoke shot into the air above the tank, with a thin shot of flame from right in the core, like a spear. "Kovalchuk is on fire!'—my heart missed a beat. I could do nothing to help this crew: I was leading 12 tanks in the advance. Another KV stopped: a shell tore out from its turret. The KV tanks were very powerful, but in terms of their speed, and manoeuvrability they were clearly insufficient.[31]

The 15th Mechanised Corps were also hit by German aviation. One of the most important targets for German aircraft were the troop command posts. At 1800 hrs on 26 June 1941 the command post of the 15th Mechanised Corps came under heavy bombardment from some 18 enemy aircraft in the area around Toporuv. Judging by the information that is available today these were *He-111*s of the *Kampfgeschwader 55 'Greif'*. The corps commander, Ignatiy Ivanovich Parpezo, suffered a serious contusion in the course of the attack and the deputy corps commander Colonel Yermolaev took up command.

While the *Schützen Brigade* of the *16th Panzer Division* beat back the attacks outside Leshnev and Scurowisce a forward detachment of the division advanced towards the approaches to Kremenets. Hube hurried to inform his command that he had entered the town. On the way however, Soviet cavalry soldiers went on the defensive on the boundary formed by the River Ikva. Back on 25 June units from the 14th Cavalry Division had reached this objective. Over the course of the day the Germans made several attempts to break through towards Kremenets using various routes. All of these attempts however were repelled by artillery fire as well as by counterattacks on the part of the tank regiment from Kryuchenkin's cavalry division. After breaking through across the River Ikva the German detachments were time and again forced to withdraw back west along the line of the river. The Soviet defence in this direction was sufficiently stable: positions occupied by the 146th and 140th Rifle Divisions, 37th Rifle Corps adjoined the 14th Cavalry's positions to the left and right. It was for the defence of these same units that M.P. Kirponos was planning to withdraw the 8th and 15th Mechanised Corps.

As mentioned above South-Western Front command had attempted to use the pause of 25th June that was caused by the delays that the mechanised corps had experienced on the march to their advantage by engaging another formation in combat. In accordance with combat order No. 0016 the 8th Tank Division was to participate in this counterattack. On 26 June however this division remained on the eastern face of the Lvov salient and was regrouping following the battles for Mageruv.

The finest hour for the 15th Mechanised Corps came right at the very end of the battle. Early in the morning of 28 June South-Western Front command issued order No. 018, which was dramatically different to the principal guidelines for the counterattacks of 24–27 June, known as directives Nos. 015 and 016. In fact all the formations located over a radius of several kilometres from Dubno received active orders. The mechanised corps were finally to be supported by infantry. The 37th Rifle Corps received an order for them to cooperate jointly with the tank units that did not have active orders from 25 June onwards. In addition to simply waiting in anticipation at their positions, which were formed of the front line to the west, the corps had begun to head north: "The 37th Rifle Corps (the 141st and 139th Rifle Divisions) are to attack from 0800 hrs and by close of play on 28 June 1941 are to have reached the edge of Bovdury, Stanislavchik and Polonichna." Bovdury and Stanislavchik was the point where the 15th and the 8th Mechanised Corps joined up. The 36th Rifle Corps were ordered to advance against the southern flank of the tip of the German *panzer* spearhead, which was breaking through. The corps was told: "To go on the offensive at 1200 hrs on 28 June 1941 to perform the task at hand, building on the success of the 8th

31 Slyusarenko 'The Last Shot' (Moscow: Voenizdat, 1974), p.12.

Mechanised Corps, advance towards the front line formed of Mlynuv, Bakuyma and Kozin."[32] The environment however had by then radically changed. Infantry divisions from the *6. Armee* were advancing from the north to meet the rifle formations. There would be no question of "Building on the success of the 8th Mechanised Corps."

The only formation that could have gone on the offensive was the 15th Mechanised Corps. On this occasion however, having ground to a halt on the crooked flank of the 6th Army it remained there, balancing in line with 'stop orders.' The area that this corps operated in was comparatively quiet—the Germans had concentrated their efforts predominantly on a dash to the north, covering the basis for a breakthrough by infantry division defence. Correspondingly the 15th Mechanised Corps could only try to break through their defence, after having arrived back at their starting point following a 'stop order.' Finally the 8th Tank Division was able to join the corps as reinforcements. However following fierce fighting aimed at holding back the units of the *17. Armee*, P.S. Fotchenkov's division had been significantly weakened. In fact a composite tank regiment did advance towards the combat area, while the motorised infantry regiment remained outside Lvov.

The order that the 15th Mechanised Corps received was written very abruptly, but succinctly: "Advance up to Berestechko by the end of the day." As we already know by 27 June Berestechko had already turned into a stronghold that was full of anti-tank armament, and a breakthrough would need to be made through the defences of the *57th Infantry Division*, and it would be much more difficult to crush this defence than to destroy the weak anti-tank shields at the point where the tank and infantry regiments joined.

The 37th Tank Division, under Colonel Anikushkin, was nominated as the leader of the 15th Mechanised Corps in this offensive. Up until this point this division had taken almost no part in the offensive battles and had been able to retain its combat capabilities. The strength of the 37th Tank Division in terms of materiel, and personnel could by 28 June 1941 be described as follows:

Personnel	
Commanders and Officer ranks	459 men
Junior Commanders and Junior Officers	553 men
Rank and file soldiers	4,055 men
Armoured vehicles	
T-34 tanks	26
BT-7 tanks	177
T-26 tanks	8
BA-10 armoured cars	11
BA-20 armoured cars	5
Artillery	
152mm howitzers	4
122mm howitzers	3
76mm tank guns	26
76mm field artillery guns	4
45mm tank guns	201
37mm anti-aircraft guns	4

32 Slyusarenko, p.12.

Clearly more than 200 tanks were serviced and supported by just 5,000 men: by way of a comparison a Red Army tank corps between 1944–1945, armed with 200 tanks, would be comprised of more than 11,000 men, twelve 122mm howitzers and forty-six 120mm mortars. Owing to a lack of mechanised transport 3,571 men from the 37th Tank Division remained in the town of Kremenets. There were just 30 trucks and special purpose vehicles for more than 3,000 men. The majority of the artillery armament in the division, in the shape of twenty one 122mm howitzers, also remained in Kremenets. The lack of transport, which had not arrived from industry by the beginning of hostilities, reduced the capabilities of the 37th Tank Division considerably and this served as an omen for the low level of capability in the 200 tanks that made up the division. In terms of their technical characteristics the BT tanks fully met the requirements of 1941. Many armies of the world, including the *Wehrmacht*, had light tanks in their inventory. The issue was whether infantry and artillery could support these tanks effectively. The latter was no less capable of supporting tanks than anti-projectile armour, by destroying anti-tank armament with its own weaponry. Unfortunately however the tank crews of the 37th Division were not given that support. Their own artillery was weak and there was a lack of support from artillery regiments that were subordinate to the South-Western Front.

One of the largest attacks by BT-7 tanks in the initial period of the war began in the middle of the day on 28 June. The 37th Tank Division crossed the first water barrier in its path—the Styr, at Stanislavchik. The crossing was captured by the 37th Motorised Rifle Regiment and the 73rd and 74th Tank Regiments were able to build on this success. The crossing of the next small river, the Ostrovka, had become an overwhelming task. The first tanks to approach this crossing were immediately destroyed. The poor artillery support did not enable the division to use their light tanks effectively. The commander of the division wrote the following in their report on the results of the combat activity: "It was comparatively easy for the enemy even with a small force to organise an anti-tank defence especially against BT-7 tanks, which were the main examples in service with units in the division. Alongside this the firepower of the BT-7 tanks in these conditions was not very effective." The poor artillery support also turned out to be fateful for the mechanised infantry in the 37th Division:

> The 37th Motorised Rifle Regiment, in their active fulfilment of the task at hand, crossed the River Styr with part of its forces and jointly with tanks in the Bordulyaki Stanislavchik sector, but was not supported by an adequate amount of artillery (just two batteries—one 152mm and one 122mm) and incurred heavy losses. According to figures supplied by the chief of staff of the Mechanised Infantry Regiment, Captain Kartsev, the regiment's losses amount to around 60 percent of the entire compliment. The commander of the regiment, Major Shlykov, and his deputy, Major Shvarts, were killed. The boundary that is held by the 37th Mechanised Infantry Regiment along the southern bank of the River Styr on the Bordulyaki Stanislavchik sector is strewn with the dead and wounded. The 37th Mechanised Infantry is seriously demoralised.

The rest of the tank formations in the 15th Mechanised Corps did not achieve any particular success. The 8th Tank Division fought on the right flank of the offensive over the course of the day. The division however was not able to break through the anti-tank defences of the German *297th Infantry Division*. We find this laconic entry in the report on this combat activity: "The battle in the area around Okhladuv. Losses—12 tanks." The 10th Tank Division was not able to break through the artillery fire from the *297th Infantry Division* near Leshnev either. This direction, which on 23 June had promised success, had become a completely hopeless one by 28 June.

The Commander of the 37th Tank Division F.G. Anikushkin (this photograph was taken after the war). In a twist of fate he was to fight in these same locations in the Ukraine in 1944, by that time as the Commander of a tank corps in the Red Army that was advancing forwards in triumph. By 1941 he was already a sufficiently experienced tank commander, having served in tank forces since the beginning of the 1930s.

A T-35 tank abandoned due to an accident involving the engine on the road between Zolochiv–Ternopil. This is a later series machine with conical shaped turrets. This tank took part in the parade in Red Square in Moscow on 1 May 1941.

The T-35 tank from the previous photo, from a different angle. The way the conical turrets match up with the vertical walls of the turret platform is evident. This is an example from the transition period.

An early production series KV-1 tank, abandoned on the side of the road from Ternopil–Pidvolochisk. The abandoned towing cables are testimony to the fact that an attempt was made to save this tank by another tank, or by a tractor.

The Commander of the 43rd Tank Division I.G. Tsibin (this photo was taken after the war). He did not enjoy a resounding career in the course of the war.

A KV-2 tank that had become stuck in the marshy ground just outside Leshnev. This machine belonged to the 12th Tank Division, 8th Mechanised Corps.

This same KV-2 from a different angle.

A Soviet BT-7 tank that has become stuck in the marshy terrain. It was not only the heavy tanks that were damaged because they became stuck on the marshy river banks.

A T-35 tank abandoned close to the village of Zhidatichi on the road between Lvov–Busk. This vehicle has cylindrical turrets and was manufactured at the end of 1935–beginning of 1936.

This same T-35 close to the vlllage of Zhidchati. This is a later photograph after the tank had been pushed to the side of the road into a ditch so as not to obstruct the flow of traffic. The protruding parts of the tank have been painted white, which shows up clearly in the twilight.

A T-34 tank that has been knocked out in the area around Sitno. This is an earlier machine with a 76.2mm L-11 gun. The tracks have most likely been removed by technicians to repair other vehicles.

BT and *Pz.IV* tanks, as well as trucks, that were destroyed in the area around Sitno.

Two T-34s of the 12th Tank Division that were knocked out in the area around Sitno. These are early series tanks armed with a 76.2mm L-11 gun.

The *Panzerjäger-Abteilung 670* on the march. In front is a *Pz.I* tank that is acting as the lead tank. Behind them the characteristic silhouettes of the anti-tank *Panzerjäger I* can be seen, fitted with trophy Czech 47mm guns.

The Commander of 'Popel's group' Commissar N.K. Popel. He fought right up until 1945 and ended the war in Berlin.

A burnt out BT-7 tank of the 34th Tank Division. Alongside is a burnt out 'Komintern' tractor.

A KV-1 tank and a ZIS-5 truck abandoned in the forest just outside Brody.

A T-35 tank abandoned close to the village of Noviy Yarychev on the road to the town of Busk.

A damaged later series T-26 tank, the circular hatch indicates that this tank was fitted with an anti-aircraft mounting.

A T-26 tank damaged in combat along with a BA-10 armoured car.

A BT-7 tank that has been disabled in combat. The track rollers that have been deformed by German shells are testimony to the tank having been hit in battle. The white stripe and the figure six are this vehicle's tactical markings.

Damaged trucks and BA-10 armoured cars on the road. In the foreground is a trapezoidal fuel tank that was attached to the wings of the armoured car.

M.F. Lukin, who commanded the 16th Army (this photograph was taken after the war). He was taken prisoner just outside Vyazma in October 1941 and released in 1945.

A T-26 tank abandoned on the road to Shepetovka. This machine most likely belonged to the 114th Tank Regiment known as 'Lukin's group'.

A T-35 that has suffered a technical failure due to engine problems and which was abandoned by its crew in the village of Zapytov (just outside Lvov). Tank crews removed the machine guns to take with them. The tank itself is a later series example with conical turrets.

Soviet BT-2 tanks abandoned on railway wagons in Ternopil. The enforced withdrawal often prevented damaged tanks from being removed for repair even if they had been loaded onto a train.

6

The Anti-Tank Hedgehog – Dubno

Back on 27 June it was the artillerists of the 108th Artillery Command (Arko 108) who, along with the logistics units of the *11th Panzer Division*, repelled the first attacks from Popel's group on the evening of that same day. The prospects for holding the town on the morning of the following day against several dozen tanks were already slim. The attack from Popel's group on Dubno was literally a few hours late. The combat journal of the *XXXXVIII Corps* sets out the time at which the German infantrymen ventured onto the streets of the town on 28 June: "At 0700 hrs the *111th Infantry Division* advanced from Mlynuv to an area east of Dubno and in the morning an advanced guard will enter Dubno. This will eradicate the immediate threat to the town."[1] Now the town's garrison, which previously consisted in the main of artillery units and logistics troops, was significantly expanded. In fact the German defensive troops in Dubno had a numerical advantage in terms of personnel over Popel's group. On the latter's side was their only advantage—tanks. However in themselves they could not compensate for the enemy's advantage in the sense of infantry and artillery.

Shortly before the offensive the 34th Tank Division was to suffer its next blow. During a reconnoitre the commander of the 67th Tank Regiment, Lieutenant Colonel Bolkhovitin, was killed. Finally at 0900 hrs on 28 June the offensive on Dubno would begin. Popel's group would encounter some fierce artillery fire both from the front line from the direction of Dubno and from the flank from the settlement of Myatin. The 34th Tank Division was to lose around 30 tanks both destroyed and set alight. They were not able to break through to Dubno. As the divisional chief of staff subsequently wrote in his report: "Individual tanks did trickle through to the edge of Dubno, but communication with them was lost and the tanks went missing without trace."[2] The howitzer regiment in the 34th Division, of which only three guns remained by that time, would use all its available ammunition and then lose its howitzers altogether to artillery fire from Dubno.

On the morning of 29 June a composite detachment from the 8th Mechanised Corps renewed their advance from Dubno. Our tank crews encountered fierce artillery fire from the edges of Dubno. The KV-2 tanks made an especially strong impression on the Germans:

> The culmination of the development of the situation in Dubno was from 0400 hrs onwards, when the Russians began a new attack using infantry and tanks, including 15cm assault tanks. The only consolation was a message from the tank group command that units in the *44th Infantry Division* were already approaching Dubno and were 15km away to the north with a mission to put the situation in the town right. Having said that the enemy evidently

1 NARA T314 R1138 f499.

2 The Central Archive of the Ministry of Defence, file 229, inventory 157, file 7 volume 1, p. 66.

> broke through on 29 June at around midday via *111th Infantry Division* positions to the south-east of Dubno, and were advancing further east.[3]

Supporting the attack with heavy tanks however could not compensate for artillery that had already been knocked out. Four KV tanks were put out of action by artillery and two of them were burnt out. In the combat journal of the 34th Tank Division the reasons behind the failure are set out very clearly. "The attack petered out due to a lack of artillery and combined-arms infantry."

Attacking forces gradually dwindle

Overall on 29 June the 34th Tank Division lost around 80 tanks. The mechanised infantry regiment lost around 40 percent of its line-up. There were 65 T-26s, five KVs (of which one was not able to fire) and two BT-7s left in the division. In the evening the commander of the 34th Tank Division would undertake an attempt to arrange cooperation with the nearby Red Army units. To this end reconnaissance troops would move south across the marshy flood plain of the River Ikva. They would however find no consolation there, reporting only that the 140th Rifle and 34th (or more accurately the 14th) Cavalry Divisions were withdrawing to the south. In the evening of 29 June Popel's group took up a defensive position along the highway running to the west of Dubno from Kleshchikha to Tarakhanov.

While Popel's group was attempting to break through to Dubno its rear guard was fighting units from the German *16th Panzer Division*. On the evening of 29 June the *kampfgruppe* under Sieckenius (consisting of the *2nd Panzer Regiment*, one battery of 88mm anti-aircraft artillery and a battalion of mechanised infantry) attempted to break through to Dubno via Werba. Despite the fact that Popel's group was not able to cooperate with aviation the encircled troops did unexpectedly receive air support. In the history of the *16th Panzer Division* this episode is described as follows: "On the way to Dubno the attack group managed to survive an air raid by Russian bombers. Wave after wave of bombers dropped bombs on columns of combat materiel. A shout was suddenly heard over the smoke of these burning vehicles "Gas!" This was a false alarm but the shout did exacerbate the general situation."[4] Having survived the air attack the *kampfgruppe* under Sieckenius advanced onwards to Ptychi and encountered Soviet tanks that had dug in.

A report written by this division on the results of the battle paints a picture of a fierce clash:

> At around 2130 hrs the tank regiment was subject to a Russian counterattack using tanks, and infantry troops. The Russians fought very hard and on several occasions they jumped onto the combat vehicles themselves, firing at the crews. Later they attached explosive charges to the tanks that had stopped. In the end the tank regiment was pushed back to an area to the south of Werba. Ten heavy combat vehicles were lost.[5]

The history of the division reveals what lay behind the tactical reversal "The tank regiment was pushed back to the south of Werba at around 2300 hrs:"

> The soldiers attempted to deploy their guns and tanks, move backwards and tried to evade fire. It seemed nobody was listening to orders and random firing broke out around us. The withdrawal partially descended into a panic. The charge of tanks and infantry could only be

3 Munzel, p.26.
4 Werthen, p.47.
5 NARA T314 R1138 f1397.

> stopped for a short time. We had to get out of Werba. There was panic in the 'Yozh'[6] camp [This was a name given to units from the *16th Panzer Division* that improvised a circular defence around Werba—author]. Following the failures near Werba and Dubno the danger of an enemy breakthrough appeared. An infantry brigade that was protecting the 'Yozh' positions had abandoned its emplacements in the night and occupied the northern front that stretched along both sides of the road towards Werba. This brigade was preparing for an enemy counterattack. Over the course of the entire night individual vehicles, as well as soldiers that had lagged behind and which were returning from the area around Dubno continued to arrive at the 'Yozh' camp.[7]

Heavy T-35s were used in these battles, which up until that point had not been lost on the marches due to breakdowns, and which had stayed in the shadows of the tank battle. The Germans wrote about this episode: "The Russians showed off their 52 tonne "Klim Voroshilov" tanks unnecessarily. Anti-aircraft and field artillery however easily dealt with these clumsy clodhoppers with five rotating turrets"[8] The name of 'Klim Voroshilov' is clearly a mistake since it was the T-35s that had five rotating turrets and 88mm anti-aircraft guns would be excessive for breaking through their armour.

Despite the successes however in repelling the attack from the *16th Panzer Division* clouds were gathering over Popel's group. Several German formations were approaching the units from two Soviet divisions that were blockaded in the approaches to Dubno from different directions. On the evening of 29 June Franz Halder wrote in his diary:

> On the front line of *Army Group South* a peculiar battle has developed in an area to the south of Dubno. The *16th Panzer Division*, having left the heights in the area around Kemenets, is attacking the enemy from the south and in the area around Kremenets the *75th Infantry Division* is advancing from the west, the *16th Motorised Division* is approaching from the south-west, the *44th Infantry Division* from the north, and the *111th Infantry Division* from the east. The 8th Mechanised Corps is active on the enemy's side. The environment around Dubno is very tense.[9]

The *44th Infantry Division* on the morning of 29 June was situated 15km to the north of Dubno and they had failed to arrive at the set location by the evening of that day. The *16th Motorised Division* had been delayed by the poor road conditions and on the morning of 29 June was situated outside Berestechko. Therefore the order given by Halder to these two formations to 'advance' did exceed expectations somewhat. The *75th Infantry Division* attacked Ryabishev's group on 29 June and withdrew from the area where Popel's group were surrounded. It was here that Halder made a simple mistake.

Up until the liquidation of Popel's group that had broken through towards Dubno, offensive operations along the central '*Panzerstrasse*' were actually halted. Both *panzer* divisions in the *XXXXVIII Motorised Corps* were stripped of their freedom of movement. The *11th Panzer Division* lay idle outside Ostrog. On the one hand Lukin's group counterattacked this division, on the other hand the battle was threatened by a breakthrough towards Dubno, and finally, bombs rained

6 In Russian 'Yozh' means 'Hedgehog'—Translator's note.

7 Werthen, pp.46–47.

8 Werthen, p.47.

9 Halder, 'Military Diary. Daily records of the Chief of the General Staff of the Land Forces' (Moscow: Voenizdat, 1971), p. 61.

down from the sky in an endless stream. In the history of this formation the following lines are dedicated to this episode:

> Over the course of three days the *11th Panzer Division*, and with it the *15th Panzer Regiment,* remained in Ostrog. At a distance of 100km from their own front line corps and left completely to their own devices they were to deal with whatever befell them here—the worst of which was the lack of ammunition. Supply by air from squadrons of *He-111* bombers did help but only for a short period, which was far from sufficient. They had to counter constant enemy attacks over this period of time on the bridgehead in Ostrog, which was under threat owing to the growing difficulties with supply. While the *11th Panzer Division*, as we have already seen, were fighting on the front line for the bridgehead in Ostrog the German military units were in combat with powerful motorised enemy troops, equipped with tanks, in Dubno itself.[10]

The overall assessment of the environment by divisional command was the same: "Up until the final reconciliation of the position concerning the logistics lines there could be no question of the *11th Panzer Division* advancing any further."[11] The *16th Panzer Division* also halted an advance on Kremenets and was forced to attack positions held by Popel's group outside Werba. The leadership of *Army Group South* complained that "Again on 29 June the motorised formations failed to attain an efficient marching speed."[12]

Despite all the difficulties in realising the plan that had been set out by Halder a sufficiently strong encirclement had formed around Popel's group by the evening of 29 June. From the morning of 30 June the artillery of the *111th Infantry Division* began to fire intensively on the positions of those in the encirclement. Several tanks were destroyed by artillery fire and specifically two BT-7s were set on fire from a reconnaissance battalion in the 34th Tank Division. The commissar of the 67th Tank Regiment, I.K. Gurov, would fall to the artillery fire, as would the chief of staff of the 68th Tank Regiment, Captain Abramikhin. By 1900 hrs on 29 June the commander of the group, N.K. Popel, had made a decision to take advantage of the successful battles among his rearward troops near Werba and break through to the south towards Kremenets. It was proposed that the road running across the marshy floodplain of the River Ikva from Ptychi to Stariy Nosovits would be used. With the onset of darkness between 2200–2300 hrs the division's rearward forces advanced onto the road and moved steadily in the direction of Stariy Nosovitsy. This movement however was detected by units from the *16th Panzer Division* and artillery fire bore down on the river crossings, which set fire to the tanks and vehicles on the bridge. Nevertheless the 34th Tank Division did break through to the south at a cost of up to 50 percent of its materiel.

Ostrog

The difficulties with supply that had arisen in connection with the breakthrough by Popel's group towards Dubno were especially challenging for the *11th Panzer Division* in connection with the unceasing attacks from M.F. Lukin's group. These tense battles gave rise to an increased use of ammunition. Over the course of the night of 27–28 June, in accordance with an order given by Colonel Sidorenko, units and sub-divisions of the 109th Motorised Division regrouped their forces for a new offensive. This however did not end well. The Germans gave the 602nd Regiment a chance to cross back over the Viliya river and advance right up to the edges of the town, after

10 Schrodek, p.133.
11 Schrodek, p.133.
12 The Combat Journal of Army Group South.

which they opened fire with artillery and machine guns and deployed tanks. The offensive by the 381st Regiment was also brought to a halt. In order to ensure its continuation the 404th Artillery Regiment joined the battle. The artillery crews succeeded in putting a number of batteries out of action as well as the enemy machine guns nests, which helped the 381st Regiment break through to the centre. Right up until the evening the regiment was engaged in combat with varying degrees of success. Only with the onset of darkness was the 381st Motorised Rifle Regiment forced to withdraw to its starting positions on the eastern bank of the River Viliya. In the official history of the *11th Panzer Division* these events are reflected using the following phrase: "With the forces we had at hand we nevertheless managed to repel an attack by the Russians on the outskirts of the town."[13]

As he was preoccupied with the environment prevalent in the offensive by his corps Werner Kempf set off for Ostrog on 28 June in a liaison aircraft. He did not see anything of comfort there. The following entry appears in the combat journal of the *XXXXVIII Corps*:

> In connection with poor conditions for radio communications only fractious reports are coming through from the *11th Panzer Division*. After returning from the front line in a 'Storch' from the division the corps commander reported that the *11th Panzer Division* were beating back constant, powerful enemy attacks on a bridgehead that had been expanded that morning and were forced to incur heavy losses from constant air attacks.[14]

These flights were typical for German corps and even army commanders. It is widely known that the commander of the *9th Army*, Walter Model, was injured on a similar flight in 1942 by ground fire from a rifle.

The War in the Air

By the end of the Border battle the Air Forces of the South-Western Front began to steadily run out of steam. On 28 June the attention of front line aviation was switched to the area around Ostrog. On 28 June the 16th Aviation Division flew 135 combat sorties and dropped 59 FAB-50 bombs. Such a miserly quantity of bombs can be explained by the fact that only five SBs and two Pe-2s remained in the division. The 17th Aviation Division was much more active. Its SB bombers from an altitude of between 200–600m bombed Ostrog and Mizoch, flying 89 combat sorties and dropping 192 FAB-100 and 180 AO-25 bombs. Pilots observed direct hits on tanks and three fuel tankers that were ablaze to the south-west of Ostrog. Losses amounted to one SB, damaged in combat with an *Me-109* and which was destroyed on landing. The 18th Long-Range Bomber Aviation Regiment flew 22 combat sorties and dropped 202 FAB-100 bombs (we note even less than those dropped by the SBs) in the area around Varkovichi, Mizoch and Ostrog. Losses amounted to one DB-3 shot down in air combat.

The real hero of the day on 28 June was the 62nd Aviation Division. If the capabilities of the other aviation formations on the front line had dropped due to losses, then the division under Colonel Smirnov received two short-range bomber aviation regiments equipped with Su-2s (the 226th and 227th), which finally constituted a formation. The results of the combat activity in this augmented line up were 159 combat sorties, in which 432 FAB-10 and 311 FAB-50s were dropped on the *11th Panzer Division*. The losses could be categorised as moderate since one SB and four Su-2s were shot down by enemy fighters.

13 Schrodek, p.133.
14 NARA T314 R1138 f510.

The attacks by enemy bombers in the 19th Aviation Division were spread over a wider area. Not only did Ostrog come into its catchment area, but also the Mlynuv, and Dubno areas. This division flew two regimental sorties, in the first of these 239 FAB-100 and seven FAB-50s were dropped, while in the second 180 FAB-100s were dropped. The division's own losses amounted to one SB, shot down in air combat.

The almost 400 combat sorties flown by the Air Forces of the South-Western Front along a relatively restricted area on a line between Ostrog, Mizoch and Varkovichi (just 40km in all) made an indelible impression on the personnel of the *11th Panzer Division*:

> The rain that had started to fall in the night gave us some hope that today would see a reduction in Russian aviation activity. This however was not the case. At dawn the rain stopped and the Soviet aircraft appeared immediately and straight away began to attack units in the *11th Panzer Division*, which had been moving towards Ostrog over the entire course of the day. [...] In order to avoid prolonged firing from the air, tank crews tried to protect themselves as follows: they excavated trenches along which the well camouflaged tanks would then pass. [...]. The fact that the Soviet enemy enjoyed **absolute superiority in the air** [I have added the bold myself—author] at least in this location, was beyond doubt.[15]

Table 6.1 The strength in terms of personnel and materiel in *JG3* on 28 June 1941

Formation	Aircraft type	Airfield	Total	Combat capable
Headquarters (*Stab/JG3*)	*Bf 109F-1/2*	Khostyne	4	3
1st Group (*I/JG3*)	*Bf-109F-1/2*	Dub	35	26
2nd Group (*II/JG3*)	*Bf-109F-1/2*	Volodymyr-Volynskyi	26	20
3rd Group (*III/JG3*)	*Bf-109F-1/2*	Khostyne	29	24
Total			94	73

The phrase about absolute air superiority may be an exaggeration but Soviet bombers did nevertheless sustain losses. The Germans however clearly had insufficient forces with which to cover their own forces. In the line-up of the 3rd fighter squadron in *JG3* on 28 June there remained approximately 70 combat capable fighters. Apart from that the fighters in *JG3*, with the exception of the *II* and *III* groups had still not changed the airfield on which they were based. As before they would take-off to cover forces from Poland, while Ostrog lay deep inside Soviet territory. Therefore the tally for aircraft shot down on 28 June was at an all-time low, just nine aircraft, including six for the *II* group in the squadron.

The following day, on 29 June, the aviation formations of the South-Western Front were tasked with missions to considerable depth, which led to a certain reduction in the number of sorties. This was clearly evident in the results of this combat activity for the 62nd Aviation Division. In the course of a day the division had carried out 116 combat sorties (as opposed to 159 on the previous day) and dropped 148 FAB-100 bombs, 195 FAB-50s and 524 AO-2.5s. The new regiments flying the Su-2s had a bloody baptism of fire—over the course of a day when eight Su-2s and three SBs were lost. Seven Su-2s were claimed by the pilots of the *III* Group in the squadron, including by their commander Walter Oesau (he was to become an ace on the Western Front with 127 victories). To begin with the Germans identified the Su-2 as an American V-11. In total on 29 June *JG3* claimed 35 Soviet aircraft destroyed for the loss of two *Bf-109F-2*s.

15 Schrodek, p.133.

It is quite difficult to indicate with any credibility who it was that attacked the *16th Panzer Division* and who supported Popel's group. The most likely candidate would be the 16th Aviation Division since the name of Werba is listed among their targets in plain sight. Apart from that the aviation regiments in this division were 'working' what were at that time typical targets—the trio of Varkovichi, Mizoch and Ostrog. In total the aviation division flew 178 combat sorties, dropping 18 FAB-100s, 110 FAB-50s and 102 AO-25s. One Yak-1 and one I-16 were shot down by anti-aircraft artillery. In a more indistinct variant, such as 'Dubno' the radius of operation for Popel's group does appear on the list of targets for the majority of the aviation divisions on the front line.

In the course of the day the 17th Aviation Division flew 220 combat sorties, dropping 286 FAB-100s, 39 FAB-50s and 18 ZAB-50s, 475 AO-25s and 180 AO-10s. The division's combat capability was at a sufficiently high level. There were 20 Pe-2s remaining in service with the 48th Regiment of the division. It was the *'Peshkas'* that dropped the highest number of bombs—some 280 FAB-100s and 20 FAB-50s. The objectives of these attacks were the roads running from Dubno out to Rivne and Ostrog: two aircraft were lost to anti-aircraft artillery. The bombers in the formation not only managed to step into the 'breach' when there was a lack of enemy fighters over Ostrog, but also to repel their attacks. Thus the SBs of the 224th Regiment were met over the target by *'Messerschmitts'* but the gunners knew how to drive them away with coordinated fire. A short, but succinct entry concerning the condition of the target appeared in a report to the aviation division: "Ostrog is ablaze." Given the large number of incendiary bombs dropped in Ostrog this comes as no surprise.

The level of activity in the long-range bombers on 29 June was not high. The 18th Aviation Division flew just eight combat sorties and furthermore one of these was a reconnaissance mission. Correspondingly the number of bombs dropped was not high either, just 70 FAB-100 bombs. There were no losses. Rivne, Dubno, Mlynuv, Mizoch and Varkovichi figured among the targets for the 19th Aviation Division. In the course of the day the division flew 76 combat sorties, dropping 210 FAB-100 and 274 FAB-50 bombs. Losses for this aviation division, compared to other aviation divisions that had switched to targeting Ostrog, were comparatively high: four aircraft failed to return from their combat sorties and three were shot down by fighters.

Over the course of the day the 14th Aviation Division, 5th Army countered enemy advances with attacks from groups of between 9–11 aircraft in the Dubno and Rivne sector and also engaged in reconnaissance. The level of activity for the aviation division was at a record low—just 49 combat sorties, with 36 serviceable aircraft. The 15th Aviation Division did not take part in the slaughter of the *11th Panzer Division* outside Ostrog either. Its aircraft only operated in accordance with orders issued by 6th Army headquarters. Not only did the 'MiGs' cover Muzychenko's troops but also operated as fighter-bombers. Pilots reported direct hits on enemy tanks outside Yavorov. It is possible that these were *'Sturmgeschütz'* self-propelled artillery mounts, which had been attached to the infantry. In total, over the course of the day, 119 combat sorties were flown, four I-16s failed to return to their home base.

The '*Panzerstrasse*' are liberated

The roads from Ptychi across the Ikva River that had been blockaded by artillery fire forced the commanders of Popel's group to seek alternative routes out of the encirclement. It was here that the commander of the 34th Tank Division, I.V. Vasilyev, made a mistake, which was to cost him his life. He decided to change the direction of the breakthrough and to break through from the western face of the 'pocket' that had formed, in a south-westerly direction, from Bolshaya Milcha to Budy. At 0730 hrs in the morning of 1 July the remnants of the division approached Bolshaya Milcha, from where they encountered artillery fire—the village was occupied by the *44th Infantry Division*. I.V. Vasilyev took a decision to fight his way through and attack Bolshaya Milcha. In this battle the division lost its remaining tanks, the artillery crews of the *44th Infantry Division* were taking out KV-2s using 150mm *sIG-33* heavy infantry guns. Some 395 men, 13 T-26 tanks and four T-34 tanks from the 12th Tank Division, as well as 12 motor vehicles, escaped the battle. Colonel I.V. Vasilyev, who participated in the battle, along with the deputy commander of the division's political unit, Regimental Commissar M.M. Nemtsev, disappeared without a trace. On the following day, in accordance with a decision that was taken by Popel's commissar along with the chief of staff of the 34th Tank Division, Kurepin, the remaining tanks and vehicles were taken out of use, all the documents were buried and the remnants of the group walked out of the encirclement on foot.

On 28 June a decision was finally taken by *Army Group South* command to use the southern '*Panzerstrasse*'. Up until the last moment Rundstedt was wavering over the direction in which Weitersheim's *XIV Motorised Corps* would enter the battle. Specifically a variant was examined, which would see the corps advance along the northern '*Panzerstrasse*' in line with the *III Motorised Corps*. Finally, on 28 June, an order was issued for the *XIV Corps* to advance via Tomashuv and Rava-Ruska. At that moment the *9th Panzer Division*, along with the motorised *SS 'Wiking' Division* became subordinate to the corps. They were due to advance along a line from Zhulkev to Zolochiv and Ternopil. Weitersheim's corps had gone on the offensive by 28 June but were delayed until 0600 hrs on 29 June due to the need to construct a 24 tonne bridge close to the settlement of Mosty-Veliki. On the evening of 29 June the 15th Mechanised Corps, which had been engaged in combat since 23 June, began its withdrawal to the front line reserves. This withdrawal was covered from the north by the 212th Motorised Division, which had occupied positions to the south of Brody. As it was stretched out along a broad front the corps was slow to turn round and depart to the east, and would steadily draw out from the narrow gap between the German infantry divisions from the north and the spearhead of the *9th Panzer Division* from the south. This interval threatened to fence them in an encirclement 'pocket' at any moment. On 29 June the situation did not turn catastrophic. The *9th Panzer Division* ran into units from the 8th Tank Division. In a report written by the latter the day's events are described briefly, but succinctly: "Through their own efforts and whilst changing from a defensive to an offensive stance the division removed the 10th Tank Division, 15th Mechanised Corps from the encirclement."[16] The 15th Mechanised Corps had completed their participation in the tank battle and gradually withdrew to the east, fighting a rearguard action with German units that had set off on their heels. In the daily report dated 30 June the *9th Panzer Division* claimed 13 Soviet tanks destroyed, including super-heavy tanks, in the battles on the approaches to Zolochiv.

The War in the Air

On the final day of June both sides were considerably worn out by the unceasing battles and were not able to maintain the previous level of activity in the air. In the history of *Kampfgeschwader 51 Edelweiss* the situation on 30 June is described as follows:

> The technical companies experienced a lack of the necessary equipment. Moreover there was a lack of cranes and hoists with which to lift the aircraft that had made emergency landings and to effect engine changes and many other instruments and spare parts were missing. By 30 June in *KG51* the number of aircraft and crews had been reduced to one third of the standard. Morale had also gone into decline, although up until that point the personnel in the squadron had only recorded victories. It was on that same day that use of the SD2 'devil bombs' was stopped.[17]

16 The Central Archive of the Ministry of Defence, fund 229, inventory 157, file 7 volume 1, p.139.
17 Dierich, 'The Bomber Squadron 'Edelweiss', The History of a German Air Force Formation' (Moscow:

The idiosyncrasies of aviation support are described in some detail in a report written by the *16th Panzer Division* on the battle of 30 June:

> Since we had been promised aviation support by way of an order from the corps and at 1100 hrs the head of the operations department [had also promised] air support the division cancelled the attack a second time to await the air support that was long overdue. At approximately 1130 hrs two fighters appeared as air support. As a result of this the attack was set for post meridian but at 1500 hrs a Russian attack came in with tank support to the east of Werba. This attack was repelled. Furthermore at the same time our attack was postponed. During the course of this pause an air raid was carried out by a squadron of *Ju-88* bombers, completely unexpectedly, and from a significant altitude. This did not achieve any significant success but at least it did not inflict any damage on the riflemen, who meanwhile had succeeded in crossing the line along which the bombs were dropped in a northerly direction [that is to say they found themselves in the area that was being bombed. – Translator's note].[18]

The missions for the aviation in the South-Western Front on 30 June remained unchanged: "Continue to destroy the enemy's motorised and mechanised groups moving towards Dubno, Ostrog and Rivne." The period of impunity however, when it was possible to bomb enemy formations that had forged ahead with minimal losses, had come to an end. The 62nd Aviation Division, having carried out 108 combat sorties in the area around Mlynuv, Goshcha and Dubno, lost 11 aircraft straight away: six Pe-2s and five Su-2s, although it was true that three Su-2s were forced to make an emergency landing on their own territory. Furthermore the bomb load that had been dropped was not that great, as it had been on previous days: 338 FAB-50s and 78 AO-10s. There were five Pe-2s, 44 SBs and 71 Su-2s (plus 16 that were unserviceable) in service with the aviation division. Here again the *III* Group *JG3* ended up being the 62nd Aviation Division's opponents. The pilots in the *III* Group claimed 23 enemy aircraft shot down, and 32 for the entire squadron, on 30 June. The V-11s again appeared on the list of those shot down. The 15th and 16th Aviation Divisions had switched to supporting the 6th Army, attacking the advancing German formations in the area around Lvov, as well as covering the Soviet forces that were withdrawing. The 16th Aviation Division also made their presence felt with an attack on the German airfield at Mlynuv. In total the aviation division flew 138 combat sorties, dropping 36 FAB-100, 36 FAB-50 and 28 AO-25 bombs. In a retaliatory strike on the airfield at Ternopil one Yak-4, one SB and one I-16 were set on fire.

The most energetic of the aviation divisions on the 30 June was the 17th Aviation Division. Their targets were the enemy's mechanised units on the road from Dubno–Rivne, as well as Ostrog, which had become a traditional target in the final few days. In total 162 combat sorties were flown and 298 FAB-100s, 50 FAB-50s and several hundred small bombs were dropped. Our own losses amounted to just one Yak-1 aircraft. The SBs and '*Peshkas*' had stopped flying without having incurred losses, not least because they were escorted by 'Yaks' of which there were 26 examples left in service. The pilots of the Yak-1s claimed one *Me-109* shot down in aerial combat.

The long-range bombers in the 18th Aviation Division flew just 20 combat sorties, dropping 71 FAB-100 bombs. Their targets were the mechanised units in the area around Berestechko and Radzekhov. First and foremost these were columns of the *16th Motorised Division* that had rushed towards Dubno. The DB-3 regiments did not incur any losses. Another front line aviation formation—the 19th Aviation Division (comprised of 60 combat capable aircraft) flew 56 combat sorties on this day, dropping 30 FAB-100s and 212 FAB-50s, as well as around 3,000 small bombs, on

Centrepolygraph, 2005), p. 90.

18 NARA T314 R1138 ff1397—1398.

their targets in the area around Dubno and Mlynuv. Losses amounted to four aircraft, which were shot down by enemy fighters.

The final counterattack

The principal enemy for the *11th Panzer Division* close to Ostrog on 30 June remained aviation: "The enemy again has absolute air superiority and inflicts considerable losses on it [the *11th Panzer Division*—author] in sustained low-level attacks using bombs and their on-board armament."[19] Overall at the tip of the German tank spearhead the environment had stabilised with the withdrawal of the *III Motorised Corps* to the boundary of the River Horyn. The Germans drew up their rearmost forces and their crossing equipment and selected points from which they would cross the river. In the combat journal of *Army Group South* these battles are reflected in the entry for 1 July: "*Panzergruppe 1* encountered a stubborn enemy defence on the Horyn River and its tank units were subject to fierce counterattacks. During the course of today the group did not posses any operational freedom of movement either."

During the build-up of front line forces the Germans had driven in an enormous wedge, or more accurately, a trapeze, by the beginning of July 1941 in the 5th and 6th Army zones. The foundation of this trapeze, on a line from Kiverets to Brody, was up to 70km wide. The trapeze extended upwards to the east to a depth of 90–100km up to the Horyn River. The upper foundation of the trapeze was formed of the *11th* and *13th Panzer Divisions* that had advanced up to 40km to a front line on the Horyn River. Soviet command decided to attack along the northern element of the trapeze using the forces of the 5th Army. The decision, which was made by the commander of the army, M.I. Potapov, envisaged the 9th, 19th and 22nd Mechanised Corps attacking in the general direction of Mlynuv, a settlement 15km to the north-west of Dubno. The 9th Mechanised Corps was to have attacked to a depth of up to 40km from Klevan to Mlynuv. The 19th Mechanised Corps was to have advanced to the south of Rivne in this same direction. The divisions of the 9th and 19th Mechanised Corps were completely worn out. For example, on 29 June, in the 85th Tank Regiment, 43rd Tank Division there were 25 T-26 tanks, while in the 86th Tank Regiment there were 35 T-26s and a single T-34. M.I. Potapov understood this very well and hence he decided to introduce the 22nd Mechanised Corps into the battle. The heart of the 22nd Mechanised Corps was the 41st Tank Division, which up until this point had only fought in the battles as individual units. On 30 June this division consisted of 106 T-26 tanks, 16 KV tanks and 12 guns. The 19th Tank Division had incurred heavy losses in the battle near Voynitsa and on 30 June only 16 T-26 tanks remained in service. The 215th Motorised Division, 22nd Mechanised Corps had also incurred losses in the first days of the war and had just 15 tanks and 12 guns. The 22nd Mechanised Corps was to have attacked in the direction of Mlynuv from the morning of 1 July, after having concentrated in the area around Ginish, Silno and Karpilovka (these were settlements near Tsuman, around 40km north of Mlynuv). The time for these attacks was very well chosen: the attention of the Germans was focused on the area around Dubno and the defence on the northern flank of the offensive had been significantly weakened. This attack however was planned separately to the overall strategy for the front line and even if it was successful, it would not have been developed.

After failing to achieve decisive success in the counterattacks using mechanised corps, front line command began to seek salvation in transferring to a passive strategy. The idea of withdrawing to the old border hung in the air: "This thought came up in every conversation: the Border battle had been lost, forces need to be withdrawn to the line of the old fortified sectors. Nobody however

19 Munzel, p.27.

thought of saying this out loud."[20] On the evening of 30 June the withdrawal to the old border was sanctioned by Moscow.

The directive from Supreme Headquarters, which was signed by Stalin, Zhukov and Timoshenko stated:

1. The enemy has captured the area around Dubno following fierce fighting using mobile units and is looking to build on this success to the east.

   At the same time large-scale enemy forces have gathered in the north-eastern region of Romania, threatening the flank of the South-Western Front. There has been a breakthrough in the area around Bobruysk, which has reached the enemy's mechanised corps.
2. The Armies of the Western Front are arranging a defence on the boundary of the fortified sectors in Polotsk, Minsk and Mozyr. The boundaries with the Western Front are as they were before.
3. The forces of the South-Western and Southern Fronts are to withdraw to the border of the fortified sectors: Korosten, Novograd-Volynsk, Shepetovka, Staro-Konstantinov, Proskurov and Kamenets-Podolsk, where an organised, stubborn defence is to be set up based on the fortified sectors using combat troops and first and foremost an allocation of anti-tank weaponry.

At 2300 hrs the South-Western Front command sent order No. 0027 to the forces under it. The introduction to the order practically repeated the directive issued by Supreme Command Headquarters. The objectives for the armies were then detailed:

> The 5th Army, whilst continuing to liquidate the breakthrough in the direction of Rivne in conjunction with the 6th Army is to dig itself in on the boundary of the first line of the Novograd-Volynsk fortified sector. The right wing of the Army is to begin a withdrawal; reaching the edge of the Sluch River by the morning of 5 July.
>
> The 6th Army along with the 24th M[Mechanised] C[Corps] of the 2nd A[Anti] T[Tank] A[Artillery] B[Brigade] is by the morning of 5 July to withdraw to a boundary formed of Ostrov, Lanotsy and Volochisk, this withdrawal is to begin from sundown on 2 July; the intermediate boundary formed of Ostrog, Kremenets, Zalozhtse and Pokropivna is to be reached by the morning of 3 July; another intermediate boundary formed of Ostrog, Kremenets, Vishnevets, Zbarazh is to be reached by the morning of 4 July.
>
> The 5th Army had been augmented by the 196th Rifle Division, part of the 7th Rifle Corps, and the 24th Mechanised Corps, and the 2nd Anti-Tank Brigade came under the command of the 6th Army.
>
> The 26th and 12th Armies were given a similar objective in terms of its content and the borders that it mentioned. The withdrawal of both armies was set for the night of 1–2 July. Over the course of 5–6 hrs the units of the four armies of the South-Western Front had to cover around 100–200km.
>
> The mechanised corps were pulled back to the reserves, it was envisaged that they would be concentrated as follows:
>
> a) The 8th Mechanised Corps—Proskurov by the morning of 3 July;
> b) The 4th Mechanised Corps—Babin (30km east of Staro-Konstantinov) by the morning of 4 July.
> c) The 15th Mechanised Corps—Staro-Konstantinov by the morning of 4 July.

20 Bagramyan, p.166.

Given such 'itchy feet' the counterattacks by the mechanised corps of the 5th Army did not have any long-term outlook, since the boundaries for the withdrawal had already been set. Nevertheless they did take place and became sufficiently successful.

The 20th Tank Division of the 9th Mechanised Corps, from the morning of 1 July, went on the offensive from the boundary formed of Klevan and Orzhev and, after having pushed enemy units back, had by 1500 hrs on 1 July covered between 10–12km and captured the boundary formed of Belyuv and Bronniki. The division claimed that up to 1,000 enemy soldiers had been killed in this battle and 10 tanks and two artillery batteries had been destroyed. Our own losses moreover reached up to 200 men killed or wounded. The enemy's *25th Motorised Division* ended up on the receiving end of an attack from the division led by M.E. Katukov. According to data provided by Major-General Heinz Guderian (the son of the well-known German military commander, who at that time was the Headquarters Officer of the *III Motorised Corps*), the 20th Tank Division really did achieve an impressive result. A powerful battalion of the *35th Regiment*, part of the German *25th Motorised Division* ended up surrounded in the area around the settlement of Bronniki. The losses for the battalion in terms of the numbers killed alone stood at 153 men. In connection with the overall withdrawal however the success of the 20th Division was not developed further. By the end of the day on 1 July the division, in accordance with an order given by the commander of the 9th Mechanised Corps K.K. Rokossovskiy had withdrawn back to its starting point.

The 35th Tank Division, 9th Mechanised Corps, advancing from the southern edge of the forest to the west of Klevan, by the end of the day on 1 July had captured the forest near Zhkovshchina and after advancing around 7km even this result was not developed further. On the night of 2 July the 35th Tank Division, in accordance with an order issued by the commander of the 9th Mechanised Corps, had withdrawn to its starting position.

The strongest blow to the flank of the German offensive was inflicted by units of the 22nd Mechanised Corps. By the beginning of the offensive there were 13,040 men in the corps, as well as 149 guns of 45mm calibre (both anti-tank and tank guns), 42 field guns of different calibres, 125 T-26 tanks (of which 19 were flame-throwers), 17 BT-5 and BT-7 tanks, 15 KV-2s and 22 armoured vehicles. In terms of personnel and tanks this approximately equates to one tank division. An attack by the 22nd Mechanised Corps was necessary on the gap between the mobile units of the *III Army Motorised Corps* that had advanced towards Goryni and the *298th Infantry Division* near Lutsk. As they were intended to cover this sector the infantry formations were mobilised on the southern flank of the German advance. The *44th Infantry Division* was involved in the destruction of N.K. Popel's group near Dubno and the infantry division was also sent south. The northern flank of the German tank spearhead was covered by what overall was a relatively fluid curtain. This made it possible for what was at that time a small formation to achieve success.

The 1 June became the baptism of fire for the 41st Tank Division under P.P. Pavlov. Up until this point the division had scrambled dejectedly through the forest and the marshes in the area around Kovel and had steadily been separated by the commanders of the rifle units. On the first day of July the division became the leader of the counterattack by the 22nd Mechanised Corps. The objective of this formation was to advance in the direction of Dolghosheya and Dubno. The exhausted German alignment on the northern flank of the advance did not become an obstacle in the path of the advance and the 41st Tank Division covered 20 kilometres. By 2200 hrs on 1 July Soviet tank crews had reached the boundary formed of Gorodnitsa and Moshkov (15km to the north of Dubno). However this success cost the division 200 men killed or wounded. By the evening two events had occurred, which nullified all the day's achievements. Firstly the 41st Tank Division received an order via the commander of the 22nd Mechanised Corps to withdraw. This order corresponded to order No. 8, issued by the commander of the 5th Army, for the army's troops to withdraw to the line formed of Novograd-Volynsk fortified sector. Specifically this stated: "The

22nd Mechanised Corps is to withdraw to an area around Podluzhnoe, Berestovets and Kostopol between 1 and 2 July 1941." Secondly the Germans reacted to the crisis situation with air raids. Bombers destroyed the bridges to the north of Olyko and over the course of a few hours were given an opportunity to rout the division on open ground to the south of the Lutsk–Rivne highway even after P.P. Pavlov's formation were formally in receipt of the option of withdrawing back and in doing so escape this attack.

The third division in the 22nd Mechanised Corps, 215th Motorised Division, which was proceeding in the second echelon behind the 41st Tank Division advanced to a boundary formed by the River Putilovka (to the north of Dolosheya) at 1100 hrs on 2 July, where they dug in, protecting both the left flank and the rear of the 22nd Mechanised Corps. The formation repeated all the adventures of the 41st Tank Division—the destruction of the bridges and the withdrawal under attack from German aviation—and incurred significant losses.

A veteran of the battle near Voynitsa, from the 19th Tank Division, who had advanced in the direction of Pokoshuv and Mlynuv, had by the morning of 2 July reached the boundary formed of Kalinov, Malsyanka and Karolina and had engaged enemy infantry in combat. By 1100 hrs on 2 July the 19th Tank Division, whilst pushing the enemy back, had advanced to a boundary formed of Mlynuv and Ozlinov where, on encountering more intensive enemy resistance, was engaged in combat until the second half of the day on 2 July. On 2 July however, in place of the *44th Infantry Division* that had departed towards Dubno, the *'Leibstandarte Adolf Hitler' Motorised Brigade* was advancing towards the *III Motorised Army Corps* to their rescue. At 1400 hrs on 2 July the 19th Tank Division were suddenly subject to a heavy blow from the *'Leibstandarte'* units on their right flank and on their rearmost forces from the direction of Ostrozhets and were forced to withdraw, incurring heavy losses, to their starting positions. The success of the counterattack by the 22nd Mechanised Corps had a limited impact. The gap between the tank and infantry divisions was rapidly closed by an *SS panzer* group advancing along the northern route of the offensive. However up until the approach of the *'Leibstandarte'* Soviet tanks had been able to generously pick feathers off of German units that were stretched over a wide front. A tank commander who was subsequently to become famous; Kurt 'Panzer' Maier, who served at the time in the *'Leibstandarte'*" recalled that Olyko was where he first saw abandoned German combat materiel.

The 1 July became the last day on which the mechanised corps would inflict counterattacks. The troops on the front line had begun to withdraw to the east, to the walls of the 'old fortress,' to the fortifications on the borders that were in place in 1939. On that day a directive was delivered from Moscow, which was an admission of a kind of the merits of the mechanised corps in the Border battle. Directive No. 00124, issued by Supreme High Command, ordered the 19th Army, under I.S. Konev, which had arrived from the Northern Caucasus and the Kharkov Military District, to withdraw from the territory of the Ukraine. It stated: "The forces of the 19th Army are to prepare, and move by rail to a new territory. The Army should be ready to board by 1800 hrs on 1 July 1941." Up until this point the 19th Army, in accordance with directive No. 0060, issued by Supreme Command Headquarters took up a defensive position in the area around Kiev. The withdrawal of I.S. Konev's army meant that command considered the position on the South-Western Front sufficiently stable. This front was still holding better than other directions were, barring large-scale catastrophes.

A Soviet amphibious T-40 tank that has been abandoned somewhere close to Dubno. Note the rupture in the armour close to the driver and mechanic's observation device.

Two *Pz.IV* tanks of the *11th Panzer Division* that have been knocked out in the Ukraine. These tanks were knocked out by shots fired at their flanks.

A column of German *Pz.III* tanks fitted with 50mm guns in the area around Dubno.

A burning BT tank in the area around Dubno. Night battle lamps have been attached above the gun barrel. In accordance with Soviet tactical thinking it was envisaged that they be used to illuminate targets at night.

A KV-2 tank that has been knocked out, as the inscription suggests, by the anti-aircraft guns of the *'Herman Goering' Regiment* just outside Dubno in 1941.

This same KV-2 from the other side. Evidently the tank was knocked out by shots fired at its flank.

A T-26 tank that has been knocked out in the area around Dubno. In the foreground is a crater made when the tank's ammunition exploded, which literally blew this heavy tank to pieces.

A T-26 tank that was destroyed by an internal explosion in the area around Dubno.

A KV-2 tank that was disabled in the area around Pelchi. Marks from the explosion can clearly be seen on the shoulder of the turret.

Another photograph of this same machine in the area around Pelchi. German soldiers are scrutinising this Russian giant.

A T-35 tank that has been knocked out just outside Werba. The pitted side screen is testimony to it having been hit with a shell.

A T-35 tank close to Werba, the Germans have already pushed this tank fully into a ditch. The skirt, which has been pitted by a shell can be clearly seen, along with traces of a shells hitting the tank's central turret. This is a 1938 manufactured machine with reinforced armour on the smaller turrets.

A T-35 tank that has been destroyed by an internal explosion in the area around Werba. The T-35 tank from the previous photograph is visible in the background.

Another destroyed T-35 tank near Werba. As a result of the explosion a small turret is all that is left. This tank is located closer to Werba than the T-35 tank in the previous two photographs.

The T-35 tank in the previous photograph, which had already been blown up by the Germans. This photograph clearly shows how all the tanks form a single group: the two T-35s can be seen in the background from the previous photographs

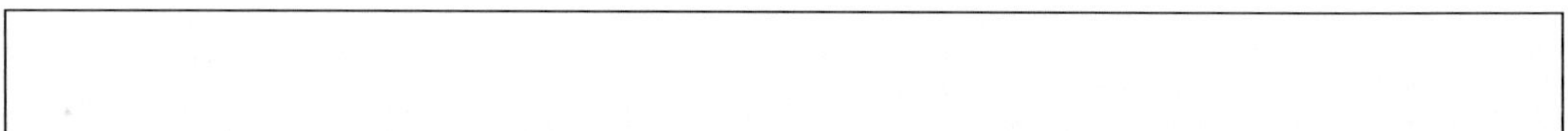

A recovered fragment of a photograph.

A further T-35 tank disabled in combat close to Werba. The front plate has been ripped off of the small turret along with the machine gun nest. In other photographs of this same tank, direct hits are visible on the turret, and armour with 76.2mm shells. This tank was manufactured in 1937 and has cylindrical turrets. It is standing on the road on the far side of Werba compared to the tanks in the previous photographs.

A German aerostat in the area around Dubno. Air superiority allowed aerostats to be used to correct artillery fire.

A T-26 tank that was knocked out in the area around Dubno. The strips on the turret suggest that this tank belonged to the 34th Tank Division: T-35s of this same division had similar tactical markings on them.

A T-35 tank abandoned by its crew in the area around the villages of Ozhidov-Olesko (just outside Lvov), due to a failure of the gearbox and brakes on 30 June 1941. The signs that have been painted on in white were applied by the Germans to avoid car accidents in the twilight hours and in darkness.

An early series BT-7 tank that has been abandoned on the road just outside Lvov. The tank is standing on wheels but it is not likely that it operated on a wheeled chassis. More than likely the tracks were removed to repair other tanks.

A T-34 tank abandoned at the disabled vehicle collection post. This vehicle is fitted with a 76.2mm F-34 gun and a cast steel turret which was manufactured shortly before the outbreak of war. It is more than likely that this machine belonged to the 32nd Tank Division (NARA).

Another photograph of this same T-34. Evidently another abandoned T-34 is standing behind this tank. Judging by the landscape in the background these vehicles have been abandoned in the town of Lvov (NARA).

German soldiers examine a Soviet T-35 tank that has been abandoned in the village of Banyunyn on the way to Brody. This is an early series vehicle with cylindrical turrets and a hand-rail antenna.

A KV-2 abandoned in Dubno, bearing the 'autograph' of the *'Herman Goering' Regiment*, that has already been cleared away from the road by the Germans so as not to impede movement of traffic.

7
Conclusion

Popular wisdom states that everything is relative. Therefore in the history of the *16th Panzer Division* the emotional assessment of the Border battle was made against a comparison of the campaign in the West. From this perspective the results of the first week of the battle were as follows:

> The Russians nevertheless managed to hold back the advance by German forces. Not only did they inflict losses on the advancing forces, and commanded their respect, but they won themselves time. We did not succeed in confusing them by using tank groups to effect a series of wedge shaped breakthroughs. The Russians also incurred heavy losses, but they managed to lead their close formations over the Sluch, Verkhniy Bug and the Dniester. The first 10 days of the campaign passed. After 10 days in France the German tanks, driving the cowardly French and English before them, had covered 800km and stood on the edge of the Atlantic. After 10 days of the 'march to the east' just 100km had been covered, and the German *panzer* attack groups were fighting an enemy that was superior in terms of its firepower, and in terms of the technology with which it was equipped, and one which would often resort to effective tactical approaches that were unproven. This time around the timescale set for a successful advance by command was not met. After the first 10 days of the war the effective breakthrough to the east had still not been completed.[1]

In the headquarters of *Panzergruppe 1* this controversial view was illustrated shortly after the completion of the Border battle by the following statistics, which combined the losses from the three battles together:

> The war in the West from 10 May–25 June 1940—some 7,268 men, or 5.6 percent;
> The Balkan campaign from 8–16 April 1941—some 1,253 men, or 1.2 percent;
> The war in the East from 22 June–10 July 1941—7,546 men, or 4.7 percent.

Moreover it is worth taking into consideration that a *panzergruppe* participated in the war in the west, which consisted of 130,000 men, and in June 1941 fought in the Ukraine with 160,000 men at arms. Nevertheless it is evident to the naked eye that the pace of losses in the war with the USSR was noticeably higher than that of the war in the West. The Red Army, which had not been fully deployed (that is to say the density of the alignment was low) fought in the same way as a fully deployed French army did between May–June 1940.

Anyone who has not limited themselves to merely studying the initial period of the history of the war would be struck by the abundance of infantry divisions on the site of the tank battles in the triangle formed of Brody—Lutsk—Dubno. This was never subsequently repeated. In the advance outside Kursk in the summer of 1943 German tank divisions were forced to plot the route in front

1 Werthen, p.49.

of them independently and from the first few days, or even hours of the battle, they were 'gnawing though' the Soviet defence. In this same location outside Kursk there was no amiable breaking in the defence as had happened in the case of the 'Molotov Line' in Ukraine in the first half of the day on 22 June 1941. Between 1944–1945 the operational support for tank formations by infantry was very poor and unregulated. Moreover, as the number of infantry formations decreased that had fought in the battle, between 1943–1945 the quality of the infantry deteriorated considerably.

Against the backdrop of the small, in terms of strength of numbers, rifle divisions in the covering armies this dense mass of infantry divisions paints a unique picture of the war as a whole. A situation in which Soviet tank formations would feverishly rush around between the islands of rifle divisions, attempting to hold back the crowd (no other word would do) of infantry divisions, or between the long spears of tank divisions stretching away into the distance, was never repeated between 1942–1945.

German infantry divisions to a considerable extent preordained the outcome of the Dubno battles. Active combat by the *17. Armee*, which consisted solely of infantry divisions, just outside Lvov forced the use of the 4th Mechanised Corps, which was the strongest to effect counterattacks, in the interests of the 6th Army. Without these counterattacks the defence on the approaches to Lvov would have just collapsed and the Germans' infantry divisions would have attacked the rear of the mechanised corps that were attacking the *Panzergruppe 1*. Also the infantry formations would have taken it upon themselves to liquidate the 'pocket' in which the 87th and 124th Rifle Divisions ended up. On the other hand these 'pockets' would have been liquidated by the motorised corps, as they sacrificed their forward advance. The battles in Hungary in January 1945 were played out in accordance with this same scenario during the course of Operation "Konrad III." After having encircled part of the forces of the 18th Tank, and the 130th Rifle Corps the *SS panzer* divisions were forced independently to blockade them, losing time, and wasting energy. In the Dubno battles it was the infantry that took on this mission.

The option of plugging the holes using infantry enabled the Germans to glaze over their blunders. For example the routing of part of the forces of the 8th Mechanised Corps just outside Brody, between 28–29 June, after the breakthrough by Popel's group just outside Dubno, was achieved by advancing infantry divisions. The capture of the supply routes for the forward subdivisions of the *XXXXVIII Motorised Corps* in an attack on Dubno was again forestalled by an infantry formation—the *111th Infantry Division*. The latter took a battering from Popel's group's tanks. The infantry covered the area on the flanks of the *Panzergruppe 1* (especially the area to the south) quite efficiently, which enabled them to move forward continuously, bringing the situation under their control.

On the contrary, Soviet command was practically stripped of the possibility of countering these crises using the forces of their rifle divisions since they were fragmented into several echelons owing to forestalling in their deployment. Soviet rifle divisions did not have the option of ending up at the right place at the right time. Correspondingly in place of these they had to introduce the tank and motorised divisions in the mechanised corps. The decidedly 'infantry like' objective of holding the *17. Armee* at the approaches to Lvov was given to the 4th Mechanised Corps. The 15th Mechanised Corps over the course of several days fulfilled this same 'infantry like' objective, when they defended the 6th Army on a crinkled flank just outside Radzekhov. Front line command was not able to replace them with rifle divisions. In the end in all these events it was not that Soviet tanks were frittered away on enemy tanks, but that they were forced to make up for the lack of rifle divisions in the covering armies.

Naturally such a multifaceted phenomenon as a week-long battle of a large number of tanks is not just limited to a clash of tanks and infantry. The enemy divisions that were armed with tanks unavoidably clashed on the battlefield. Complex factors determined the winner in these battles, but first and foremost it was the organisational structure of the tank forces on both sides. Here the

Wehrmacht's infantry and artillery, though this time they were motorised, were a match for the tanks of the Red Army. This enabled the pulverisation of enormous numbers of light tanks and the attacks by T-34s and KVs to be countered.

Thus we come to the main reason behind the failure of the mechanised corps of the Red Army in the Dubno battles—the lack of refinement in their organisational structures. By the outbreak of the war Soviet command did not have any experience of the practical use of independent tank formations, that is to say of tank operations away from rifle corps and divisions. The mechanised corps in the course of the Border battle in the Ukraine had to fight in accordance with this same scenario: a breakdown far from their home base, a march on the flank of the German *panzer* spearhead and an advance in isolation from other units. Action of this nature requires a certain amount of autonomy and the knowledge of how to solve all kinds of problems without outside assistance. In itself the tank is a steel box with a very poor, restricted, view of the outside world. If tanks broke through to enemy positions on their own they would be fired upon by heavy artillery and Molotov cocktails would be thrown at them. Therefore protecting tanks with thick armour provides little security if they are to move successfully since their movements need to be protected by their own infantry. The infantry that are protecting the tanks are able to do so not just by firing the tank's machine guns but by winning the duel with artillery. Otherwise the howitzers, against which tanks are invulnerable in masked positions, would mow down the infantry, or force them to lie low, leaving the tanks exposed. If furthermore our tanks do not have thick armour then the burden of the battle with the enemy's anti-tank guns lies on the shoulders of the artillery. In the latter case aside from the howitzers, anti-tank guns would also be used, driving back the 'colleagues' on the other side of the front line in the course of a tank attack. The mechanised corps of the Red Army were formed on the basis of some pre-war theoretical conclusions and clearly they were not sufficiently equipped with artillery. A German *panzer* division without any reinforcements had twenty-four *105mm ieFH18* light field howitzers and twelve *150mm sFH18* heavy field howitzers (four of which were often replaced with 105mm *K18* guns). An artillery regiment in a Soviet tank division would as standard be equipped with twelve 152mm M-10 howitzers and twelve 122mm M-30 howitzers, which conceded to the enemy both qualitatively (in terms of the M-10, which was not as powerful as the *sFH18*, and *K18*), and quantitatively. The situation was exacerbated by what were typical problems for 1941 linked to transport, when the artillery regiment in a tank division that was part of a mechanised corps would be partially immobilised (as per the 32nd and 37th tank Divisions, or the tractors would break down on the march (as per the 34th Tank Division). In this case masses of tanks would be left without artillery support and would be beaten back en masse by German artillery. Anti-tank armament, that is to say guns for firing at close range, were absent as a class of weapon in the tank divisions of the Red Army, and there were only 48 of them in the *Wehrmacht's* divisions, which enhanced the efficiency of the formations in both defensive and offensive battles. The lack of mobility in the Red Army formations added fuel to the fire, when part of the artillery fleet was unable to escort the division in its manoeuvres owing to the lack of tractors. A typical example of this was an incident with the 15th Mechanised Corps, when an attack by a very large number of tanks was literally only supported by individual guns. If truth be told the weakness of the artillery fleet was the scourge of our tank formations up until the summer of 1943 inclusive. Another problem was that the mechanised formations in the Red Army did not wait until the summer of 1943 but made itself known very evidently in the summer of 1941—the fact that the mechanised corps were not sufficiently equipped in terms of infantry. For a standard strength of 375 tanks a Soviet tank division had approximately 3,000 men in its mechanised infantry, while a *panzer* division in the *Wehrmacht* had 6,000 men in its mechanised infantry. If a recount is done strictly on the battalions then for every six tanks (not counting the two battalions of chemical tanks) our tank divisions had just three battalions of mechanised infantry. This works out to a ratio between tanks and infantry of 2:1 in favour of tank battalions. In a German tank division for every two or three tank battalions there were four or five (if the motorcycle battalions are included as well) battalions of mechanised infantry, that is to say 1:2.5 or 1:1.7 in favour of infantrymen. Such a large number of men armed with machine guns and rifles enabled the Germans to effectively use the results of a tank attack even just to mollify the defence ahead of a tank attack by making use of an infantry strike. The different results of the battle between the German *14th Panzer Division* and the 87th Rifle Divisions on the one hand and the tank divisions of the 8th and 15th Mechanised Corps against the German infantry divisions on the other are of no surprise. To a large extent the fact that given such a mass of tanks the mechanised corps of the South-Western Front lost the Dubno battles should come as no surprise to us, but that given such poor manoeuvrability in terms of artillery and such an insignificant numerical strength in terms of mechanised infantry that they were able to do anything at all. They did however achieve a great deal: the German advance was, albeit temporary, forced away from both '*Panzerstrasse*' and the pace of the advance was significantly reduced. The efficient counterattacks of the mechanised corps even saved the majority of the 6th Army from being routed and encircled and delayed the entry of the *XIV Motorised Corps* into the battle along the southern '*Panzerstrasse*'. The order that was issued for counterattacks, and for the encirclement and destruction of the main German attack force, using the forces and weaponry that the headquarters of the South-Western Front had at their disposal would appear impossible even if the environment were ideal for the fulfilment of all the directives. Even given a favourable confluence of circumstances the mechanised corps would be able to intercept the communications of the *III* and *XXXXVIII Motorised Corps*, but it is unlikely that they would be able to hold them back under the weight of the infantry divisions of the 6th Army.

In addition it would have made no sense to deny the fact that the command of the South-Western Front did make mistakes. Leaving the 4th Mechanised Corps subordinate to the commander of the 6th, Muzychenko, restricted its use in the battles just outside Brody and Dubno. A vigorous attack on the 23 June on Radzekhov could, if not have led to the routing of the *11th Panzer Division* then at least it could have made the conditions for the advance of the *XXXXVIII Motorised Corps* more difficult. Furthermore the 6th Army's fluid front line could have been supported by the 8th Mechanised Corps that was moving across to fall in line with it, away from the 26th Army. The transfer of the latter to Muzychenko was also superfluous and led to an unnecessary detour in marches carried out by Ryabishev's corps. The ambivalence with the 'stop-order' dated 26–27 June cannot be credited to either Kirponos or Purkayev.

The slow shakedown of the front line air forces raises a great many questions. After obtaining a sufficiently clear picture of the situation between 1600–1700 hrs on 22 June front line command issued succinct orders that were truly worthy of praise out to the mechanised corps. In addition however front line aviation was actually idle in the remaining hours of the evening of 22 June. E.S. Ptukhin only issued orders to the pilots late in the evening of 22 June (probably under orders from G.K. Zhukov). Correspondingly on 23 June the Air Forces of the South-Western Front were still not functioning fully. Vigorous air attacks were capable of significantly slowing the pace of the advance of the *11th Panzer Division* and of enabling the 'remote' formations to advance to the objective of the Ikva and the Styr before the enemy was able to break through to this boundary. That is to say up until the moment the *11th Panzer Division* reached Mlynuv and Dubno they would have been held stubbornly by the 228th Rifle Division.

There is a significant fault however running through all these analyses: the fact that it was not only the Soviet commanders and leaders who made mistakes, but the enemy made them too. The mistakes that *Army Group South* permitted were also ample in number. One could start with the delays in the tank divisions of the *III* and *XXXXVIII Motorised Corps* reaching their starting points on 22 June. They were only introduced into combat in the second half of the day on 22 June and were not able to advance to any depth on the first day of the war. Allowing Popel's group to get through to attack Dubno, as a result of which the central '*Panzerstrasse*' was recaptured for several days, would equally appear absolutely unforgivable. It was only liberated after a great deal of work as a result of the aforementioned abundance of infantry divisions.

Mistakes made by one side were to some extent balanced out by the mistakes of the opposing side. What result a variant of any battle in which there were 'no mistakes' (on either side) would have been one can only guess. In any case if similar variants concerning the way the German *panzer* divisions were countered are examined, then it is highly ambiguous to suggest what could be done with the mass of German infantry. Infantry divisions, just like a herd of buffalo, would have trampled on any endeavours on the part of the mechanised corps.

When we began to count the cost one of the principal indicators of any battle are the losses that are inflicted. Given all the ambiguity and the difficulties of interpreting this indicator the data provided by both sides on their losses naturally requires examination. Even in the initially untenable situation in which the Kiev Special Military District found itself in, its units and formations still attacked the enemy and moreover in a series of cases these attacks dealt a painful blow.

In accordance with the documents, on 5th July 1941 the condition of the tank fleet in the *Panzergruppe 1* was characterised by the following statistics (see the table below).

Therefore following the Border battle approximately 60 percent of the combat vehicles remained in the *Panzergruppe 1*. Furthermore the fact that several of the tanks that had been damaged in the period from 22 June up until the beginning of July 1941 had already been successfully repaired also needs to be taken into consideration. Unrecoverable losses were comparatively low, around 10 percent of total strength. However the movement of the front line to the east worked in the German's favour. Those tanks, which were listed as being in the workshops, were out of danger. They were not under threat of capture by advancing Soviet forces as often happened between 1943–1945 and even in 1942. A natural curiosity gives rise to the question: "Who was it that suffered the most?" Unfortunately the very earliest data concerning the losses among the tanks and divisions is in the combat reports written by the *Panzergruppe 1* and dates only from 11 July 1941. That is to say the distribution of losses in the Border battle is somewhat overshadowed by the losses incurred during the breakthrough across the 'Stalin Line'. Nevertheless this data is undoubtedly of interest (see the second table below).

The table clearly illustrates that the *16th Panzer Division* had become the absolute leader in terms of the number of tanks lost among the formations in Kleist's *panzer* groups. The explanation for this is obvious: Hube's division fought against units in the 8th Mechanised Corps, which had a greater number of the newer types of tanks. Also the *16th Panzer Division* was forced to advance on Popel's group and come under fire from tank guns of all calibres. Furthermore Hube was lucky again that his tanks that became Soviet trophies were abandoned and not blown up or set ablaze. It is interesting how indicative the situation in the *11th Panzer Division* was. This division did not lose that many tanks, but then the division did lose 129 motorcycles, 5 tractors and as many as 187 automobiles. Not one German division lost that much of its mechanised transport. The answer to the question 'Why?' is obvious. The combat vehicles and motorcycles in Crüwell's division became, first and foremost, victims of Soviet aviation.

The tank divisions in Mackensen's corps were in the most favourable position. They practically never encountered the newest tanks and those tanks that were knocked out in combat with the 1st Anti-Tank Brigade and the 19th Tank Division were repaired. Aviation on the South-Western Front did not bother them with their presence either. They therefore became outsiders in respect of their losses of materiel.

Overall the data that has been provided correlates with known facts on the course of the war. What is not entirely clear is how the discrepancy came about in the number of 'units' that were listed as having been unrecoverable losses in comparison with the previous table. If a rise in the losses among other types of tanks was noted in comparison with those of the previous date, then the number of *Pz.I*s, in contrast, falls from 11 to nine. In both cases the source of the information is the same: a report written by the *Oberkaurtermeister* of the *Panzergruppe 1*. It is possible that there was a reclassification of the losses, since the units were quick to get rid of the *panzers* that demonstrated questionable combat capability, while the technical subdivisions on the other hand nevertheless considered it necessary to repair them. In the end the miracle of military industry in the *Vaterland* was returned to the *panzer* crews, who greeted them with a vinegary smile.

Losses of personnel had a deep significance for German aviation in 1941. Last but not least the attack capabilities of the *Wehrmacht* were reduced down to almost nothing in the autumn of 1941 owing to reductions in the strength of numbers in the combat formations. Moreover losses among highly trained combatants with combat experience can only be recovered at great cost on both a qualitative and quantitative sense. The start of this process was laid down during the Border battle. Losses in terms of personnel in the mobile formations of the *Panzergruppe 1* are characterised by the following statistics (see the third table below).

Based on these statistics the leader of the German advance in Ukraine, namely the *11th Panzer Division* is also the leader in terms of losses. If the losses in the armoured vehicles in Crüwell's division could be assessed as moderate, then the losses in terms of personnel in this formation rarely rise above the average. The contributions of both by the Red Army units (just outside Radzekhov, Dubno and Voynitsa) and Soviet aviation are included. Undoubtedly 'Stalin's falcons' could claim the majority of the losses inflicted on the division. Aside from that the losses among the formations that came into the battle just before the end also leave an impression. After fighting for literally just a few days but having been caught up in the final Soviet counterattack, the *25th Motorised Division* lost more than the *13th* and *14th Panzer Divisions* that had been fighting since the first day of the war. In terms of the numbers lost without trace the *25th Motorised Division* comes top of the list. The losses in the *9th Panzer Division*, which encountered the remaining elements of the 4th and 15th Mechanised Corps that were retreating via Zolochiv, head to head, also leave an impression.

How did the tanks get through? The statistics in the table under the 'Total', considering the strength of the mechanised corps of the Red Army that took part in the battle are spellbinding. Even more spellbinding is the number of the new types of tanks. Alongside the legends that were prevalent in Soviet times concerning the invulnerability of the T-34 and KV tanks there is a need to search for any unorthodox reasons behind the failure. Indeed the invulnerability of the T-34 and KV tanks was highly relative. The reader would have already noticed above that the losses among the new types of tanks during the course of attacks were very run of the mill. In a report by the Commander of the 10th Tank Division we note the following description of the shortcomings in the tanks that had recently been received from the manufacturers:

> Concerning the T-34 tanks:
> a) The armour on the engine and on the tank body could be penetrated from a distance of 300–400m with a 37mm armour piercing shell. The vertical plates on the sides could be penetrated by a 20mm armour piercing shell. When cresting a ditch the tank digs in due to it being low set. Contact with the ground is insufficient owing to the relative smoothness of the tracks.
> b) The driver's forward hatch caves in after a direct hit from a shell.
> c) The tracks are weak and any shell would be able to break them.

Therefore the T-34, given certain conditions, could be taken out even by a 37mm armour piercing PAK-35/36 shell, or a 20mm or 37mm anti-aircraft machine gun. Furthermore the new types of 50mm PAK-38 shells could be effective against tanks. There were two of these in each regiment in the infantry divisions that became the opponents of our tank crews in the Dubno battles. Given the poor artillery and infantry support the T-34 could have become a victim of the 105mm *leFH18* field howitzer, as an armour piercing shell from one of these guns was able to penetrate 60mm of homogenous armour from a distance of 500m. The KV tanks however were 'a tougher nut to crack' but even they could reliably be hit by 88mm anti-aircraft guns or 105mm *K18* corps guns. The latter were present both in several of the tank divisions as well as in the corps units. In accordance with a recommendation by the inspectorate of mobile forces, dated 29 June 1941, it was possible for 50mm PAK-38s guns to hit '50-tonne' Russian tanks from 400m; and for 50mm tank guns from 200m; and for 47mm Czech guns from 200m; and finally for 88mm anti-aircraft guns from 1,000m. Finally there remained anti-tank mines and Molotov cocktails, which would be thrown in the engine compartment of a T-34 or KV tank as a last resort by infantrymen. Put simply the combat losses of the T-34 and KV tanks in the Border battle should come as no surprise. They happened and have been confirmed by both sides in the conflict.

It is also worth noting that a detailed study of the Dubno battles reveals that the title of 'the greatest tank battle in the history of war' is discoloured somewhat. Despite what were nominally high figures in terms of the strength of the mechanised corps on the South-Western Front, a comparatively small number of combat vehicles were successfully introduced simultaneously into the juxtaposition of enemy tanks. All too often the tank formations ended up split between different echelons and were introduced into combat piecemeal. The 75 tanks from the 12th Tank Division, 8th Mechanised Corps, which reached their starting positions for the counterattack on 26 June, out of the almost 300 that were listed, could be considered the apotheosis of this.

One of the significant live factors in the Dubno battles were the technical shortcomings of the new Soviet tanks. They possessed a whole set of 'teething problems' which made the fulfilment of standard and even day-to-day manoeuvres for a mechanised corps significantly more difficult. If we are to call a spade a spade then the quantity of the standard output from the indigenous military industrial complex for 1941 left much to be desired.

Serious complaints were prevalent in the military relating to both the KV and the T-34. In his report to the Principal Automobile and Mechanised Tank Directorate of the Red Army the Head of the 3rd Department of this same directorate in the South-Western Front Military, Engineer Second Class Ganopolskiy, wrote: "One of the most basic and widespread defects with the T-34 vehicle has to be the warping of the main clutch discs. Out of the 24 vehicles in the 34th Battalion, 64th Regiment, 32nd Division, that had completed their combat operation, it was not possible to change gear on four of them for the above reason."[2]

Attempts to eradicate this defect at grass roots level by reassembling the main clutch discs after cleaning them was very rarely successful. More often than not this required the replacement of components, which given a catastrophic situation with respect to spare parts at the beginning of the war, caused a big problem. It is worth noting that this shortage of T-34 tanks had not been fully solved even by 1945. A post-war report written by the deputy commander of the maintenance unit of the 18th Tank Corps states the following amongst a dossier of proposals for design changes to the T-34: "The main clutch plates need to be refined as instances of their warping have been noted."[3]

2 The Central Archive of the Ministry of Defence, fund 229, inventory 157, file 36, p.141.
3 The Central Archive of the Ministry of Defence, fund 243, inventory 2928, file 369, p.142.

Table 7.1 The condition of the tanks of the *Panzergruppe 1* on 5 July 1941[4]

	Pz.I	*Pz.II*	*Pz.III*	*Pz.IV*	Total
Combat-ready	25	151	200	55	431
In the workshop	13	47	106	34	200
Unrecoverable loss	11	14	49	11	85

The problems with the T-34 were not limited to the main clutch plate. The 'family trait' of the machines that were constructed in Kharkov were the problems with the gearboxes. A gearbox with three forward gears was used on the BT tanks and at the beginning of its production the T-34 was fitted with a so-called 'four-speed gearbox'. Even if we were not to compare this with the *Pz.III*, one of the modifications of which saw it being fitted with a gearbox that had 10 (!!!) forward gears, this number was clearly insufficient. The fewer gears meant that there were large gaps between the gears, and the stick force on the gear lever was high. As a result the pivot joints on the gear shifting gates would wear out quickly. The bending of the linkages, as well as wear in the pivot joints, led to the gear lever and the sliding pinions in the gear box being in the wrong place. Furthermore this could lead to a situation in which two gears would be engaged at once. This inevitably led to the failure of the gearbox and to the main clutch plates catching fire.

The lack of time for the assimilation of new vehicles meant that even small failures could lead to the loss of a tank. The head of the Principal Automotive Battalion Tank Forces, 6th Army, Colonel Dedov wrote: "The crews of the KV and T-34 tanks and 'Voroshilovets' tractors for the most part lack experience and are in no position to eradicate even the smallest of technical failures."[5] These combat vehicles initially ended up on the side of the road in columns of vehicles and wagons along with their dejected looking crew. Subsequently the tank would run the risk of turning into a sculpture, against which the occupying troops would be photographed.

Through this prism of all these technical problems the 75 tanks that were ready for an offensive out of the 300 in the 12th Tank Division, 8th Mechanised Corps is testimony in itself. On 29 June 1941 there were nine KVs in service in the formation in the division, 12 had been lost in battle and 37 were listed as stragglers. In relation to the T-34 this was the picture that emerged: there were seven tanks in the formation, 27 had been disabled and 66 were listed as stragglers. As far as other types of tanks and vehicles were concerned the situation was more or less the same. During the overall withdrawal of forces belonging to the South-Western Front back to the old border the tanks that had been scattered along the roads, or which had been gathered together in the workshops, but which had yet to be repaired were, naturally, considered unrecoverable losses.

There is however no sense in thinking that everything was going perfectly well for the enemy either. On the one hand the Germans did manage to retain the combat capability of their own *panzer* formations, due in no small measure to the fact that they returned *panzers* that had been knocked out to service. It cannot be said however that there were no disadvantages in this situation. Thus a report by the *Oberkaurtermeister* of the *Panzergruppe 1* that had been drawn up on 13 July 1941 indicated:

4 NARA T313 R15 f7241967

5 The Central Archive of the Ministry of Defence, fund 229, inventory 157, file 36, p.153.

The *16th Panzer Division* had still not been restored following the heavy losses in terms of materiel by way of returning tanks to the formation that needed to be repaired. Apart from the fact that for the *panzers* unrecoverable losses were high (60 vehicles), the division does not have the required number of specialists who are capable of repairing damaged tanks rapidly.[6]

Table 7.2 Losses in terms of personnel in tank, and motorised formations in the *Panzergruppe 1* in the period from 22 June to 6 July 1941[7]

	Killed	Injured	Missing without trace	Taken ill	Total
9th Panzer Division	175	232	36	8	451
11th Panzer Division	287	766	179	2	1,234
13th Panzer Division	86	249	26	–	361
14th Panzer Division	89	303	28	5	425
16th Panzer Division	132	407	105	–	644
'Wiking'	48	39	–	–	87
The 25th Motorised Division	82	228	207	67	584
The 16th Motorised Division	6	14	–	11	31

Understandably, if the Germans were to have held back, then they would have been in this same position as the mechanised corps of the South-Western Front had been in the Border battle. Of course, allowing for the fact that the 'teething troubles' that were previously encountered in the production of tanks had been overcome, the mechanical reliability of tanks was at high level for the Germans in 1941. In the case of the front line moving westwards and not eastwards, the materiel that had broken down would have to be abandoned. Specifically the Germans were forced to act in this way between 1943–1945, when they were even forced to abandon the formidable and notorious 'Tigers' on the sides of the roads and in the workshops, because of the need to 'straighten out the front line.'

By way of a comparison I would allow myself to present information concerning the combat activities of one of the participants in the Dubno battles, the *14th Panzer Division*. Two and a half years later, in the autumn of 1943, the division arrived on the Eastern Front, in October 1943, from France where it had regrouped and reformed. The formation acted in a similar way to the method it had employed in 1941, practicing a manoeuvring, defensive warfare to the north of Krivoy Rog. The division joined the battle on 28 October and consisted of 49 *Pz.IV* tanks, 44 *StuGIII* Self-Propelled Artillery Platforms, seven flamethrowing (*Flamm*) tanks and nine commander's vehicles, and conducted combat operations as part of the *1. Panzerarmee*. Losses in the division's tank fleet over the 16 days of the battle are reflected in the table.

We note that in this case this refers to vehicles that have been in production for some considerable time and on which the chassis had been debugged. The deployment of the newest kinds of tanks, and self-propelled artillery platforms, gave rise to a situation that bore an even greater similarity to the story of the initial failures in the mechanised corps.

6 NARA T314 R1138 f166.
7 NARA T313 R15 f7241704.

Table 7.3 The structure of losses in the *14th Panzer Division* in the autumn of 1943

Classification of the loss	*Pz.IV*	*StuGIII* Self-Propelled Artillery Platforms	*Flammpanzer*	Commander tanks
Battle damage (those that caught fire etc)	9		0	0
Tanks that required factory repairs as a result of battle damage	6		0	0
Tanks that were left damaged on enemy territory as a result of battle damage	5	6	2	0
Tanks that were left damaged on enemy territory as a result of technical failures	6	4	0	0
Tanks that failed as a result of lengthy marches, and which were abandoned due to a lack of equipment to tow them behind the lines	7	2	1	0
Total	33	25	3	0

Table 7.4 The condition of tanks in the *14th Panzer Division* 7 December 1943

Combat capable	8[1]	6	2	4
Tanks that required a field repair lasting up to 14 days	8	8	2	4
Tanks that required a field repair lasting more than 14 days	4	5	0	1

Note

1 This includes four new *Pz.IV* tanks that were delivered from the factory in the course of the battle.

Aviation

It is worth noting that air attacks by aircraft of the South-Western Front were concentrated first and foremost on the enemy *panzer* divisions that had surged ahead. The many infantry divisions could easily be overwhelmed by hundreds of those same FAB-100s although this would have had less of an effect. Despite the poorly organised structure of the Red Army Air Force of that period, air force command, as well as the commanders of the aviation divisions, could concentrate the considerable forces of bomber aviation on the narrow strips of the '*Panzerstrasse*'. The effect of these air strikes was obvious and was acknowledged by the enemy. Moreover this was not just an instant effect, but a long lasting one. In July 1941 the *Oberkaurtermeister* of the *Panzergruppe 1* reported: "Due to the high losses in terms of trucks, especially in the *11th Panzer Division* (these amounted to 200 machines), which on top of everything else makes the situation with respect to supply much more difficult, the division is in no position to deploy additional materiel from the Governate-general."[8]

In turn the efficiency of the action by German aviation needs no exaggeration. As far as the landmarks that were to be used for air strikes the German command announced, for example, the following (in a report written by the *16th Panzer Division* dated 27 June):

8 NARA T314 R1138 f166.

> "Combatting enemy tanks using the forces of the *Luftwaffe* is absolutely necessary. Since tanks are mobile it is impossible to define the boundaries for the bombing. All the time the division is on the road there is no danger of them ending up under their own bombs. You will be informed immediately in the event of any departure from the road."[9]

The air controllers in the forward units were used to the '*Stukas*' (the *Ju-87* dive-bombers), which were simply absent from the line-up of the *V Fliegerkorps* in June of 1941. Correspondingly the level of cooperation with land forces in the Air Forces of the South-Western Front and the *V Fliegerkorps* was not very strong. The difference was more marked in the relationship between land forces and aviation and the considerable attention paid to designating our own forces as well as the forward edge.

Losses for the Air Forces of the South-Western Front were sufficiently high, but they could not be called catastrophic.

At the headquarters of the Air Forces of the South-Western Front a table was prepared of the losses incurred between 22–30 June, although it had more of a propaganda than a practical purpose. In accordance with this between 22–25 June the air forces of the front line incurred 228 unrecoverable losses and a further 222 were damaged. Over the next five days from 26–30 June losses stood at 70 aircraft (66 of which had been destroyed and four had been damaged). Correspondingly this painted a rosy picture of life which had played out following Astakhov's replacement with Ptukhin. These figures however do not match with either the enemy's data or the reports from the aviation formations themselves.

In accordance with the combat journal of the Air Forces of the South-Western Front unrecoverable losses between 22–24 June stood at 448 aircraft, while between 25–27 June a further 173 aircraft were lost. As of 30 June there were 871 aircraft remaining in the front line aviation divisions (see the appendices). This figure does not include the 63rd Aviation Division and the 36th Aviation Division of the Kiev Air Defence System, which had been attached to the Southern Front. This allows the following calculations to be made. Excluding the 2,003 aircraft that were in service as of 22 June with the 63rd and 36th Aviation Divisions gives us a figure of 1,789 aircraft. If the 871 aircraft that remained in the line-up of the front line air forces as of 30 June are subtracted, then we are left with 918 combat aircraft that were lost between 22–30 June. Claims by *JG3* pilots of Soviet aircraft destroyed in air combat amount to 258 examples. The figures for the *Luftwaffe* claims for aircraft shot down in air combat in this period match up well and can be taken as a basis on which to assess losses in the air. By deducting the losses that are known to have taken place from the combat journal of the Front Line Air Forces from 22–27 June, this gives a figure of 297 aircraft lost in the period from 28–30 June. The number of aircraft shot down in air combat over these few days, according to claims made by *JG3* pilots, was 76 aircraft. Correspondingly there is every chance that 222 aircraft damaged between 22–25 June, and which were left on airfields owing to the difficult conditions of the overall withdrawal of forces from the front, have been included in this figure of 297. A very clear picture of the air war emerges: the heavy losses on the airfields in the first few days were followed by heavy losses in the air, and the final blow was the withdrawal, which forced damaged materiel to be abandoned en masse.

German aviation was definitely in a more advantageous position. Its airfields were practically free from bombing and there was no need to withdraw and abandon aircraft that had been forced to make emergency landings or that had been damaged. It cannot be said however that the air battle over the triangle formed of Brody—Lutsk—Dubno came at a low cost to the *Luftwaffe*. According to an assessment by the well-known indigenous aviation historian D.B. Khazanov, up until June 1941, in the air above the Ukraine, *Luftflotte 4* lost between 150–160 aircraft of all types

9 NARA T314 R1138 f1179.

(84 aircraft from the *V Fliegerkorps* were lost over the front line, or were considered 100 percent total losses in accordance with the German classification, including a single *He-111*, which was shot down in error by its own fighters).

Communication

This is named as one of the main reasons behind the failure of the Red Army in the initial period of the war. "Thus, for example, the 36th Rifle and the 8th and 9th Mechanised Corps did not have radio communications as they advanced in the area around Dubno."[10] Even if the mobile network 'Kievstar' were transferred from the 21st Century to the area around Dubno in June 1941 it is unlikely this would have helped the commanders of the 8th and 19th Mechanised Corps. By the time the 8th Mechanised Corps had received the order to advance towards Dubno N.V. Feklenko's corps had already been pushed back to the approaches to Rivne. If recent information is anything to go by Tsibin had not yet broken through towards Dubno, and even if Kievstar had been available he would not have had the technology to say to Ryabishev on his 'mobile': "Get over here, I am on the edge of Dubno, let's beat these blasted fascists!" The formations of the South-Western Front received all the required orders, and communication problems cannot in any way provide an explanation of the Red Army's failure. Communication problems were just one of the reasons but not the most significant one. The roll out of a radio communication system for troops was merely tactical. The front line was managed by traditional cable communications:

1. Cable communications can be repaired after destruction by any means and for front line communications they are the most resilient method of ensuring management.
2. Radio equipment can only ensure limited management in the absence of cable communications (due to a lack of capacity)[11]

Communications performed poorly in the first few days of the war due to the corresponding formations not having been mobilised. By the end of June the communications units had been given the necessary manning and were able to support the operability of the front line communications network with comparative efficiency.

In order to significantly affect the course of combat operations the level of management should first and foremost be characterised in a qualitative sense. For example an upbeat entry in the combat journal of the *XXXXVIII Motorised Corps* states: "Since no messages have been received this evening from the division [the *11th Panzer Division*], corps headquarters is not aware of its position."[12]13 There are a great number of entries such as these, which testify to serious delays in the receipt of information from one formation or another in the corps' combat journal.

In summing up all of the above, it is possible to reach the following conclusion: The mechanised corps under the Kiev Special Military District (South-Western Front), owing to the fact that the Red Army had not been deployed, or mobilised fully, found themselves in a very difficult position. They were forced to waste a great deal of energy on fighting the enemy's infantry formations. Nevertheless it was thanks to these same tanks and aviation that the South-Western Front managed to avoid a catastrophic escalation of events in the form of an encirclement of the Lvov Salient and was able to withdraw in a relatively controlled manner to the objective of the old border.

10 Anfilov, *The Beginning of the Great Patriotic War (22 June–To the Middle of June 1941) A Military History Essay* (Moscow: Voenizdat, 1962), p.170.
11 *Collection of Combat Documents from the Great Patriotic War*, Issue No. 36, p.108.
12 NARA T314 R1138 f515.

Soviet trucks and buses abandoned at a river crossing (this is a still from a newsreel).

A KV-2 tank that has been blown up in Mikolayuv. The tank suffered a technical failure. As the Germans approached Mikolayuv the tank crews engaged them in combat and were killed.

A hotchpotch of military technology abandoned by a river crossing including BA-10 armoured cars. Alongside them, approximately in the centre of the photograph, is a breakdown truck (the one with the box suspended above the cab; a workshop on wheels).

Abandoned BA-10 armoured cars in close up. There are at least five armoured cars of this type in this photograph. The machine guns have been removed from the ball mounting next to the driver's position.

A T-35 tank that has been abandoned on the road between Sasov–Koltov during the course of the overall retreat. Behind the T-35 is a burnt out BT-7.

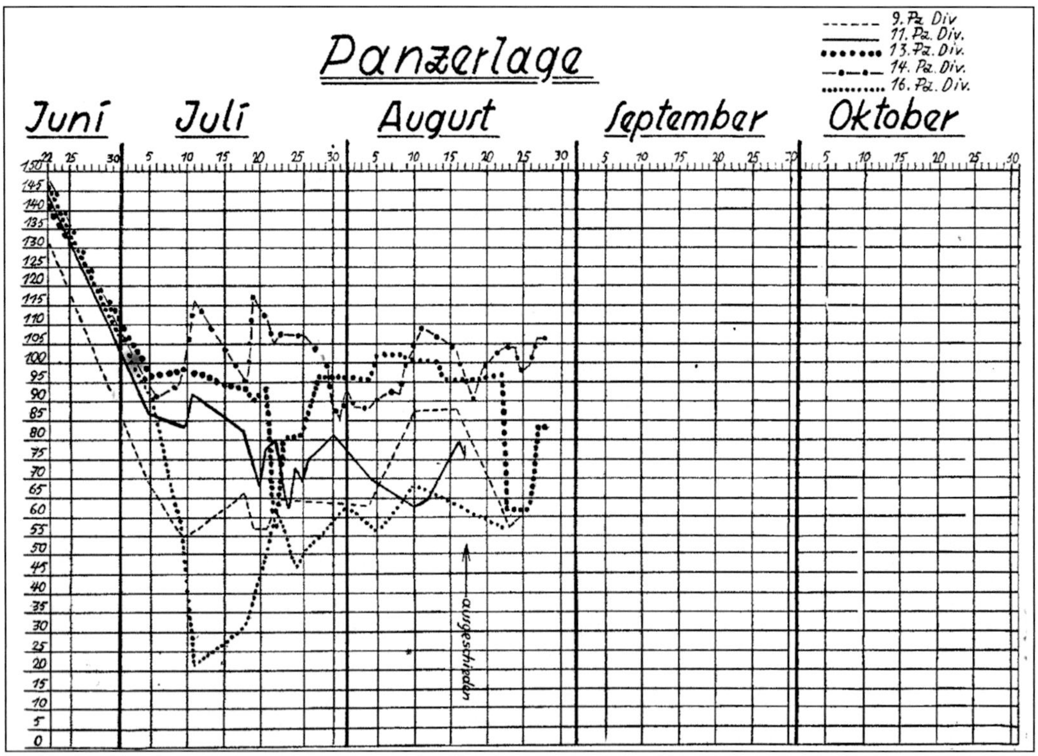

The diagrams showing the number of combat capable tanks in the formations of the *Panzergruppe 1* in the summer of 1941. Clearly the border battle caused a sharp drop. These losses were not made good.

A KV-2 tank that had failed and was abandoned in Lvov, as it had not been possible to evacuate this tank. This vehicle is from the 8th Tank Division's fleet, 4th Mechanised Corps. To the right of the KV-2 stands a flamethrower variant of the T-26 tank.

A T-34 tank abandoned at the disabled vehicles collection point as it had not been possible to evacuate this vehicle.

Soviet tanks that have either failed, or have been damaged in combat stood for some considerable time where either an enemy shell or a technical failure had left them. This T-35 tank was abandoned on 2 July 1941 close to Zagrobeli (a suburb of Ternopil) due to the failure of its differential drive. Photographed either in the winter of 1941–1942 or of 1942–1943.

Appendix I

The Combat Order Written by the Air Forces of the South-Western Front No. OP/1 23 June 01.00[1]

1. The enemy, by driving the M [Mechanised] formations in the direction of Ustyluh, Volodymyr-Volynskyi and Krystynopol–Radzikhov[2]2 on the 5th Army's front line has created the threat of a breakthrough of our defensive units.
2. On the 6th and 26th A[Army's] front line the enemy's attacks have been beaten back and the forces are holding the objective of the S[State] border.
   On 22 June our airfields were subject to bombing by enemy air forces operating in small groups at low level.
2. 22 June Front line mobile units from the 5th and 6th A [Armies] will inflict a concentrated blow with the aim of destroying the enemy alignment in the area around Sokal and Grubeshuv.
3. The Air Forces of the front line on 23 June are in operation against the enemy's motor [mechanised] units, in support of the advance by front line forces in the area around Sokal and Grubeshuv.
4. The Air Forces of the 5th A[Army]/14, and the 62nd A[Air] D[Division] and the 18th A [Air] D [Division], in cooperation with the 22nd M [Mechanised] C[Corps] (by 1100 hrs on 23 June the 22nd M[Mechanised] C[Corps] was being concentrated in the area around the stations at Voynitsa, and Turiysk), are destroying the motorised and mechanised units in the area around Ustyluh and Grubeshuv.[3]
   a) The 18th A [Air] D [Division] from the dawn of 23 June using successive attacks in echelon formation is to attack the concentration of enemy tanks in the area around Ustyluh, Grabeshuv[4] and Korytnitsa.
      Labour—one sortie as a division.
      On completion of the above mission, be at No. 2 state of readiness in order to fulfil the next mission.
      From the morning of 23 June onwards the 90th Long-Range Bomber Aviation Regiment operating from Bronniki airfield is to redeploy to airfields in accordance with the operational plan:

1 The Central Archive of the Ministry of Defence, fund. 229, inventory. 161. file. 5, pp. 3–5. Original version, submitted for publication in The Journal of Military History, No.7, (1989), pp. 28–29.
2 This is how it is rendered in the document—the correct rendering is Radzekhov.
3 This is how it is rendered in the document.
4 This is how it is rendered in the document.

b) The 62nd A[Air] D[Division] (the 52nd and 94th H[High] S[Speed] R[Regiments] are equipped solely with SB aircraft), in conjunction with the 22nd M[Mechanised] C[Corps] is to destroy the motorised and mechanised enemy (which are uneven) units around Ustyluh, Grubeshuv and Korytnitsa, and is to prevent them from reaching the area around Volodymyr-Volynskyi.
Labour—one sortie as a division.
On completion of this mission be at No. 2 state of readiness in order to attack an alignment of enemy tanks in this same direction.
c) The 14 A[Air] D[Division] is to cover the 22nd M[Mechanised] C[Corps] in the area in which it is concentrated (close to Turiysk and Voynitsa) and the 18th and 62nd A[Air] D[Divisions] are to protect combat operations by patrolling in this area.

5. The Air Forces of the 6th A[Army] (the 15th and 16th A[Air] D[Divisions] along with the 33rd H[High] S[Speed] B[Bomber] R[Regiment], 19th A[Air] D[Division] are to destroy the enemy alignment in the area around Sokal, Krystynopol and Parkhach.
   a) The 33rd H[High] S[Speed] B[Bomber] R[Regiment] from dawn on 23 June is to destroy the enemy alignment using successive attacks in echelon formation at a certain time and altitude, around Sokal, Krystynopol and Parkhach.
   On their return flight to their home base they are to land on Romanovka airfield (Berdichev) in case they need to be loaded up for their next flight on to their home base (of Gorodishche).
   Labour—one sortie as a regiment (just flying Ar-2s, and SBs).
   On conclusion of this mission be at No. 2 state of readiness for the following action in this same area:
   b) The 16th A[Air] D[Division], in conjunction with the 4th M[Mechanised] C[Corps] is to destroy the German enemy ground troops in the area around Krystynopol in successive attacks in echelon formation. The task of the 86th H[High] S[Speed] B[Bomber] R[Regiment] is to cover the 92nd F[Fighter] A[Air] R[Regiment].
   Labour for the bombers—one sortie as a regiment.
   c) The 15th A[Air] D[Division] is to provide cover in the area around Lvov and the area in which the 4 M[Mechanised] C[Corps] are to be concentrated and the 3rd Cavalry Division.
6. 17th A[Air] D[Division] (the 20th and 91st F[Fighter] A[Air] R[Regiments]) are to provide cover for the railway junctions at Proskurov, Shepetovka, Novograd-Volynsk and are not to allow the enemy air forces to break through to this area.
   The 48th H[High] S[Speed] B[Bomber] A[Air] R[Regiment] (equipped with Pe-2 aircraft) is to be redeployed to operational airfields along with the withdrawal of airfields across the border, which are to be carefully camouflaged.
7. The 64th A[Air] D[Division] (comprised of the 12th, 149th, and 166th F[Fighter] A[Air] R[Regiments] is to protect the concentration of the 12th Army in the area around Stanislavuv and Chernovitsk, from enemy air attacks, destroying the enemy air forces.
8. The 44th A[Air] D[Division] is to redeploy the 88th F[Fighter] A[Air] R[Regiment] to Kochubeyev and Pudlovtsy airfields and is to hand over the regiment to the disposal of the commander of the 64th A[Air] D[Division].
9. The 138th and 136th S[Short] R[Range] B[Bomber] R[Regiment] in my reserve are to be at No. 2 state of readiness in order to fly missions against enemy ground forces.
10. I will be at the command post in Ternopil.

The Commander of front line Air Forces Vrid, the Chief of Staff of front line Air Forces Lieutenant-General PTUKHIN, and Colonel TAYGREBERT.

Appendix II

A Report on the attacks on reinforcements on the mound at Sokal in the combat zone by the augmented [German] 199th Infantry Regiment on 22 June 1941 and the attacks on the reinforcements to the north-east of Sokal (the 75th Infantry Division) and to the east of Poturzitsy (the 179th Infantry Regiment) on 23 and 24 June 1941[1]

1. An assessment of the terrain. The *51st Sapper Assault Battalion* that were used in the attack on the front line of the *199th Infantry Regiment* should have crossed the Bug river, which at this point reached a width of 40m, ahead of the attack on the reinforced line. The bank from our side, and particularly from the other side, is in a number of locations covered in a liquid mud and is marshy. The depth of the Bug was between one and a half to three metres on average. The bridge that was in the zone of the advance of the *51st Sapper Battalion* was of a wooden construction and was 101m long with 14m spans and a capacity of around 20 tonnes. On the road leading to the bridge small houses stood on the left and right (these were part of the village of Zhabitse).

   On that side of the river close to the bridge are the villages of Sokal and Babinets with long streets that extend out of sight and rows of houses dropping away down to the river. Beyond them is a chain of hills, the height of which increases right up to the Sokal mound. On the outside this chain of hills that run parallel to the front line are dissected by ravines running in different directions.

1 NARA T314 R1138 frames 746—768.

This entire terrain is engaged in agriculture, part of the area is covered in cornfields while other areas are covered in other, smaller crops. In the foreground, around the Sokal heights, is a sufficiently large forest thick with scrub.

Between the first and second line of hills, in the last ravine on the way to the Sokal mound, an anti-tank ditch was located with a multitude of twists and turns.

2. Reconnaissance ahead of the attack. The reconnaissance information that was to hand was not sufficient, since air reconnaissance had not been carried out and there were no aerial photographs, neither was there any information from agents. From the towers of the Sokal monastery, from which reconnaissance was first and foremost conducted, only some of the structures were visible, which for the most part had been camouflaged, as well as the anti-tank ditch.

   It was impossible to establish the construction, nor the level of armament of the individual sites. The fields of fire for the pillboxes and the location of the armoured turrets were not established. Many of the structures on the opposite slope, and the well-camouflaged field reinforcements were also out of sight.

3. Preparatory measures. The preparation for this attack had to be carried out with extreme caution and only on the last night since it would be clearly visible to the enemy. The materials necessary to construct the river crossings were delivered during the short nights starting from 19 June. Only the nights of 21 and 22 June remained to reach the objective of the infantry positions. Since we had to consider the possibility that the enemy may destroy an exceptionally valuable bridge, every effort had to be made to ensure the bridge was captured complete and if the bridge were nevertheless destroyed—to ensure that it could be replaced as soon as possible or that a crossing could be constructed that was capable of taking assault armament.

   In the event that the bridge was destroyed the following measures would be taken, which were aimed at ensuring that the crossing could be rebuilt as soon as possible.

   1) In order to prevent the bridge, half of which was under Russian control, being set on fire, several days prior to the start of combat operations a sapper platoon under Lieutenant Schlingmann was posted next to the bridge, watched over by the fire brigade. This platoon was equipped with a small fire pump, fire extinguishers, buckets, boat hooks, saws and inflatable rafts, which were stored in locations close to the bridge.
   2) If the enemy did nevertheless succeed in destroying their end of the bridge, or one or two spans, the crossing was to be manufactured initially using a multitude of angled poles, which would be angled towards the surviving part of the bridge and which would rest on the sandbank that was located on the Russian side. By this time the pre-prepared bridging boards would have been delivered, which would enable the sappers and the infantry to cross with their light weaponry.

      In order to make it possible for light transport vehicles weighing around four tonnes to cross, sections of the bridge material 'S' would be prepared adjacent to the bridge, which would be used to arrange an access ramp from the surviving part of the bridge onto the sandbank on the enemy's side. A bridge building battalion was on hand to ensure that the bridge was reconstructed properly and also to reinforce the structure.
   3) Since the bridge was extremely important to the successful development of the advance, all efforts had to be made to ensure that it was captured undamaged. The 2nd Company, *51st Sapper Assault Battalion* was ordered to prepare to take the bridge rapidly, and undertook the necessary training. In addition to constantly watching the enemy bank and updating information on the strength of numbers among enemy forces, steps were taken to clear the bridge's surfaces, which on the German side were prodigiously partitioned

with barbed wire. Under cover of darkness the wire was cut through so that it could be easily pushed to one side during the attack. Since all these preparations had to be hidden from the Russians, this work needed to be completed very quickly in the few hours of darkness. A loud power station that stood on the bank of the river helped to a great extent to muffle the noise from this work and the sound of the tools. After the wire had been cut through it had to be fastened once again so that the enemy would not notice a change to the usual picture. Measures however had to be taken not just to ensure that the bridge was taken quickly. Since the bridge could only take no more than 16 tonnes in weight, a second crossing had to be constructed for the 22 tonne assault guns, with which it was envisaged the attacks by the assault groups would be supported. This crossing could only be manufactured by wading into the river. Not every location on the Bug, which had an average depth of between one and a half to two metres, was anywhere near suitable for a crossing of this nature. In the regiment's section a fording site had to be found that would be no more than 70cm deep. The intelligence that the battalion had indicated that several of these fording points existed, which on closer inspection turned out to be unsuitable.

In connection with this Lieutenant Schlingmann was ordered to subtly check the depth of the river in various locations as he was swimming. Initially he was not successful in achieving the desired result but on 21 June close to the regiment's boundary on the right hand side a section was found with a relatively flat riverbed. As they were swimming the soldiers were able to approach the opposite bank to a distance of up to 20m and established that a fording point did exist with a depth of between 70–80cm and where the riverbed was sandy. This location was chosen as the crossing point for the assault guns. In order to prepare for the possibility that the depth may be greater in the remaining 20m that have still not been scrutinised the *51st Construction Battalion* prepared 30 water fascines with a thickness of between 40–50cm, which would be lowered into the water at the deepest points. Tests conducted on the previous day with these fascines illustrated that as the assault guns went over them they did not give way or spread easily and would allow a vehicle to travel over them 30cm from the bottom. Thus there was hope that the assault guns would be able to cross successfully. In order to prevent the fascines floating to the surface, the option of anchoring them with a metal cable that would pass through an eyelet in each of the fascines was examined. It subsequently emerged that they would float very easily despite the use of wood that had only just been cut down and that it would have been better to set lengths of rail into the fascines. Since these lengths of track were not delivered on time the fascines had to be weighed down with metal chains and a large quantity of cable.

All the heavy equipment, the inflatable rafts, fascines and the sections of the bridge material 'S' were delivered to the bridge on the night of 21 June. On the final part of the journey the trucks had to be towed by hand so as not to alert the enemy. The materials were placed behind the houses and were camouflaged from the air. On the night before the offensive this was all moved out to the starting positions by companies that were to attack in the first wave.

During the reconnaissance and deployment the narrow nature of the river at this point, and the excellent possibilities this afforded the enemy in terms of observation, caused a great number of difficulties. Despite all the precautions the preparations could not be hidden from the enemy given their careful observations from their side.

4. Deployment. After all the preparatory measures had been taken the deployment of the *51st Sapper Assault Battalion* began for the attack. Two assault groups were formed for the attack on the *199th Infantry Regiment*. The right assault group under the leadership of the

commander of the *51st Sapper Assault Battalion* consisted of the following: the augmented *51st Sapper Assault Battalion*, two platoons of the 14th Company, *199th Infantry Regiment*, the 3rd company, *197th Sturmgeschütz Battalion* (minus one platoon), two rifle platoons from the *1st Battalion, 199th Infantry Regiment* (to provide firing cover during the crossing of the Bug river), and specifically the *1st Battalion, 199th Infantry Regiment.*

The left hand assault group was under the command of the Commander of the *2nd Battalion, 199th Infantry Regiment.* This attack was to be conducted as follows:

The augmented *51st Sapper Assault Battalion* were to prevent the enemy destroying the bridge as quickly as possible and cross the river Bug in multiple locations at the same time, capturing the village of Babinets, and in doing so creating a small bridgehead on the eastern side of the river. Behind this first wave would come the two augmented assault companies, who, having advanced from the bridgehead in two separate detachments were to encircle the Sokal mound from the right and left flanks, and capture Height 237, liquidating defensive structures on the way. After this first target had been achieved this formation's advance was to enter the forest to the east of the heights and reach its far edge. The *1st Battalion, 199th Infantry Regiment*, which were to follow the *51st Sapper Assault Battalion* up until the Sokal heights had been captured, would then pass through the sapper's combat formations and move forward through the forest since, in all probability, the principal mass of the *51st Sapper Assault Battalion* would be delayed in their suppression of resistance from individual fortifications.

One platoon each from the 14th Company, *199th Infantry Regiment*, one platoon each of assault guns, as well as one rifle platoon each of the *1st Battalion, 199th Infantry Regiment* were attached to each of the augmented assault companies attacking the Sokal mound.

This deployment of the *51st Sapper Assault Battalion* was conducted on the night of 22 June 1941. The battalion, with its transport, departed from the camp and took towards the southern exit from Zhabitse, reaching it at approximately 2230 hrs. It was here that the companies alighted and reached their starting positions along with their armament. The 2nd Company gathered in the houses immediately adjacent to the bridge. The augmented 3rd Company was concentrated directly behind the 2nd in houses to the south of the road leading to the bridge, while the 1st Company were located to the north of the road. As they were moving out towards the starting positions the subdivisions that had been attached to the companies joined them and as such the journey to the starting positions went smoothly. The assault guns attached to the battalion were not taken out to the battalion's starting positions in view of the noise that this would create but remained considerably to the west of the railway line. Prior to, and during, the troop movements out to their starting positions a great number of observers and communications officers from the artillery and rocket launcher subdivisions began to arrive at the command post. The commander of the assault gun battery was also located close to the battalion's command post and commanded his platoons from this location by radio.

In order that the right hand assault group crossed at a point past the bridge, the survival of which could probably never be relied upon, they had nine large and 12 small inflatable rafts, as well as two assault craft. The six large and 24 small inflatable rafts that were promised by company of engineers never arrived. The lack of these rafts did not have a significant effect on the development of the attack since the sudden attack on the bridge was successful and it fell into our hands undamaged.

In order to engage the enemy targets on the opposite bank of the Bug as soon as possible the *1st Battalion, 199th Infantry Regiment*, as well as two platoons of army anti-aircraft guns (with a calibre of 2cm) and four anti-tank guns that were not used in the first wave, but which were from the 14th Company, *199th Infantry Regiment* were on hand.

The battle with the enemy positions that were a considerable distance away was to fall to the field and anti-aircraft artillery as well as to the rocket launchers.

The *51st Sapper Assault Battalion*'s journey to their starting positions had been completed, more or less, by 0100 hrs. This process was completed so quietly that the enemy on the opposite bank of the river Bug did not notice anything.

5. The attack. At 0315 hrs the preliminary artillery bombardment began and with it the crossing of the Bug river. The first company in the sapper battalion to cross the border was the 2nd Company under the command of Oberleutnant Steinkamp. Its orders were as follows:
   1) Take the bridge quickly.
   2) Create a bridgehead, and capture the village of Babinets.
   3) In the event that the bridge is blown up, create a river crossing for the soldiers, and their light transports.
   4) Provide a river crossing for the 1st and 3rd Companies, *51st Sapper Assault Battalion* and the units subordinated to it from the *199th Infantry Regiment.*
   5) Prepare a fording point for the assault guns to cross the river.
   6) Make contact with your neighbouring unit on the right hand side, the *179th Infantry Regiment.*

In order to achieve this the company was structured as follows:

The 1st Platoon: Was to cross the Bug river in four assault groups upriver of the bridge and one of these groups was to prevent the destruction of the bridge in an assault craft. The three remaining groups, which had one inflatable raft each in a sector where it was approximately 300m wide, capture the village, form a bridgehead on its eastern side and create a starting position for the other two assault companies for the subsequent offensive. The commander of the platoon was Lieutenant Ruhlemann.

The 2nd Platoon: Their orders were similar, but downstream of the bridge where the river was 250m wide. The commander of the platoon was Lieutenant Brandt.

The 3rd Platoon: The platoon's assault group was to reach the other side of the bridge and prevent it from being blown up, or organise along with another group, the construction of a river crossing for the infantry and for light vehicles in the event that the bridge is destroyed. The commander of the platoon was *Oberfeldwebel* Weissenborn.

A group of six sappers and the infantry platoon attached to them were to reconnoitre a fording point for the assault guns to cross the river, mark it, and where necessary blanket the deeper sections with fascines. The commander was Lieutenant Schlingmann.

Following the artillery raid at 0315 hrs the assault group of the 3rd Platoon, under the command of *Feldwebel* Putticher, rapidly overcame their own barbed wire fences, reached the other side of the bridge and cut all the cables that were in place.

Both of the Russian customs men standing at their end of the bridge were shot by soldiers who were specially tasked with this objective at the very start of the attack.

The platoons that were deployed to the right and left of the bridge reached the riverbank at the double, cut through the barbed wire, and launched the inflatable rafts out onto the water. The soft and marshy soil made transporting the inflatable rafts difficult so that from the very start men were jumping into the river to enable the raft to be launched into the water more quickly. After the raft had reached the other side the barbed wire that was there was cut through and the assault groups were able to rapidly break through to the surrounding countryside. Enemy resistance in some houses in different locations was quickly put down with the help of flame-throwers and hand grenades. Some 20 mins later the 2nd Company had the starting positions for the 1st and 3rd Companies at their disposal. The company's losses at that point in time amounted to one injured soldier. Since the company managed to take the bridge in a sudden attack the other companies were so quick to follow them that the 2nd Company, in order to avoid any nasty surprises, received an order from battalion command to mop up the houses around the bridgehead.

The creation of the fording point that had originally been envisaged turned out not to be necessary since the assault guns were able to cross the river via the bridge.

By 0352 hrs the 2nd Company had contacted the *179th Infantry Regiment*. During the course of the mopping up of the village by the 2nd Company, the 1st and 3rd Companies began their advance in their allotted directions. The 2nd Company received an order to move back behind the 3rd as a reserve detachment. At 0430 hrs the company reached the Sokal mound via Height 237.

Immediately after the crossing by the 2nd Company, the 1st Company, which was situated on the right flank of the augmented *199th Infantry Regiment*, also crossed the Bug River. This company's orders were to advance to the south of Height 237, break through the defensive line that was located there, and the turn towards the city of Sokal and, given weak enemy resistance, reach the eastern edge of the forest located to the east of the mountain. In order to achieve this task a rifle platoon was attached to the company, as well as a platoon of anti-tank guns and a platoon of assault guns. The company itself was split into three assault platoons, each of which consisted of two assault groups each, and one mop-up group each, and apart from that each platoon had a machine gun detachment. With the start of the artillery bombardment at 0315 hrs the company set off towards the river with their inflatable rafts, crossing the Bug River partly upriver from the bridge, and partly via a bridge that had been captured by the 2nd Company. The 1st Assault Group, with the help of a single assault gun, succeeded in suppressing weak enemy resistance south of Sokal (Babinets), and commence a rapid advance towards the defences to the south-east of the city. Immediately behind them were the other two assault platoons accompanied by the second line of assault guns. Thanks to the vigour of both of the forward assault detachments the enemy was quickly dislodged from the forefield and in 45 mins had reached the defensive line of the pillboxes, covering a distance of 2km. The rifle platoon followed in an echelon formation to the right to cover the right flank. With the onset of the immediate attack the rifle and machine gun platoons were used, in line with the anti-tank ditch, to cover the front line and the right flank. While the 1st Assault Platoon attacked pillbox No. 3, the 2nd Assault Platoon moved away from the anti-tank ditch towards pillbox No. 4.

The 3rd Platoon was engaged in mopping-up the field defences in the forefield. Since pillbox No. 4 had already been attacked by the 3rd Platoon, *51st Sapper Assault Battalion* the 2nd Assault Platoon passed it by and proceeded towards bunker No. 4 and attacked this latter defensive position.

In order to provide covering fire for the attack by both of the assault platoons against the pillboxes they had two assault guns at their disposal, which were very active in their support of the attack. The platoon of anti-tank guns was very late in coming because of the rapid advances made by the sappers and the rough ground, and actually arrived so late that it did not take part in the battle. Moreover the construction of the bunkers was such that it would be doubtful that any kind of anti-tank guns could have been used against them. All this time the 1st Assault Platoon had attacked bunker No. 3, which had a machine gun and an artillery gun port, and apart from that it had an additional machine gun in the armoured turret. Thanks to the distribution of the fortifications, which to our surprise turned out to be outstandingly skilful, there was a possibility of joint covering fire from the pillboxes, which would make an attack much more difficult. The bombardment of the pillboxes and gun ports using assault guns had proved almost useless thanks to the high quality concrete and the low positioning of the gun ports with their powerful, spherical screens. Under covering fire from assault guns the 1st Assault Platoon was able to approach one of the pillboxes and first and foremost, to take the armoured canopy out of action using 6 kg of explosives. Since the enemy put up a determined resistance and was supported with effective covering fire from the other fortifications, only after a battle lasting two hours and predominantly by using explosives, was it possible to take the gun ports out of action and to suppress the resistance at the entrance to the bunker in a swift attack. Moreover four men were taken prisoner, one of whom died a short time later. A fifth member of the defence lay dead in the pillbox. The survivors, who had all lost consciousness, were brought out of the pillbox by soldiers of the 1st Assault Platoon, after which this defensive installation was blown up from the inside.

The 2nd Assault Platoon meanwhile had begun to advance between pillboxes nos. 3 and 4 and came under intense fire from the other two pillboxes, as a result of which they were forced to lie low for some time. Only with the support of a second assault gun was the platoon able to crawl forward another 500m that separated it from pillbox No. 4. The assault gun that had been attached to the platoon was able to suppress the anti-tank fire coming from the pillbox with its own fire, so the men in the defensive installation were just left with their machine guns.

Despite the exceptionally heavy fire from the pillbox, and the fire coming from the flanks from the two other pillboxes, the assault platoon succeeded in approaching the pillbox, suppress the gun ports with a couple of explosions and break through the garrison's defences. After this the 2nd Assault Platoon continued to advance in their allotted direction and came under fire from houses in the Collective Khorbkov (in Vostok). In the course of the fighting another four people were taken prisoner by the enemy.

The 3rd Assault Platoon, following the mop-ups in the forefield, passed to the left of the 2nd Assault Battalion and attacked pillbox No. 46. Moreover it was met with fire coming not only from the front line but also from their right flank and the platoon was only able to move forward after it had sent flares to the assault gun which supported them with fire. Only after a fierce battle that lasted an hour, and after having lost several men, was the platoon able to suppress fire from this pillbox.

Since the subsequent advance of this company was threatened by three pillboxes in their neighbouring sector on the right flank, the commander of the company ordered units in the 3rd Platoon to attack the closest pillbox; No. 3. Despite the fact that tank and assault guns were already busy with something else the soldiers succeeded in approaching the pillbox and setting off a series of explosions, which temporarily took it out of action. Furthermore they came under fierce fire from the majority of the pillboxes on their flanks, which made it impossible to completely destroy them without support from assault guns or from another type of heavy weaponry. In order to avoid any further casualties in this battle, which was undertaken without any covering fire, the commander of the battalion ordered the attack on the pillboxes be stopped, which apart from anything else, were located in the zone of another regiment's advance. The losses, which the company incurred, were as follows: one non-commissioned officer was killed and seven men were injured, several of them seriously.

After a re-grouping the company was used to cover the right flank and without any heavy fighting covered 2km through the forest up to Height 247, located seven kilometres south-west of Sokal. Immediately after this point was reached the company was withdrawn from the battle and was subordinated to the *75th Infantry Division*. It had reached the north-western exit from the Sokal on foot by 1800 hrs.

The 3rd Company, *51st Sapper Assault Battalion*, which had been augmented by a platoon of assault guns, a platoon of anti-tank weapons and a rifle platoon received an order to suppress enemy defences on the banks of the Sokal mound and in the event of weak enemy resistance was to reach the eastern edge of the forest located to the east of the heights.

With the beginning of the attack at 0315 hrs this company, along with the other companies, set off for the captured bridge on the eastern edge of the village of Babinets, which it reached at 0325 hrs. From here it embarked on a non-stop march to Height 237. At this point the company encountered weak machine gun fire, which did not present a significant obstacle to the advance. At 0325 hrs the assault platoon under Lieutenant Hartung, which had acted as an advance guard for the company, reached tank trap No. 1 on the opposite side of the mound. This tank trap consisted of .a wall that had been cut in two lengthways on a slope and which was about four metres high, the approach to which was visible and indeed was located within the field of fire of pillbox No. 169. A further advance aimed at attacking this defensive installation came under fire from this same pillbox which, it later emerged, was firing from a pair of machine guns from the main gun port, as well as from open positions next to the pillbox itself. When the platoon had come within 150m it suddenly came under fire from the side from pillbox No. 128. In connection with this the platoon was forced, in a field of wheat, to dig in.

Meanwhile the other units in the company, following a mop-up of the forefield, were drawn up to this tank ditch. After they had come under fire from pillbox No. 169 the machine gun platoon was used to suppress fire from gun ports in the pillbox. At the same time an assault platoon under Lieutenant Velker was given an order to capture pillbox No. 128 in an assault. Lieutenant Velker carried out this order, conducting a number of explosions next to the gun ports and the doors of the pillbox. The garrison, which consisted of three men, was destroyed by throwing several hand grenades inside and pillbox No. 128 fell silent at approximately 0430 hrs. After this the assault platoon under Lieutenant Hartung was able to continue the advance to pillbox No. 169. It was supported by assault weaponry, which immediately had an immobilising effect on the enemy, since it was not able to hit the gun ports effectively, or the concrete walls of the pillbox. This defensive position had a machine gun port and a defensive position next to the entrance to the pillbox.

Having blown-up a combination of these two Lieutenant Hartung was able to silence the pillbox by throwing hand grenades inside and destroy the garrison which consisted of three men. The liquidation of pillbox No. 169 had been completed by 0515 hrs.

Thanks to the liquidation of pillboxes Nos. 128 and 129 the subdivisions in the battalion were able to advance along the ravine between the Sokal mound and Height 237 to the defensive installation No. 24.

During the battle for pillboxes Nos. 128 and 129 the other subdivisions in the company were drawn up that had passed along the tank trap which, after a further 100m, would turn into an anti-tank ditch. It was from the extended corner of the anti-tank trap No. 1 that the assault group under *Feldwebel* Korch attacked defensive installation No. 24. It was supported by one assault gun and one anti-tank gun. The assault group succeeded in coming another 60m closer to the pillbox, after which it came under machine gun fire from a position located next to the defensive installation. Hand grenades proved successful in forcing the enemy back inside the pillbox. After a few shots the enemy disappeared behind the walls of the defensive installation. An anti-tank gun used by *Feldwebel* Korch to fire at the gun port was taken out of action by a direct hit from a 5cm shell. By 0445 hrs the assault group had approached the pillbox. The attempts they had made to force the pillbox into silence by explosions inside the gun port had not been successful. Specifically they had not managed to get the explosives far enough inside the gun port that the explosion would damage the equipment inside. The pillbox continued to fire with its 5cm gun and its machine gun, covering tank trap No. 2. When Korch had used up all his explosives by 0530 hrs units from the 2nd Company, under

Lieutenant Steinkamp, approached the defensive installation and took it out of action. The 2nd Platoon, 2nd Company was ordered to finally finish off the pillbox. Thanks to the unexpected tenacity of the Russians, who fought to the last, the battle for the pillbox took quite some time. Despite the artillery bombardment some people did manage to approach the gun port. However owing to the high quality of the Russian materials the explosions were unsuccessful. During the course of the subsequent use of flamethrowers and explosives the entrance door was blown open, after which the soldiers were able to climb onto the pillbox. After blowing up the periscope aperture and the subsequent use of smoke grenades and explosives the soldiers managed to enlarge the aperture such that it became possible to lower explosives inside.

Apart from that petrol and fuel for the flamethrowers were poured inside. The resultant explosion completely destroyed the inside of the pillbox. After that the soldiers were able to be sure that the garrison in the pillbox had all been killed. At 0600 hrs the company reported to the battalion that the bunker had been captured.

At 0700 hrs the battle moved on to the Kol. Khorbkov and the company was employed between the 1st and 3rd Companies to provide cover on the flank from the south-east. During the final liquidation of defensive installation No. 24 by the 2nd Company, the assault platoon, under Lieutenant Hermal-Trager, had crossed the ravine that stood between tank ditches Nos. 1 and 1a, which was under fire from pillbox No. 4, as well as from the field defences. As they approached tank ditch No. 1a the group came under fire from pillbox No. 3. Making use of the fissures in the trench they managed to approach the pillbox. Lieutenant Hermal-Trager met Lieutenant Portshteffen from the 1st Company, which had already sent units from its assault group to attack the pillbox. The assault group led by Lieutenant Hilze initially set off for pillbox No. 169. However on seeing Lieutenant Hartung's men there he transferred to pillbox No. 129, which was only armed with a single machine gun. The enemy was evicted from the pillbox and escaped into the forest. After this the assault group under Lieutenant Hilze joined up with Lieutenant Hartung's men to attack fortification No. 181.

Lieutenant Hartung's assault group moved towards fortification No. 181 following the liquidation of pillbox No. 169. This pillbox had two 7.6cm guns, which were used to fire on units in a battalion of the *199th Infantry Regiment* on the left flank.

The assault group were fired upon from field positions as they approached. At approximately 0545 hrs they reached the fortification. Lieutenant Hartung, along with several soldiers, climbed onto the fortification and tried to take the gun ports out of action with explosives. As this attempt failed smoke grenades and hand grenades were thrown into the fortification via the observation dome. This was not successful either. Some time later some of the garrison, approximately 10 men, came out in a sortie and tried to push Hartung's men back with rifle fire and hand grenades.

This sortie was liquidated with fire from two machine guns as well as with hand grenades. All 10 men were killed. Lieutenant Hartung now began to fight the pillbox, throwing smoke grenades and hand grenades inside it through the ventilation shafts. The fortification continued to fire all this time. Only after half an hour was the pillbox silenced. This happened at around 0700 hrs. It subsequently emerged that the pillbox was manned by three crews, had two 7.6cm guns and three machine gun ports and fortifications around the entrance. The garrison consisted of 20 men and they were all killed. The enemy had defended the pillbox stubbornly and fiercely, offering resistance right up until the last moment. The suppression of this pillbox took three hours. It was the biggest one in the *199th Infantry Regiment*'s section.

On the southern slope of the Sokal mound meanwhile the following was unfolding:

After the suppression of pillbox No. 128 the assault group under Lieutenant Velker had set off for the tank trap No. 1a. He reached it at 0445 hrs at the same time that Korch's assault group began to attack fortification No. 24. Since Korch, as it appeared, had silenced the fire from the flanks coming from fortification No. 24 on the tank trap No. 2, and Lieutenant Portshteffen had attacked pillbox No. 3 Lieutenant Velker began, with the support of one assault gun, to attack pillbox No. 4. At that moment the firing from fortifications Nos. 24 and 128, which had previously been relatively weak, suddenly became much stronger, such that the group was forced to lie low. Firing also began from pillbox No. 24 from a 5cm gun. At approximately 0510 hrs a machine gun platoon were approaching tank trap No. 1a, which was being used to support the assault group under Lieutenant Velker, who at that moment were also coming under fire from the field fortifications between the pillboxes that had previously remained hidden. A few minutes later the assault gun drew near to pillbox No. 24 and began to fire at it. Lieutenant Velker managed to overcome tank trap No. 2 with three of his soldiers and approached pillbox No. 4.

There he met Lieutenant Turman from the 1st Company, who had already begun to attack this pillbox. Under covering fire from an assault gun the commander of the company drew up a machine gun platoon towards tank trap No. 2. This platoon managed to break through the zone of fire from the flank, which had still not been supressed, close to tank trap No. 2 and was able to reach pillbox No. 4. Furthermore *Unteroffizier* Vinnike was injured along with *Gefreiter* Arnold, while from the assault group under Lieutenant Velker, *Obergefreiter* Jungmann was injured. After this the assault group and the machine gun platoon were used to guard the edge of the forest east of Kol. Khorbkov. This took place at 0615 hrs. A reconnaissance group that had been sent into the forest for the purposes of reconnaissance reported that the enemy was absent from the edge of the forest. Up until 0715 hrs the other units in the company gathered to the east of Kol. Khorbkov and were used to guard the area.

On the orders of the commanders of the *199th Infantry Regiment, 51st Sapper Assault Battalion* was not supposed to pass through the forest to the east, but remain on the Sokal mound to cover the regiment that was advancing forward and for defence against possible attacks by the enemy from the north-east.

At around 0730 hrs our infantry began to move through the forest to the east. The 3rd assault company was used initially to cover the regiment's right flank and then to carry out this same task on the other side of the forest. Moreover there were no military clashes. Two men were taken prisoner. The company's losses up until this point in time amounted to one killed and nine injured.

On the following day the company was ordered to return to Babinets, where the battalion was being concentrated.

At 1230 hrs, in accordance with an order from the *199th Infantry Regiment*, all three assault companies were used behind the *1st Battalion, 199th Infantry Regiment* on Height 247, to the north of Ksaverovka, to cover the flank from the south and south-east. These companies were lined up one behind the other—the 3rd, 2nd, and 1st—at a distance of around 200m from one another. The advance by the *1st Battalion, 199th Infantry Regiment* towards Tartakov developed slowly and at this time the companies were coming under artillery fire and were forced to dig in. The reconnaissance groups established contact with their neighbours to the right.

The first company received a new order and in connection with this was subordinated to the *75th Infantry Division*, reaching the northern outskirts of Sokal by 1800 hrs. The 2nd Company received an order at 2020 hrs to take up positions in Poturzitse and establish communication with the *3rd Battalion, 179th Infantry Regiment*. At a dog-leg to this battalion the company were to liquidate all the pillboxes in the *3rd Battalion, 179th Infantry Regiment*'s sector as they proceeded in this battalions' formation. This company only arrived at 0030 hrs and re-started the advance at 07000 hrs on 23 June. In order to fulfil these orders two platoons of assault guns were attached to the company, together with one 8.8cm anti-aircraft gun.

After reconnaissance and the issuing of orders each of the platoons attacked one pillbox each. Under covering fire from anti-aircraft guns the sappers approached the pillboxes from the rear. Thanks to the fact that the assault gun crews took it upon themselves to suppress the fire from the flanks the assault groups were free to approach the pillboxes. These same pillboxes had already been attacked the night before by infantry, and had incurred some damage, but had not been liquidated. In connection with this the enemy had again occupied their combat positions and began to fire fiercely on the advancing units. As with the previous day's assault on the pillboxes the ventilation shafts were blown up as a priority. After that the assault groups, supported by flamethrowers, approached the gun ports covering the entrance and then they first blew the gun ports and then the entrance door. After the passage inside had been opened in this way the soldiers mopped-up the individual positions and put the armament beyond use. The battle inside the pillboxes unfolded slowly owing to the level of smoke inside them and took quite some time. Only after 1100 hrs were the first three pillboxes suppressed. By 1400 hrs each platoon had silenced one pillbox. In total pillboxes Nos. 15, 25, 29 and 105 were knocked out, together with another example that is not shown on the map.

In each of the pillboxes there were on average three officers, a non-commissioned officer and four soldiers, the majority of whom were either killed or seriously injured. Several of the slightly injured were taken prisoner.

After everything that was urgent had been completed and they had regrouped and re-armed, the 2nd and 3rd companies were again used in combat to mop-up the fortifications since it had emerged that firing had again resumed from some of the pillboxes that had been listed as having been liquidated.

During the course of this mopping up it was established that some of the garrisons had been able to escape the fortifications and hide in a wheat field. Now these men had returned and had resumed firing. During the course of the mopping-up and the suppression of a further two pillboxes the 2nd Company lost an *Unteroffizier* and three rank and file soldiers, who were killed close to fortification No. 102.

While the *3rd Battalion, 179th Infantry Regiment* were making use of the 2nd Company, the 1st Company were being used in the *75th Division*'s zone against the fortifications north of Kol. Tartakov. Ahead of these fortifications were units from the augmented infantry regiment, as well as artillery and anti-tank artillery, which had already sustained very heavy losses in this location but had still not managed to liquidate the fortifications. After the information had been acquired from the commander of the infantry battalion, the company commander managed to complete the reconnaissance for the attack in the gathering darkness and the attack was set for the following morning owing to the lateness of the hour. In order to prevent a night time breakthrough by the garrison the company, along with other subdivisions, surrounded the pillboxes to some depth.

At 0430 hrs the company began to attack the fortifications, after which, between 0300 hrs and 0400 hrs, they were fired upon by a single 21cm mortar battery and one howitzer battery. Despite this powerful artillery fire its impact on the pillboxes was very insignificant. Thus one of the mortars fired 22 times on a three-storey artillery and machine gun pillbox and only managed to chop off a piece of the concrete wall; which was approximately 60cm deep, one and a half metres tall and one metre wide; but did not damage any of the gun ports. Since the company's attack was not supported by any heavy armament, apart from artillery, it was forced to go on the attack despite the heavy fire from defending units. Immediately after the end of the artillery bombardment fierce firing began from the gun ports so the assault platoons were forced to crawl up to the pillbox metre by metre.

Reconnaissance had shown that there was a weak link in this system of fortifications and it was to this location that the 1st Assault Platoon managed to reach without incurring any heavy losses.

The assault platoon took two and a half hours to suppress pillbox No. 18 fully. This fortification consisted of two storeys and was armed with two anti-tank guns and four machine guns. Only after the liquidation of this pillbox was it possible for the other assault platoons to destroy another seven pillboxes between 0400–1800 hrs, during the course of fierce fighting in which the company exceeded all conceivable indicators of forbearance and courage since they had not eaten or drunk anything, or slept, for over 50 hrs.

The division was especially interested in the suppression of these pillboxes which, from a tactical perspective, were located in a very favourable position in as much as they possessed a large quantity of both anti-tank and other weaponry. The point being that these pillboxes were keeping the main road, running between Sokal–Tartakov, under fire from a variety of armament, including anti-tank armament. Aside from the heavy losses in terms of officers, *Unteroffiziers* and soldiers, these fortifications had set several vehicles on fire in the subdivisions that were travelling behind the infantry, and they were completely destroyed by direct hits from two 8.8cm anti-aircraft guns.

6) A description of the fortifications. The location of the Russian border fortifications has to be acknowledged as exceptionally clever, especially in terms of the skilful use of the terrain. The majority of the pillboxes were not visible from the front line and the gun ports were designed to fire from the flanks or from the rear. This explains why the majority of the fortifications had not been found by the start of the attack. Only those fortifications that were designed to fire forwards were known about prior to the attack. The Russians placed, very skilfully, a number of field fortifications and ground fortifications between these same concrete fortifications which made the entire system that much stronger. It was from these field fortifications, which for the most part went unnoticed by reconnaissance, and the gun ports, which were only visible several feet away due to vegetation, that the Russians would fire on the attackers with impunity. In the majority of cases the assault groups that came within a minimum distance of the pillboxes saw the Russians who had rushed inside.

The garrisons for the most part consisted of young soldiers, belonging to the young communist organisations and as such they fought with a particular tenacity.

The Russian soldiers offered outstanding resistance, only surrendering if they were injured, and fighting to the very last.

Individual elements of the augmented Russian line were exceptional in terms of their materiel and their armament. The concrete consisted for the most part of a mix of granite, cement and steel and was very strong and able to withstand fierce artillery fire.

The majority of the pillboxes consisted of a combat area and a recuperation area situated one above the other, but some of them were even three storeys in height. The pillboxes were armed with machine guns, light and heavy anti-tank armament and partly with 7.6cm guns; it was possible to change the armament and the spherical screens. The barrels of the machine guns did not protrude beyond the screens. Any gun barrels that did protrude outside were covered by special tubes fitted to the screens. The only weakness in the design, it appeared, was the ventilation ports. The gun ports in the pillboxes were very deep, which made firing into them very difficult. Apart from that they were located comparatively close to the surface, which made finding them and suppressing them difficult. Work to construct and camouflage these pillboxes had still not been completed.

For anyone attacking these pillboxes it was hard to break through the line of fortifications, especially since very little was known about Russian fortifications and their defensive capabilities. A rapid breakthrough could only be achieved by skilful and innovative actions undertaken by each soldier who was not beaten back by any obstacles. Since attempts to suppress the guns that were located behind the spherical screens were, in the majority of cases, unsuccessful, our sappers had to approach the firing points that had not been suppressed stealthily and take them out of action with whatever they had to hand. Thus, in this case, more was expected of the sappers in both a moral and a technical sense than in previous attacks on the pillboxes.

7. Experience gained so far. Experience of attacking fortifications showed that the use of anti-tank armament, which by virtue of its design has to be able to move around on an uneven terrain, creates significant difficulties and their timely use can lead to failure. Anti-tank armament is not effective when firing at the gun ports with their spherical screens. The high quality of the concrete makes artillery and anti-tank bombardments ineffective.

   Assault guns may not destroy the enemy but it can delay their fire. Blowing the gun ports up using three kilogramme explosive charges is not usually successful. A six kilogramme charge would usually be used to take a machine gun port out of action, but a 10 kg charge would be needed to completely destroy it. The 10 kg charges were used to take the gun ports out of action but they only destroyed the barrels, the actual gun ports were not damaged.

   Experience has shown that the best way of combatting the Russian pillboxes was by throwing smoke grenades, explosives, petrol and fuel for the flamethrowers in via the ventilation systems.

   Surrender by the garrisons in these Russian fortifications could not be relied upon even if all the armament had been knocked out and the structure was filled with smoke. A permanent and well-armed guard of all the doorways is needed. Even the injured in pillboxes that had been completely destroyed would take up the fight again if they got their hands on a weapon. Individual Russian soldiers who had been inured inside a fortification and whom were thought to have been killed, or who could get out of the fortification, would occupy captured pillboxes for several days, taking up the fight again. There were instances when Russian soldiers who had been injured several times in the chest, or who had penetrating wounds the size of a fist and had lost massive amounts of blood without having received medical assistance, would take up a weapon again some 10–15 hrs later.

   In order to avoid surprises a fundamental and systematic mop-up of these fortifications was needed. Furthermore each of these pillboxes, including the lower storeys, was to be defended with explosives and combustible material. The field fortifications and pillboxes needed to be treated appropriately.

   Furthermore a full encirclement is necessary using serried ranks of infantry around the larger defensive areas as well as a mop-up. Work brigades, consisting of prisoners or drawn from the civilian population, need to fill in all the field positions immediately following a mop-up.

   Even if the encirclement and mop-up require a large number of soldiers, this will be worth it, since small groups of Russians cause, and will continue to cause, large scale disruption to supplies as well as losses in logistics units, which will mean wasting effort on organising cover for each of the subdivisions and on eradicating the source of the problem.

Lieutenant-Colonel, Battalion Commander / signature/

Appendix III

Strength of Aviation Regiments under the command of the Air Forces of the South-Western Front, 22 June 1941

Aviation Divisions	Aviation Regiments	Aircraft availability		Availability of personnel	
		Type	Number	Pilots	Pilot observers
14th Aviation Division	Directorate	I-16	2	3	–
	17th Fighter Aviation Regiment	I-153	50	–	–
		I-16	1	54	–
	46th Fighter Aviation Regiment	I-16	25	–	–
		I-153	28	–	–
		I-15	2	66	–
	89th Fighter Aviation Regiment	I-16	66	68	–
	253rd Ground-Attack Aviation Regiment	–	–	7	–
	Total	–	174	198	–
15th Aviation Division	Directorate	MiG-3	2	–	–
		I-16	1	5	–
	23rd Fighter Aviation Regiment	MiG-3	48	–	–
		I-153	10	–	–
		I-16	7	–	–
		I-15	1	60	–
	28th Fighter Aviation Regiment	MiG-3	48	–	–
		I-16	12	60	–
	164th Fighter Aviation Regiment	I-16	14	–	–
		I-153	28	–	–
		I-15	2	51	–
	66th Ground-Attack Aviation Regiment	I-15	58	–	–
		Il-2	5	69	–
	Total	–	236	245	–

Aviation Divisions	Aviation Regiments	Aircraft availability		Availability of personnel	
		Type	Number	Pilots	Pilot observers
16th Aviation Division	Directorate	SB	2	5	5
	86th Short-Range Aviation Regiment	SB	35	–	–
		Pe-2	9	66	90
	87th Fighter Aviation Regiment	I-16	60	–	–
		MiG-3	4	88	–
	92nd Fighter Aviation Regiment	I-153	63	–	–
		I-16	5	–	–
		I-15	4	75	–
	Total	–	182	234	95
17th Aviation Division	Directorate	Yak-1	1	–	–
		I-153	1	–	–
		SB	1	7	8
	20th Fighter Aviation Regiment	I-153	26	–	–
		Yak-1	63	70	–
	91st Fighter Aviation Regiment	I-153	59	64	–
	48th Short-Range Bomber Aviation Regiment	Pe-2	34	–	–
		SB	8	67	82
	224th Short-Range Bomber Aviation Regiment	SB	13	60	75
	225th Short-Range Bomber Aviation Regiment	SB	11	70	65
	242nd Short-Range Bomber Aviation Regiment	–	–	55	57
	244th Short-Range Bomber Aviation Regiment	–	–	12	–
	Total	–	217	405	286
18th Aviation Division	Directorate	DB-3F	3	8	9
	90th Long-Range Bomber Aviation Regiment	DB-3F	59	54	79
	93rd Long-Range Bomber Aviation Regiment	DB-3F	57	55	83
	Total	–	119	117	171
19th Aviation Division	Directorate	SB	2	7	10
	33rd Short-Range Bomber Aviation Regiment	Ar-2	23	–	–
		Pe2	10	–	–
		SB	527	73	83
	136th Short-Range Bomber Aviation Regiment	SB	4	58	63
	138th Short-Range Bomber Aviation Regiment	SB	27	60	96

Aviation Divisions	Aviation Regiments	Aircraft availability		Availability of personnel	
		Type	Number	Pilots	Pilot observers
	Total	–	142	198	252
36th Aviation Division	Directorate	I-16	1	4	7
	2nd Fighter Aviation Regiment	I-16	41	–	–
		I-153	16	46	5
	43rd Fighter Aviation Regiment	I-16	42	–	–
		I-153	12	57	4
	254th Fighter Aviation Regiment	–	–	6	–
	255th Fighter Aviation Regiment	–	–	–	–
	Total	–	112	113	16
44th Aviation Division	Directorate	I-16	4	2	7
	88th Fighter Aviation Regiment	I-16	71	31	–
	248th Fighter Aviation Regiment	I-153	29	20	–
	249th Fighter Aviation Regiment	I-16	20	–	–
		I-153	12	21	–
	252nd Fighter Aviation Regiment	I-153	15	–	–
		I-15	15	11	–
	Total	–	166	85	7
62nd Aviation Division	Directorate	–	–	2	5
	52nd Short-Range Bomber Aviation Regiment	Pe-2	15	–	–
		SB	21	60	86
	94th Short-Range Bomber Aviation Regiment	SB	63	59	72
	226th Short-Range Bomber Aviation Regiment	Su-2	55	61	56
	227th Short-Range Bomber Aviation Regiment	Su-2	59	65	86
	243rd Ground-Attack Aviation Regiment	–	–	–	–
	245th Ground-Attack Aviation Regiment	–	–	–	–
	Total	–	213	247	305
63rd Aviation Division	Directorate	–	–	4	1
	62nd Ground-Attack Aviation Regiment	I-15b	9	–	–
		I-153	55	92	–
	165th Fighter Aviation Regiment	I-16	4	–	–
		I-15b	8	–	–
		I-153	26	71	–
	Total	–	102	167	1
	Directorate	–	–	1	–

Aviation Divisions	Aviation Regiments	Aircraft availability		Availability of personnel	
		Type	Number	Pilots	Pilot observers
	12th Fighter Aviation Division	I-16	19	–	–
		I-153	47	–	–
-		I-15	12	66	4
	149th Fighter Aviation Division	MiG-3	56	–	–
		I-16	13	–	–
63rd Aviation Division		I-153	49	59	4
	166th Fighter Aviation Division	I-16	42	67	–
	247th Fighter Aviation Regiment	MiG-3	1	–	–
		I-153	48	46	–
	246th Fighter Aviation Regiment	–	–	–	–
	Total	–	287	239	8
	315th Reconnaissance Aviation Regiment	SB	20	66	85
	316th Reconnaissance Aviation Regiment	Yak-2-1	31	–	–
		SB	2	45	82
Total acc. to the Air Forces of the South Western Front		2003		2,355	1,307

Appendix IV

Vehicle losses of the 10th Tank Division

No.	Nature of the losses	The number of losses for each type of tank						Total
		KV	T-34	T-28	BT-7	T-26	Armoured vehicles	
1	Taken out of operation and burnt out on the battlefield	11	20	4	53	7	13	108
2	Suffered a technical failure in the course of a mission and was left on territory occupied by the enemy	–	1	4	2	2	4	13
3	Failed to return along with its crews from the battlefield following an attack	11	3	–	3	3	7	27
4	Burnt out as a result of bombing	–	–	–	1	–	4	5
5	Remained with their crews in an enemy encirclement due to a technical failure, or due to a lack of oil and lubricating materials	2	–	6	1	–	–	9
6	Remained behind due to a lack of oil and lubricating materials, and that it was impossible to deliver them since the tanks' locations had fallen into enemy hands	–	–	4	2	–	–	6
7	Lost without trace along with their crews	–	–	3	–	–	–	3
8	Destroyed at a collection post for disabled vehicles as they could not be evacuated during the withdrawal	7	1	6	–	–	6	3
9	Abandoned during a unit's withdrawal for technical reasons, and because it was impossible to either repair, or evacuate them	22	6	15	28	10	14	95
10	Foundered on obstacles with no way of pulling them out, or of evacuating them	3	1	2	10	2	3	21
	Total	56	32	44	100	24	51	307

Appendix V

Strength and losses of combat vehicles in the 8th Mechanised Corps as of 20 July 1941

	Listed as of 22 June 1941	At a repair base, or at the manufacturing plant	Left in their winter quarters	Taken forward into battle	Transferred to other units	Lost in combat	Abandoned on the way	Disappeared without trace	Loaded onto freight trains	Available as of 20 July 1941
1	2	3	4	5	6	7	8	9	10	11
KV	71	5	6	60	11	13	15	9	12	–
T-35	48	–	10	38	–	30	8	–	–	–
T-34	100	–	5	95	22	18	16	24	15	–
T-26RC	141	5	3	133	7	65	21	28	11	1
T-26 battle	139	4	4	131	–	84	13	34	–	–
T-26 2b	10	2	7	1	–	1	–	–	–	–
T-26 Ftr.	50	3	1	46	–	22	19	5	–	–
Su-5	2	1	1	–	–	–	–	–	–	–
T-26 tractor	2	1	1	–	–	–	–	–	–	–
T-27	80	14	66	–	–	–		–	–	–
BT-7	242	42	48	152	39	62	49	4	28	2
BT-5	20	3	13	4	–	–	4	–	–	–
BT-2	15	1	9	5	–	1	4	–	–	–
T-37	23	3	20	–	–	–	–	–	–	–
T-40	17	–	–	17	–	6	4	–	5	2
BA-10	99	–	–	99	2	21	19	9	1	33
BA-20	75	5	5	65	7	18	19	8	8	13
BA-6	3	–	1	2	–	–	–	–	–	2
FAI	7	2	3	2	–	–	–	2	–	–

Notes

The Central Archive of the Ministry of Defence, fund. 229, inventory. 161, file. 89, p. 90.
This table was compiled by 8th Mechanised Corps Headquarters (the document is signed by the Deputy Corps Commander in charge of the Technical Unit, Engineer 1st Class Gorchakov). Correspondingly, all the tanks that left with Popel's group are either listed as lost in combat, or missing without trace.

Appendix VI

The Order of Battle of the Air Forces of the South-Western Front, 30 June 1941

	Regt.	MiG-3	Yak-1	I-16	I-153	I-15bis	Pe-2	Ar-2	Su-2	Yak-4	SB	DB-3
14th Aviation Division	46			4/2*	4/1							
	17				8/4							
	89			14/8								
62nd Aviation Division	52						5				5	
	94										39	
	226								25/7			
	227								46/9			
15th Aviation Division	23**	19		5	5	18						
	28						1				3	
16th Aviation Division	86		2	30								
	87			2	23							
	92											
64th Aviation Division	12			15	17							
	166			17								
	149	13		7								
	247			2	5	8						
17th Aviation Division	48						15					
	224										10	
	225										12	
	20		26									
	91				32							
18th Aviation Division	90											31/16
	93											17/21
19th Aviation Division	136									27/16		
	33						8/1	11/4			14/5	
	138										9/12	
44th Aviation Division	88			56/8	1/1							
	243				9							
	248				12/3	25/4						
	249			16/6	28/5							
Total		32	28	167/22	154/14	71/14	29/1	11/4	71/16	27/16	92/17	48/37

Notes

The Central Archive of the Ministry of Defence, fund. 229, inventory. 181, file. 33, p. 23.

* The numerator denotes the number of serviceable aircraft, while the denominator denotes the number of unserviceable aircraft.

** The number of aircraft is actually given across the aviation division as a whole, including the 164th Fighter Aviation Regiment, and the 66th Ground Attack Aviation Regiment.

Appendix VII

Photographs of the Battlefields today

The 'Glinska Brama' gate in Zhovkva (now known as Zhulkeva) as it is today.

The central Market Square in Zhovkva. In the centre of the photo is the 'Glinska Brama' gate. To the left of the 'Glinksa Brama' is the town hall, then the tower of the XVI Century castle, to the right is the Catholic Church of St. Lavrentiy.

A school in Zhovkva, opposite which two abandoned KV-2 tanks once stood.

A house on the road to Zhovkva, where in 1941 the abandoned T-28 once stood.

'The Court House' in Nemirov. This building was built in the 1930s in the constructivist style and was used as a court house, the judges lived on the first floor. Now it is an ordinary domestic dwelling.

A panorama of the town of Nemirov, the view is taken from high ground above the town to the south. Soviet tanks attacked from east to west (that is to say from right to left). In the centre of the photograph is the 'court house' and to the left the dome of the Greek Catholic Church is visible, while in front of the church is Market Square.

A contemporary view of Market Square on which the BT-7 tank stood bearing the designation 'A2'. Today it is just a crossroads in the town of Nemirov. The Greek-Catholic Church can be seen in the foreground.

The Catholic Church and a domestic dwelling on the southern edge of Nemirov. It was next to this house that the T-28 tank was knocked out. Only the satellite dish is testimony to this being a 21st Century courtyard. The Catholic Church was recently restored with the help of the Polish authorities.

Yazuv Stariy. This was the location where three T-34 tanks were knocked out, including one, which had been turned upside down.

Bibliography

Anfilov, V.A., *Бессмертный подвиг* ['Immortal Feat'], Moscow: Nauka, 1971.

Anfilov, V.A., *Начало Великой Отечественной войны (22 ию-ня – середина июля 1941 г.). Военно-исторический очерк* ['The beginning of the Great Patriotic War (22 July–The middle of July 1941). Military history essay'], Moscow: Voenizdat, 1962.

Anon., *1941 г. Документы* ['1941 Documents'], Moscow: International Fund "Democracy", 1992.

Anon., *1941 год – уроки и выводы* ['1941: Lessons and Conclusions'], Moscow: Voenizdat, 1992.

Anon., *Тактика танковых войск* ['Tactics of tank troops'], Moscow: Voenizdat, 1940.

Anon., *Боевой и численный состав ВС СССР в период Великой Отчественной войны. Статистический сборник № 1* ['Combat and numerical strength of the USSR Armed Forces during the Great Patriotic War. Statistical collection number 1'], Moscow: Institute of Military History of the RF Ministry of Defence, 1994.

Anon., *Киевский Краснознаменный. История Краснознаменного Киевского военного округа. 1919–1972* ['The Kiev Red Banner. History of the Red Banner Kiev military district. 1919–1972'], Moscow: Voenizdat, 1974.

Anon., *Полевой устав РККА (ПУ-39)* ['Field regulations of the Red Army (PU-39)'] Moscow: Voenizdat, 1939.

Anon., *Сборник боевых документов ВОВ. Выпуск № 33* ['Collection of Combat Documents from the Great Patriotic War, Issue No.33'], Moscow: Voenizdat, 1957.

Anon., *Сборник боевых документов ВОВ. Выпуск № 36* ['Collection of Combat Documents from the Great Patriotic War, Issue No.36'], Moscow: Voenizdat, 1958.

Arkhipov, V.S, *Время танковых атак* ['Time of tank attacks'], Moscow: Voenizdat, 1981.

Bagramyan, I.Kh., *Так начиналась война* ['So the War began'], Moscow: Voenizdat, 1971.

Boog et al, *Germany and the Second World War Volume IV*, Stuttgart: Deutsche Verlagsanstalt, 1983.

Braun, J., *Enzian und Edelweiss. Die 4.Gebirgsdivision 1940–1945*, Bad Nauheim: Podzun, 1954.

Dierich, W., *Kampgeschwader 55 Greif*, Stuttgart: Motorbuch-Verlag, 1973.

Egorov A.V., С *верой в победу* ['With faith in victory'], Moscow: Voenizdat, 1974.

Glantz, Col David M. (ed.), *The initial period of war on the Eastern Front 22 June–August 1941. Proceedings of the Fourth Art of war* Symposium, London: Frank Cass, 2001.

Grams, R., *Die 14.Panzer-Division 1940*–1945, Bad Nauheim: Verlag Hans-Henning Podzun, 1957.

Gretsov, M.D., *На Юго-Западном направлении* ['In the South-West direction'], Moscow: Voenizdat, 1965.

Halder, F., *Военный дневник. Ежедневные записи начальни ка Генерального штаба Сухопутных войск* ['Military Diary. Daily records of the Chief of the General Staff of the Land Forces'], Moscow: Voenizdat, 1971.

Jentz, T., *Panzertruppen* volume 1, Atglen PA: Schiffer Military History, 1997.

Kalinin N.V., *Это в сердце моем навсегда* ['It's in my heart forever'], Moscow: Voenizdat, 1967.

Kalinin, N.V., *За каждую пядь земли…* ['For every inch of the earth …'], Moscow: Voenizdat, 1983.

Khorkov, A.G., *Грозовой июнь* ['Thunderstorm June'], Moscow: Voenizdat, 1991.

Lannoy, François de, *Panzers en Ukraine. Juin–Dècembre 1941*, Bayeux: Heimdal. 2001.

Lanz, H., *Gebirgsjäger. Der 1.Gebirgsdivision 1935–1945*, Bad Nauheim: Podzun, 1954.

Mackensen, Eberhard von, *Vom Bug zum Kaukasus, Das III.Panzercorps im Feldzug gegen Sowjetrußland 1941/42,* Neckargemünd: Kurt Vowinckel Verlag, 1967.

Malygin, K.A., *Малыгин К.А. В центре боевого порядка* ['In the center of the battle formation›], Moscow: Voenizdat, 1986.

Munzel, O., *Panzer-Taktik. Raids gepanzerter Verbaende im Ostfeldzug 1941/42*, Neckargemünd: Kurt Vowinckel Verlag, 1959.

Ott, E., *Jaeger am Feind. Geschichte und Opfergang der 97. Jaeger-Division 1940–1945*, N.p.: Verlag der Kameradschaft der Spielhahnjäger, 1966.

Popel N.K., *В тяжкую пору* ['In a difficult time'], St. Petersburg: Terra Fantastica, 2001.

Prien, J., *Die Jagdfliegerbände der Deutschen Luftwafte 1934 bis 1945. Teil 6/I*, Eutin: Rogge, n.d.

Riabyshev D.I., *Первый год войны* ['The first year of the war'], Moscow: Voenizdat, 1990.

Schmitz, G., *Bildband der 16.Panzer-Division 1939–1945*, Bad Nauheim: Podzun, 1956.

Schrodek, G., *Ihr Glaube galt dem Vaterland. Geschichte des Panzer-Regiments 15 (11.Panzer-Division),* München: Schild Verlag, 1976.

Slyusarenko Z.K., *Последний выстрел* ['The last shot'], Moscow: Voenizdat, 1974.

Tuzov, A.V., В *огне войны. Боевой путь 50-й гвардейской дважды Краснознаменной орденов Суворова и Кутузова стрелковой дивизии* ['In the fire of war. The Combat path of the 50th Guards twice Order of Red Banner, Order of Suvorov, Order of Kutuzov Rifle Division'], Moscow: Voenizdat, 1970.

Vladimirsky A.V., *На киевском направлении. По опыту ведения боевых действий войсками 5-й армии Юго-Западного фронта в июне–сентябре 1941 г.* ['In the Kiev direction. The experience of the troops of the 5th Army of the South-Western Front in June-September 1941'], Moscow: Voenizdat, 1989.

Werthen, W., *Geschichte der 16.Panzer-Division 1939–1945*, Bad Nauheim: Verlag Hans-Henning Podzun, 1958.

Zamlinsky, V.A. (ed.), *Лето 1941. Украина. Документы и материалы. Ход событий* ['Summer of 1941. Ukraine. Documents and materials. Course of events'], Kiev: 'Ukraine' Publishers, 1991.

Index

INDEX OF PEOPLE

INDEX OF PLACES

INDEX OF GERMAN MILITARY FORMATIONS & UNITS

INDEX OF SOVIET MILITARY FORMATIONS & UNITS

INDEX OF GENERAL & MISCELLANEOUS TERMS